THEORIZING THE

George J. Sefa Dei and Suleyman M. Demi (Eds.)

ISBN 978-1-64504-075-0 (Paperback)

ISBN 978-1-64504-076-7 (Hardback)

ISBN 978-1-64504-077-4 (E-Book)

Library of Congress Control Number: 2020939103

Printed on acid-free paper

© 2021 DIO Press Inc, New York

https://www.diopress.com

This book is part of the *Race, Indigeneity and Anti-Colonial Studies Series*.
Series Editor: *George J. Sefa Dei*

DIO Press International Board

ACKNOWLEDGEMENTS AND DEDICATION

First, our thanks go to the Creator for his continuing mercies, the gift of life and wisdom that has nourished us to bring to fruition such academic work. This book was inspired by critical class discussions in George Dei's upper level graduate class on: *'Anti-Colonial Thought: Pedagogical Implications'* at the Ontario Institute for Studies in Education of the University of Toronto, in the Fall of 2018. In class discussions, students brought critical analytic lens to understanding of colonization and its continuing global impacts. There is a saying among the Akan people of Ghana that "somebody's life key may open somebody life door". This proverb means that people can share similar life stories and find success. Yet, another proverb says, "if you advertise your sickness, you get a cure." The import of these sayings is that wisdom does not reside in one person's head. Hence, this book is dedicated to those whose struggles paved the way for us to have these discussions.

Consequently, we want to recognize the passing of a civil right icon, the legendary Honorable John Lewis [may his soul rest in absolute peace] and all those who fought to make the world better than we came to meet it. We acknowledge that we are leaving in an unusual time with this deadly COVID 19 pandemic. There is much pain and suffering. But we must count on hope winning at the end of this all. Consequently, we dedicate this book to victims of COVID 19 and their families, the frontline workers and all others who have sacrificed their lives daily for humanity. We equally acknowledge all the victims of the police brutality worldwide. We also acknowledge the protestors who defy all odds. We express our heartfelt thanks to DIO Press for the opportunity to come to voice. We thank all the individual contributors for their diligence and patience and devotion to excellence.

Suleyman M. Demi and George J. Sefa Dei

Toronto, July 2020.

ENDORSEMENT

This is a compelling collection of insightful essays about the vicious pervasiveness of colonialism, but also about the persistent and creative resistance to colonialism. This gives us much hope that this ugly beast will finally be tamed and neutralized so that the world's wretched can begin or continue healing.

Ama Mazama, Professor of Africology, Temple University

Theorizing the anti-colonial presents a rigorous and thoughtful examination of the multiple forms of violence of colonialism, issuing a powerful call to interrupt colonial practices and investments that sustain this violence today. The book invites readers to confront harmful geographies and practices of colonialism and to build anti-colonial relational responsibilities that can resist the colonial economies in everyday life.

Vanessa Andreotti,

Professor and Canada Research Chair in Race, Inequalities and Global Change, Department of Educational Studies, University of British Columbia

Situating anti-colonial theory, pedagogy and praxis as a pathway to realize the goal of decolonization, contributors to this project provide diverse interventions that push forward this important groundwork. At a time where the destructive legacies of colonialism and racism are felt globally, this timely collection attends to these challenges and offers ways to imagine alternative futures.

Jasmin Zine, Professor, Wilfrid Laurier University

Table of Contents

Chapter One

Reframing the "Anti-Colonial" for New Futures: An Introduction

George J. Sefa Dei and Suleyman M. Demi

George Dei remembers an encounter with his dad growing up in Ghana. His late father, a soldier in the British colonial army who fought in India, always had stories to share regarding his sojourn in the army. He would couple his stories in Burma, India with the stories of Africa's anti-colonial nationalist leaders and the struggles for Independence from the "Whiteman." Even at that time it was not difficult for a son to identify with the heroism of the "anti-colonial" thinkers and activists. To be anti-colonial has always been a badge of honor for those fighting against European tyranny, oppression and injustice. The Whiteman was associated with colonialism, and one cannot fight African colonialism without being anti-colonial. Colonialism has always been a plaque upon all houses. This was an important lesson that was to live with many of us in later years. Through time we have learned how colonialism manifests itself in several forms and strands besides an occupying imperial force on other people's lands. Colonialism has been a virus that is difficult to cure. Colonialism has been a brutal force of human encounters. There is a saying that "the more things change the more they remain the same!" Arguably, what has not changed is the knowledge that colonialism and anti-coloniality are powerfully intertwined. This is the story of the anti-colonial struggle.

A number of subversive writings have revealed the links between colonialism and anti-colonialism, highlighting important points of convergence and divergence in these contested knowledges. Radical intellectual thought has sought to present an anti-colonial discursive framework as fundamentally about questions of philosophy, theory, and method (Dei & Kempf, 2006; Dei & Lordan, 2016; Maldonado-Torres, 2017; Dyke, Meyerhoff, & Evol, 2018). The links between Indigeneity and anti-colonialism have also been articulated to critique learning spaces in the search for new academies and educational futurity (Cannon, 2012; Dyke, Meyerhoff, & Evol, 2018; Fast & Drouin-Gagné, 2019; Grande, 2004; Simpson, 2007; Tuck & McKenzie, 2014; Smith, Tuck, & Yang, 2019). There is an emerging global epistemic resistance that sheds light on the curricular and pedagogical challenges, as well as possibilities of anti-colonial praxis, for decolonial solidarity. A current preoccupation in the pursuit of the anti-colonial is engaging in the grammar of decoloniality (Christie & McKinney, 2017; Mignolo, 2011, 2009, 2000; Mignolo & Walsh, 2018; Ndlovu-Gathsheni, 2015). The anti-colonial language of global human struggles asserts the significance of Land, difference, identity, subjectivity, and representation. Land and the cartographies of knowledge reveal the complex impacts of colonialism and settler colonialism in local and Indigenous populations (Cannon, 2011; Cannon & Sunseri, 2018; Tuck & Yang, 2012; Smith, Tuck & Yang, 2019). In seeking to flesh out the philosophical and practical underpinnings of anti-colonial theory and praxis for contemporary times, our goal is to reflect on new thinking that centers the question of Land, cartographies of Indigeneity, and spirituality in the understanding of anti-colonialism.

In this work we articulate the convergences of the "anti-colonial" and the "decolonial." It is argued that the anti-colonial is a path to follow to reach a decolonial end. While it may appear "impossible" to reach that end, we are hopeful that we can reach it eventually. We anticipate difficulty; however, the journey can be faster if we recognize that no one has ever been decolonized. Thus, we must examine new decolonial and anti-colonial futurities through counter-hegemonic knowledge practice that heralds the significnace of dreams, visions, and spiritual praxis to frame new educational futurities for learners (Dei, 2018; Sium, 2014; Snaza et al., 2014). In seeking to reframe the anti-colonial praxis, we take up theory and knowledge as weapons of change with an insistence that there is a place for the intellectual warrior in combat. The psycho-existential realm has been and must continue to be a good starting point for anti-colonial re-theorizing. In fact, Fanon's thoughts on the "psycho-existential contradictions of colonialism" (Robinson, 1993, p. 79) offers an opening for understanding human social realities. If the colonized body is "an essentially pathological personality" (Robinson, 1993, p. 80), how do we reclaim our humanity with an anti-colonial praxis steeped in our intellectual, spiritual, and political awareness of self and community? There is the enduring problem of cultural and intellectual alienation of the colonized/colonial subject that requires we insist on the urgency of an anti-colonial project to ensure the "dis-alienation" of the human soul (Dei & Jaimungal, 2018).

Anti-colonial is about social practice. It is also about communities and differences. Making claims of community and difference is contradictory but rather empowering. Making such claims serve to reinforce an understanding of difference as not monolithic. Similarly, what we claim as "community" is also an amalgamation of differences. But such a practice of claiming community and difference must be political. We must theorize anti-colonial in ways that does not conflate race, class, gender and colonialism, but rather emphasize a more sophisticated analysis of intersections, while maintaining the relative autonomy of race/gender/sexuality/class, etc. We note that some "postcolonial" scholars with good intentions sometimes fall into the trap of unilateral difference—as if the world is all about individual expressions, what we each choose to do, and the recognition of our individual differences. We exist within communities and collectivities. As individuals we are scripted by communities we belong or identify with even as we continually exercise our individual agencies. Therefore, we must understand the broader macro-political structures that undergird and script us all even as we resist. Clearly, as anti-colonial scholars, we need to be critical of ourselves, our practices, and what these mean in the context of Euro-hegemony and White supremacy that define Euro-modernity (e.g., conceptions of Western beauty as standards of global beauty).

No knowledge is apolitical, and the places from which we theorize our knowings are not neutral spaces. Politics, desires, location, history, and contexts shape our coming to know. Arguably, postmodern and post-colonial theories and modes of thought dominate the (Western) academy. Such thinking has been viewed as "critical" thinking for surviving academia. These prisms and discursive frames also offer a measure of the "intellectual validity" or prowess of knowledge that is judged as "scholarly." We want to interrupt this reading! We need to be mindful of the moments when oppositional discourses are erased, denied, or discredited. We need to be aware of the dangers of fitting different frameworks (sometimes incompatible frameworks) (e.g., Indigenous/anti-colonial) into Western prisms or lens that only serve to reify Eurocentricity. In today's neoliberal context, there is much clamor for the globalizing of "education for all," yet we are haunted by the "global coloniality" of race: that is, the way race materially, ideologically, and politically organizes our present world (Escobar, 2004; Grosfuguel, 2007). Dei (2018) notes that anti-colonial and decolonial lessons point to the relevance of explaining social life in multiple ways. These lessons also point to the power of political advocacy and the ways to imagine the possibilities of new futures and new worlds. As Shultz (2015) has noted, referencing the works of decolonial theorists such as Mignolo (2000, 2009), Odora Hoppers and Richards (2011), and Santos (2007), "the deep onto-epistemic divide created by colonialism as an *abyssal line,* where knowledge of any significance to humanity was seen to exist only in the 'Western' mind" (p. 97) is still a challenge for us to deal with. Many of these pioneering writers of the anti-colonial would argue that in decentering the Western hegemony of knowledge production we must "make visible those epistemologies hidden by colonialism" (Odora Hoppers & Richards, 2011, p. 97). But how is this possible when other bodies of knowledge are denied or there is a dominant center that continually insists on having all the intellectual space onto itself? We must take up anti-colonial theory for its multiple epistemes and cartographies of knowledge, so as to produce, validate, and sustain counter-hegemonic and oppositional knowledges about our worlds. By shedding light on the visibility and tensions of colonialism and resistance, on the visibility and tensions of the experiences of race, gender, different sexualities and class backgrounds, we subvert the "normal" and taken-for-granted knowledges. Similarly, pointing to the visibility of material and spiritual consequences for learners who embody multiple and different knowledges, educators and critical social and community workers can begin to reshape the hegemonic structure of education and our institutions, and also demonstrate the power of thinking "outside the box" (Dei, 2018).

We begin with a simple question: What is colonialism, and how do we understand the mechanics and poetics of colonization? This question is important to examine because it does shape how we approach anti-colonial praxis. While colonialism is not a historical accident but something that was well-planned, it is also not an event or a mere occurrence. Colonialism is a system with social and institutional legacies. Colonialism was not uniform across geographical spaces in nature, context, time, space, and impact. But the different colonialisms speaking to specific geographies share certain ideas in common. While we cannot argue for a uniform theory of colonialism or colonization, we can draw the convergences and synergies of colonialism and colonization across multiple spaces and boarders to inform anti-colonial practice. Elsewhere the "colonial" has been conceptualized as more than "foreign" or "alien" to include anything "imposed" and "dominating" (Dei, 2000; Dei & Asgharzadeh, 2001). The practices through which colonialism as a system allowed an imperial occupying force to exercise its control and domination of local peoples is the process of colonization. Colonialism is ongoing and its consequences are felt in all human societies. Many of us have never known a world outside of colonialism. Colonialism was and is a process with an ongoing afterlife. Colonialism and colonization are tied in terms of the undistinguishable binding of imperial force and the impact of its power. This explains why we use the two terms interchangeably. If colonialism is a system, then colonization is a process to achieve desirable outcomes of the system. Colonization is also ongoing. But to answer the question we posed earlier, we strategically rely on the writings of anti-colonial theorist Aimé Césaire to situate the contributions this book makes to the existing literature.

We have been in conversations where the question is asked whether colonialism brought some benefits to colonized peoples. Not only do we find such a question not worthy of answers, we also doubt the question has any merits at all, for we believe the disasters of colonialism are there for all to see. It is important to quote at length Césaire (2001) in his *Discourse on Colonialism* to help us understand the many faces of colonization:

> In other words, the essential thing here is to see clearly, to think clearly—that is, dangerously—and to answer clearly the innocent first question: what, fundamentally, is colonization? To agree on what it is not: neither evangelization, nor a philanthropic enterprise, nor a desire to push back the frontiers of ignorance, disease, and tyranny, nor a project undertaken for the greater glory of God, nor an attempt to extend the rule of law. To admit once and for all without flinching at the consequences, that the decisive actors here are the adventurer and the pirate, the wholesale grocery and the ship owner, the gold digger and the merchant, appetite and force, and behind them, the baleful projected shadow of a form of civilization which, at a certain point in its history, finds itself obliged, for internal reasons, to extend to a world scale the competition of its antagonistic economies. (p. 32–33)

There is no ambiguity about colonialism being an evil system. Everywhere, colonization of Indigenous populations was pursued purely for economic interests. The colonizers wanted Land, resources, and material wealth and pursued this desire under the guise of evangelization. In the process, humans were denied their humanity and were made to think of themselves as a "thing," as either property or worthless. This is an undeniable fact. Colonization was about exploitation and brutal force to subject the labor of the colonized for the benefits of the colonizer. Césaire (2001) remarks that "between colonizer and colonized there is room only for forced labor, intimidation, pressure, the police, taxation, theft, rape, compulsory crops, contempt, mistrust, arrogance, self-complacency, swinishness, brainless elites, degraded masses" (p. 42). Césaire (2001) states that colonization was "no human contact, but relations of domination and submission which turn the colonizing man into a classroom monitor, an army sergeant, a prison guard, a slave driver, and the Indigenous man into an instrument of production" (p. 42). His mathematical equation that colonization = "thingification" was very apt.

Colonization was about the destruction of economic life and human existence. Césaire (2001) insists that:

> I am talking about natural *economies* that have been disrupted— harmonious and viable *economies* adapted to the Indigenous population—about food crops destroyed, malnutrition permanently introduced, agricultural development oriented solely toward the benefit of the metropolitan countries; about the looting of products, the looting of raw materials. (p. 43)

But clearly the effect of colonization has been more than economic. As a system, colonialism has seeped into mental, spiritual, psychological, and other, physical realms. The consequences of the processes of colonization as revealed in the occupying/imperial force for local communities cannot be diminished with talk of examining its "contributions" to colonized communities. Coming into contact with disastrous outcomes for all local populations. Colonialism can only be seen as an interrupter; it is unproductive even to think of the "positive" aspects of colonization. Colonization, through its processes of restricting human lives, divided communities "rather than colonization really *placed civilizations in contact.* Or, if you prefer, of all the ways of *establishing contact,* was it the best? I answer *no"* (Césaire, 2001 p. 33). In speaking about the effects of colonization, Césaire (2001) raises the double-sidedness of dehumanization. He writes:

> They prove that colonization, I repeat, dehumanizes even the most civilized man; that colonial activity, colonial enterprise, colonial conquest, which is based on contempt for the native and justified by that contempt, inevitably tends to change him who undertakes it; that the colonizer, who in order to ease his conscience gets into the habit of seeing the other man as *an animal,* accustoms himself to treating him like an animal, and tends objectively to transform *himself into* an animal. (p. 41)

This is about the savagery and barbarism of colonialism. The colonizer himself is not left unscathed. Their barbarity is an affront to their own self-worth and basic human decency. Colonialism was never about any "civilizing mission" intended on bringing some value to colonized peoples. We remember colonialism for its inhumanity. We also theorize colonialism to understand the power of the human subject as an anti-colonial Being, one able to bring their own humanity into existence. The lessons of colonialism are not to repeat it. Writing that "I see less clearly the contributions it has made," Césaire (2001) considers the possibilities: "Security? Culture? The rule of law? In the meantime, I look around and wherever there are colonizers and colonized face to face, I see force, brutality, cruelty, sadism, conflict, and, in a parody of education, the hasty manufacture of a few thousand subordinate functionaries, 'boys,' artisans, office clerks, and interpreters necessary for the smooth operation of business" (p. 42). We cannot repeat these evils of the past. We must acknowledge the truths behind the lies of colonialism. Césaire (2001) warns, "I hear the storm. They talk to me about progress, about 'achievements,' diseases cured, improved standards of living" (p. 42). The goal is to divert our attentions away from these inhumane acts. But Césaire (2001) shows no ambiguity and is not fooled: "I am talking about societies drained of their essence, cultures trampled underfoot, institutions undermined, lands confiscated, religions smashed, magnificent artistic creations destroyed, extraordinary *possibilities* wiped out" (p. 43). The theft and lies of colonization were accompanied by its brute force to achieve its full effects.

Decolonization is giving up stolen Lands and property to the rightful owners literally and metaphorically (de Leeuw & Hunt, 2018; Sium, Desai & Ritskes, 2012; Trask, 1991; Tuck & Yang, 2012). It is regaining our cultures and heritage. We should never be distracted from such struggles for restitution, including repatriations. The colonizers are good at distractions. As Césaire (2001) notes:

> They throw facts at my head, statistics, mileages of roads, canals, and railroad tracks. I am talking about thousands of men sacrificed to the Congo- Océan. I am talking about those who, as I write this, are digging the harbor of Abidjan by hand. I am talking about millions of men torn from their gods, their land, their habits, their life—from life, from the dance, from wisdom. (p. 43)

The denials, negations, erasures, and omissions of colonialism that make its impacts even more profound. Rather than improving human lives, colonization denied life. The colonized have always sought life over death; it is the colonizer who seeks death and destruction. While local populations wanted to live, colonizers had plans to ensure our physical, social, and spiritual extermination. We chose life, and the colonizer chose death for us. The paradox of colonialism is that in seeking life, the colonized is made to desire what the colonizer has but will not relinquish. As Césaire (2001) argues, "the proof is that at present it is the Indigenous peoples of Africa and Asia who are demanding schools, and colonialist Europe which refuses them; that it is the African who is asking for ports and roads, and colonialist Europe which is niggardly on this score; that it is the colonized man who wants to move forward, and the colonizer who holds things back" (p. 46). To the colonizer we are only good for our labor. We do not deserve what we had nor what the colonizer possessed during the colonial encounter. The colonizer deserved what we have and only they get to keep what they have. This is the other equation of colonization: Colonization is evil and is equal to death [Colonization = Evil =Death].

We need to understand these facts about colonialism and colonization to develop intellectual arguments in support of anti-colonial praxis. In the search to reclaim our humanity and life, the colonized cannot demand White/European schools. We must create our own. The colonizer never meets our demands, and we cannot afford to be perpetual dependants on them. This understanding is very important for anti-colonial praxis. For far too long the effects of colonialism are not simply denied, but the colonized have been made complicit in colonizing encounter and ensuing relations. So, we hear a discourse of responsibility and accountability that often leaves the colonizer off the hook. We hear denials of the colonizer/colonized binary with seductive postmodern arguments that we are all colonized and have all become colonizers. While this paradigm is important in a search for collective futures, we must still maintain a critical gaze on the colonial dominant who still wields power, privilege, and position of influence over and above the colonized, irrespective of intersections of class, gender, sexuality, and (dis)ability. This counter-reading maintains a gaze of White supremacy and White supremacist capitalist logics that dictate and determine the terms of social and political engagements. We need a reframing of anti-colonial praxis that can challenge the two prisms or gazes and never leaves the colonial dominant off the hook in a liberal discourse of pluralism, such as the slogans that we are all oppressors, or we have all been oppressed.

Anti-colonialism is an intellectual, spiritual, and political struggle for human life. The colonial violence on human dignity has necessitated a struggle to reclaim our humanity. This response does not mean that we are reacting to or been reactive to the colonizer. It means we are reclaiming our Indigeneities as a necessary process of our own decolonization. The fact of the matter is that local peoples are still living with the conditions and consequences of colonization. Colonization has morphed into new forms, but the effects on communities have been the same. We need a new theory of the mind that helps us not only understand colonialism and colonization, but also to carve a new path to decoloniality. This is the anti-colonial path.

There is an irony in all of this. Given its brutality and inhumanity, why would we want to continue with colonizing relations and colonial practices? Why do we want to possess the inhumanity of the colonizer in our own Being? How do we explain the ongoing processes of colonization of peoples and their Lands? And how have race, gender, class, ableism, sexuality etc., as powerful markers of identity and difference, become entry points for domination and oppression of individuals and groups in our societies today? In recent years, and particularly within academia, there has been a resurgence in anti-colonial theorizing for radical politics. It is also important for us to ask: In what ways are current framings of anti-colonial theory different from previous ones? How are these framings drawing on the convergences and divergences with early theorizing of anti-colonial theory linked with nationalist struggles for independence in the Global South? What new and emerging forms of coloniality and colonial relations inform such debates? How does recent theorizing draw on the synergies of theory and social practice to articulate radical framings of anti-coloniality that center questions of identity, Indigeneity, race, and social difference? These are profound questions for investigations. In moving the discussion further along, we highlight some concrete questions that inform our book: How do we reframe anti-colonial theory as an approach to theorizing issues emerging from colonial and colonized relations in new geopolitical spaces and landscapes? Can we articulate new cartographies of anti-colonial praxis that borrow from local, national, regional, global, and transhistorical lessons? How do we present anti-colonial theory as a subversive pedagogy and instruction for the classroom learner and community activist to bring about educational and social change?

Each of the essays assembled in this collection adds to the growing literature on reframing anti-colonial praxis and the implications for social change and educational transformation. Contributors examine the challenge of articulating anti-colonial theory as "an epistemology of the colonized anchored in the Indigenous sense of collective and common colonial consciousness and the conceptualization of power configurations embedded in ideas, cultures and histories of marginalized communities" (Dei & Asgharzadeh, 2001, p. 299). The essays bring nuanced understanding of global Indigeneities as part of multi-epistemes and anti-colonial pedagogical practice, contending that the pursuit of agency, resistance, and subjective politics through anti-colonial praxis is critical for social transformation. Similarly, the investigation of the power and the politics of knowledging, as well as interrogations of the embedded meaning of social practice and action are all crucial for surviving colonial and colonized encounters. The essays agree on the necessity of identifying the historical and institutional structures and contexts that sustain our intellectual anti-colonial pursuits.

Emerging dialogues see the anti-colonial as intimately connected to decolonization, and by extension, decolonization, cannot happen solely through Western (scientific) scholarship (see Dei, 2016). The coloniality of Western scientific scholarship, and its role in the everyday practices of education, needs to be interrogated. For example, how have schools used Western science knowledge to articulate hegemonic viewpoints that favor dominant interests and goals? How has the school curriculum reproduced colonial relations of schooling through the use of text, pedagogies, and other instructional practices that do not accord agency to Black, Indigenous, and racialized learners? How do the power hierarchies in schools reproduce dominant-subordinate relations? We must look for particular ways educators, researchers, and policy makers can provide anti-colonial education that helps develop in learners and community workers a strong sense of pride, identity, self, and personhood, as well as mutual respect, agency, and empowerment. We must equip learners with critical thinking of anti-colonial praxis to subvert colonial hierarchies embedded in conventional relations of ruling and relations of domination in multiple spaces. We must also re-envision schooling and education to place at their center such values as anti-colonial justice, resistance, and decolonial responsibility. We need new forms of education to respond to emerging challenges of educational futures informed by discourses on the cartographies of Indigeneity, Blackness, and Diasporiac identity formations and subaltern subjectivities. An important contribution we bring to the flourishing anti-colonial debate is the necessity for anti-colonial research methodologies to draw on the connections with Indigenous research practice and approaches in order to generate new knowledge for collective empowerment and existence.

This book presents chapters on wide range of issues in an attempt to re-theorize the anti-colonial. Izza Tahir's chapter highlights her journey in discovering an anti-colonial prism. She traces the journey of shedding her post-colonial intellectual stance for an anti-colonial prism. Tahir examines the experience of her "Native Land," Pakistan as both a colonized, and later, a post-colonial state, arguing that the Islamic revivalist movements that emerged in post-colonial Pakistan should, in fact, be seen as anti-colonial movements. This position is contested by some scholars who paint the Islamic revival as a rebellion against modernity. It has also been seen as re-colonization by local elites and Western powers in pursuance of their own interests. Tahir concludes by drawing out the implications for anti-colonial framings by imagining possible ways of decolonizing and energizing the Islamist revivalist movement as nascent anti-colonial struggle.

Zainab Zafar's paper takes a closer look at science education in most schools today, arguing that such "science knowledge" is not innocent knowledge. She calls for a critical interrogation of the current science knowledge, which is mostly based on Western science. Zafar points out that Eurocentric science has its own culture basis, standards of knowledge production, and processes of knowledge validation. The Western knowledge system has been used to justify historical atrocities, including the negation of the Indigenous knowledges. Thus, Zafar critiques "Science Education" through an anti-colonial discursive framework, arguing that the framework allows for a more nuanced examination of the current practices of "Science Education." The discussion brings a new understanding of "Science Education" through the lens of Indigeneity.

Using Critical Race Theory (CRT) (Crenshaw, Gotanda, Peller, & Thomas, 1996) and the anti-colonial lens (Angod, 2006; Dei & Asgharzadeh, 2001), Hellen Taabu suggests ways of contesting and creating paradigmatic shifts within nursing practices in the Canadian context. She critiques the much-touted Eurocentric concept of "Culturally Competent Care," revealing how nursing is irredeemably colonized and thus in desperate need of decolonization. She interrogates racism in the nursing and healthcare sector, its impact on racialized minorities, and how this undermines the efforts to decolonize nursing. Taabu presents her discursive interrogation as a way to foster resistance and reimagine collective futures in the nursing profession. She contends that this task is a collective responsibility to find different vantage points that inform resistance.

In her chapter, Shamugapriya Thanuja Thananayagam explores how capitalism perpetuates colonial practices in the corporate world through everyday organizational strategies. The author uses her experience as a manager in the corporate sector in Canada and elsewhere in order to bolster her argument on the wrongs of capitalism. The Canadian context shows how settler colonialism is the beginning of capitalism. The author links capitalism to the destruction of the ecology, arguing that depletion of the quality of natural resources such as air, water, soil, and the destruction of the natural habitat as well as the extinction of wildlife are masterminded by capitalism. This chapter is premised on the plight of the planet and how current patterns of consumption of Earth's natural resources pose a threat to global survival. The chapter draws our attention to human colonial projects under capitalism and our collective responsibility to resist global coloniality.

Coly Chau revisits the Afro-Asian Bandung Conference of 1955 to question how it informs contemporary liberation efforts and constructions of Being. It is argued that the Bandung Conference's invocation of Indigenous/local cultural knowledges, expression and embodiment of poetic knowledge, and assertion of decolonial solidarities and futurities, all serve as disruptors to Western and colonial paradigms. Chau reflects on the general lessons from the Bandung Conference, using her present-day experiences in community settings in Toronto.

We cannot talk about colonialism and forget the question of language, which has always been the big question in colonial encounters. In Cherie Daniel's chapter on the English language's futurity in the post-colonial nation state, she asserts that English, as the language of the dominant, has been the standard for identifying success in the Western world. This chapter highlights the power of language to unify or divide people. Drawing upon scholarly works as well as her own experiences as a lawyer, the author discusses language and its meaning in society and educational settings. She shows the ways language has been used as a tool for dominance and for anti-colonial resistance.

In speaking about colonial encounters, lived experiences are important. Arthi Erika Jeyamohan draws upon her personal experience—specifically an encounter at a bar in Toronto—to explore what it means to unlearn in the Western academy. She reflects on the educational experience through: a) unlearning and relearning from an anti-colonialism lens, b) creating spiritual "trialectic space" for learning (Dei, 2012), and c) the significance of creating strategic alliances. From her anti-colonial framework, Jeyamohan brings anti-racism theory into conversations with education, examining "refusals" and their implications for a "politics of refusal" (Simpson, 2017; Wood & Rossiter, 2017). The chapter is significant for the political and intellectual project of de-linking the academy from modernity and coloniality using Indigenous cultural knowledges and the politics of Indigeneity.

The tensions, dilemmas, and contradictions of lived experiences within colonial and colonizing contexts is poignantly addressed in Ciro William Torres-Granizo essay. He argues that once a person is deemed a colonized body, she/he never stops being seen as such. He supports this argument using his personal stories of racialization, alienation, and "thingification" (Césaire, 2001). Torres-Granizo reflects on his personal journeys from the life trajectory of his acceptance in Turtle Land (i.e., Canada), learning three languages, excelling in education inside and outside Canada and earning a university degree, working in menial jobs, achieving Canadian citizenship, and eventually applying for employment. He noted that all his efforts at integration into Canadian society have been met with an endemic refusal. He is left with a sense of hopelessness and despair and a longing to return to Ecuador, his Native Land. But these experiences, together with his anti-colonial gaze on education, have given him a strong sense of the relevance of place in the identity of Indigenous people.

How are current global forces shaping discourses of identity, human survival, and Euro-colonization? In her chapter, Heba Khalife highlights some pertinent questions regarding Arabs and Muslim identity in the West. She examines how the notions of neoliberalism and multiculturalism affect Arabs and Muslims and their claims to an authentic identity. She teases out ways nation state policies perpetuate coloniality. Khalife shows how some Arabs "benefit" from a White supremacist system by becoming complicit in perpetuating the colonial system. Khalife questions the effectiveness of Arabs in anti-oppression, resistance, and decolonization. As a first-generation Lebanese Canadian, Heba Khalife uses her intervention for the purpose of decolonization, questioning herself and others to take responsibility for our complicities and to unlearn our deeply-held thoughts and practices in order to constitute forms of anti-colonial resistance.

The tentacles of Euro-colonizations reach human food security and sustenance measures. Suleyman M. Demi assesses the resistance of Ghanaians against the introduction and commercialization of Genetically Modified (GM) crops in Ghana. Using a qualitative research method, the author interviewed 20 smallholder farmers, one extension officer, and one representative of the Peasant Farmers Association of Ghana. The study critiques the use of GM crops, which were introduced without considering the unique cultural settings, beliefs, and financial status of smallholder farmers in Ghana. The study reveals, among other things, that farmers are worried about the possibility of seed companies taking control of their food systems and about possible neocolonization. Furthermore, farmers complain about their inability to afford "improved seeds," which makes them vulnerable to seed companies. The chapter, therefore, provides insights into the plight of smallholder farmers amidst the introduction of GM crops in Ghana.

In presenting these discussions the goal is to show how the "anti-colonial" is both theorized and experienced in different and divergent contexts, and how such understandings are critical for reframing social movement politics and practice. Understanding the "anti-colonial relation" is about building relational responsibilities as well as undoing our relational investments to upend colonial injustice. To come to the anti-colonial understanding is to take up the philosophical ideas of anti-colonialism and to see how it applies or can be applied to our understanding of the everyday realities of human existence. While we note that doing anti-colonial work is more about social practice, we also maintain that the effectiveness of our practice will depend on how we learn from converging and diverging experiences that are revealed in multiple geo-spaces and Lands. We may each bring different interpretations to anti-colonial theorizing. However, the end goal is to understand and subvert colonial practice; thus we can each see ourselves as contributing to the decolonial end. Colonialism is ongoing and our knowledge of the coloniality of Being and practice from the different social locations must create a powerful understanding that we can resist the geographies of colonization.

References

Angod, L. (2006). From post-colonial to anti-colonial politics: difference, knowledge and R v R.D. S." In. Dei, G. J. S. & A. Kempf (eds.), *Anti-colonialism and education: the politics of resistance*. Sense Publishers, Netherlands, pp. 159-174

Cannon, M. & Sunseri, L. (eds.). (2018). *Racism, colonialism and indigeneity in Canada* (2nd ed). Oxford University Press.

Cannon, M. (2011). Ruminations on red revitalization: Exploring complexities of identity, difference, and nationhood in Indigenous knowledge education (pp. 127–141). In G. Dei (ed.), *Indigenous philosophies and critical education*. Peter Lang Publishing.

Cannon, M. (2012). Changing the subject in teacher education: Centering indigenous, diasporic, and settler colonial relations. *Cultural and Pedagogical Inquiry 4*(2), 21–37.

Césaire, A. (2001). *Discourse on colonialism*. New York University Press.

Christie, P. & McKinney, C. (2017). Decoloniality and "Model C" schools: Ethos, language, and the protest of 2016. *Education as Change Vol. 21*(3), 1–21. https://doi.org/10.17159/1947-9417/2017/2332

Crenshaw, K., Gotanda, N., Peller, G. & Thomas, K. (eds) (1996). *Critical race theory: The key writings that formed the movement*. The New Press.

de Leeuw, S. & Hunt, S. (2018). Unsettling decolonizing geographies. *Geography Compass*, 1–14. *https://*doi.org/10.1111/gec3.12376.

Dei, G. J. S. (2000). Rethinking the role of indigenous knowledges in the academy. *International Journal of Inclusive Education 4*(2), 111–132. https://doi.org/10.1080/136031100284849

Dei, G. J. S. (2012). "Suahunu," the trialectic space. *Journal of Black Studies, 43*(8), 823–846. https://doi.org/10.1177/0021934712463065

Dei, G. J. S. (2016). Indigenous philosophies, counter epistemologies and anti-colonial education. In W. Lehman (ed.), *Education and Society* (pp. 190–206). Oxford University Press.

Dei, G. J. S. (2018). Reframing education through indigenous, anti-colonial and decolonial prisms. In P. McLaren and S. Soohoo (eds.), *The radical imagine-nation* (pp. 214–235). Peter Lang.

Dei, G. J. S. & Asgharzadeh, A. (2001). The power of social theory: Towards an anti-colonial discursive framework. *Journal of Educational Thought, 35*(3), 297–323. https://www.jstor.org/stable/23767242

Dei, G. J. S. and Kempf, A. (eds.). (2006). *Anti-colonialism and education: The politics of resistance.* Sense Publishers.

Dei, G. J. S. & Lordan, M. (eds.). (2016). *Anti-colonial theory and decolonial praxis.* Peter Lang.

Dei, G. J. S & Jaimungal, C. (eds.). (2018). *Indigeneity and decolonial resistance: Alternatives to colonial thinking and practice.* Myers Educational Press.

Dyke, E., Meyerhoff, E. & Evol, K. (2018). Radical imagination as pedagogy: Cultivating collective study from within, on the edge, and beyond education. *Transformations: The Journal of Inclusive Scholarship and Pedagogy, 28*(2), 160–180. https://doi: 10.5325/trajincschped.28.2.0160.

Escobar, A. (2004). Beyond the Third world: Imperial globality, global coloniality and anti-globalisation social movements. *Third World Quarterly, 25*(1), 207–230. DOI: 10.1080/0143659042000185417

Fast, E. & Drouin-Gagné, M.-E. (2019). We need to get better at this! Pedagogies for truth telling about colonial violence. *International Journal of Child, Youth and Family Studies 10*(1), 95–118 https://doi: 10.18357/ijcyfs101201918808

Grande, S. (2014). *Red pedagogy: Native American social and political thought.* Rowman & Littlefield Publishers, Inc.

Grosfuguel, R. (2007). The epistemic colonial turn: Beyond political economy paradigms. *Cultural Studies, 21*(2), 211–223. DOI: 10.1080/09502380601162514

Maldonado-Torres, N. (2017). On the coloniality of human rights. *Revista Crítica de Ciências Sociais, 114,* 117–136. https://doi: 10.4000/rccs.6793.

Mignolo, W. (2000). *Local histories/global designs: Coloniality, subaltern knowledges, and border thinking.* Princeton University Press.

Mignolo, W. (2009). *Darker side of Western modernity: Global future, decolonial options.* Duke University Press.

Mignolo, W. D. & Walsh, C. E. (2018). *On decoloniality: Concepts, analytics, praxis.* Duke University Press.

Mignolo, W. D. (2011). Epistemic disobedience and the decolonial option: A manifesto. *Transmodernity, 45–66.* https://doi.org/10.1177/0263276409349275

Ndlovu-Gathsheni, S. J. (2015). Decolonization as the future of Africa. *History Compass 13*(10), 485–496.

Odora Hoppers, C, & Richards, H. (2011). *Rethinking thinking: Modernity's "Other" and the transformation of the university.* UNISA Press.

Robinson, C. (1993). The appropriation of Frantz Fanon. *Race and class, 35*(1), 79–91. https://doi.org/10.1177/030639689303500108

Santos, B. D. S. (2007). Beyond abyssal thinking: From global lines to ecologies of knowledges. *Review XXX*(1), 45–89. https://www.jstor.org/stable/40241677

Shultz, L. (2015). Decolonizing UNESCO's Post-2015 education agenda: Global social justice and a view from Undrip. *Postcolonial Directions in Education, 4*(2), 96115. https://www.um.edu.mt/library/oar/handle/123456789/19921

Simpson, A. (2007). On ethnographic refusal: Indigeneity, "voice" and colonial citizenship. *Junctures, 9,* 67–80.

Simpson, A. (2017). The ruse of consent and the anatomy of "refusal": Cases from indigenous North America and Australia. *Journal of Postcolonial Studies, 20*(1), 18–33. https://doi.org/10.1080/13688790.2017.1334283.

Sium, A. (2014). Dreaming beyond the state: Centering indigenous governance as a framework for African development. In G. J. S. Dei & P. B. Adjei (eds.), *Emerging perspectives on 'African development': Speaking differently* (pp. 63–82). Peter Lang.

Sium, A., Desai, C. & Ritskes, E. (2012). Towards the 'tangible unknown': Decolonization and the Indigenous future. *Decolonization: Indigeneity, Education & Society 1*(1), I-XIII.

Smith, T. L, Tuck, E., & Yang, K. W. (eds.). (2019). *Indigenous and decolonizing studies in education: Mapping the long view.* Routledge.

Snaza, N., Appelbaum, P., Bayne, S., Carlson, D., Morris, M., Rotas, N… & Weaver, J. (2014). Toward a posthumanist education. *Journal of Curriculum Theorizing, 30*(2), 39–55.

Trask, H.-K. (1991). Coalition-building between Natives and non-natives. *Stanford Law Review, 43*(96), 1197–1213. https://doi: 10.2307/1229037

Tuck, E., & McKenzie, M. (2014). *Place in research: Theory, methodology, and methods.* Routledge.

Tuck, E.. & Yang, W. K. (2012). Decolonization is not a metaphor. *Decolonization: Indigeneity, Education & Society, 1*(1), 1–40.

Wood, P. B. & Rossiter, D. A. (2017). The politics of refusal: Aboriginal sovereignty and the Northern Gateway pipeline. *The Canadian Geographer, 62*(2), 165–177. https:// doi.org/10.1111/cag.12325

Chapter Two

From Post-colonial to the Anti-colonial: Decolonizing the Re-colonized Anti-colonial in Pakistan

Izza Tahir

Introduction

This is a travelogue. It is a chronicle of my journey—still underway— in transitioning from a post-colonial academic-in-training towards adopting a more anti-colonial stance in my thinking and my work. In charting this journey, I will begin by positioning myself as a colonized body that has been firmly entrenched, because of my personal and academic experiences, in a post-colonial discursive framework. I will then document my transition away from this framework towards an anti-colonial one, which came with the realization that such a transition required a 'return to my native Land': a quest to rediscover my Indigeneity, my identity, my language, and my roots, from which, I recognized, I had been gradually alienated. As I started on this quest and began to explore my history and cultural past—in a new light this time—I began to ask questions of myself for which I initially had no answer. For example, given my colonial history, why did I subscribe to a post-colonial view rather than an anti-colonial one? Why did I not realize that I was still being colonized, and why have I not, until now, been exposed to anti-colonialism? This led to a shift in my gaze towards my literal native Land, Pakistan, and my musings coalesced into the overarching questions guiding this chapter: Given the colonial history of my country, why is there very little recognition of continuing coloniality in the public consciousness in Pakistan, and why are there no visible stirrings of anti-colonialism, especially in education, as in other post-colonial states?

To obtain some semblance of an answer, I explored the colonization of education in colonial India and post-independence Pakistan. This brief exploration, as documented in this paper, revealed that there *was*, in fact, an anti-colonial movement at work in Pakistan. Moreover, it had been active even during British colonial rule, preceding the actual decolonization of the Indian subcontinent into independent India and Pakistan. This anti-colonial movement took the form of a movement for Islamic revival. Today, Islamic revivalist movements take a shape vastly different from those of the colonial era, but their aims are essentially the same: freedom from Western hegemony over education, the economy, and other aspects of social and cultural life, and a return to the Indigenous Islamic way of life.

I will argue that the reason Islamic revival is not automatically recognized as an anti-colonial movement but painted instead as a rebellion against (Western) modernity, is because it has been re-colonized by the local elites who, by virtue of aligning themselves with the Western powers in order to serve their own goals and agendas, have assumed the role of the colonizer that was left vacant by the British when they "granted" independence to Pakistan. I discuss this re-colonization, not only of "my native Land," but also of myself, as a product and reflection of this land, and conclude by imagining possible ways of decolonizing and energizing this anti-colonial movement.

Post-Colonial Beginnings

This chapter is the result of a course I took on *Anti-colonial Thought and Pedagogical Challenges* at the Ontario Institute for Studies in Education of the University of Toronto (OISE/UT), in 2018. I came to this course as a post-colonialist. The reasons for this self-identification were twofold. First, I had grown up in a newly independent post-colonial state. Pakistan's colonial past was recent enough that our grandparents were able to tell us many first-hand stories of life under colonial rule. The remnants of colonialism, from the structure of our economic, legal, political, and educational systems down to the naming of our roads, hospitals, and educational institutions after 'distinguished' colonialists, were still present in enough detail for me to catch glimpses of the old colonial order.

This colonial heritage played a significant role in my education. As I started school at the age of three in Montessori, I was taught popular nursery rhymes in English instead of my native language of Urdu. I sang "London Bridge is Falling Down" without having ever seen a bridge; I sang "Rain Rain Go Away" living in a semi-arid climate; I sang "Hot Cross Buns" having no clue what these were; and I sang "Ringa Ringa Rosies" not realizing for years that the poem was in fact "Ring a Ring o' Roses." This emphasis on English at the expense of Urdu remained to be the case throughout my elementary and secondary education, with the result that today, I am more proficient in English than I am in Urdu. This was the case with other forms of Indigenous knowledge as well. It is difficult to overstate the role that the religion of Islam plays in Pakistani society, envisaged as it is as an all-encompassing way of life, and yet, in mainstream education, both in the public as well as private sectors, it is relegated to a single class on *Islamiyat*, or Islamic Studies. I had not yet realized that the colonizer's attacks on the language and identity of the colonized are strategic, as it is through Indigenous languages and identities that the possibility of new futurities and solidarities are envisaged. The colonizer consciously aims to take away the identity of the colonized, to make it a site of contestations. My Indigenous identity *was* taken away. As I stand today, I am alienated from my language, my culture, and my religion. I have lost my authentic self. I feel dismembered, adrift.

I thus grew up as a colonized body. However, for a long time, I simply accepted this as the burden of belonging to a post-colonial state, and hence identified as a "post-colonial" in its most literal sense. I did not realize that I was, in fact, being re-colonized through my education. For instance, I completed my elementary and secondary education in an elite private school which had adopted the British system of education. Thus, I acquired my Ordinary and Advanced Level certifications (O' and A' Levels) through the external education program of the University of Cambridge in the United Kingdom. At the time, I was not aware that this example of the export of education was, in fact, a new form of colonialism, enforcing and maintaining the geopolitical hegemony of Western knowledge production. Education has always been a tool *par excellence* of colonization. Colonization is achieved through the imposition of certain ideas and practices with the end of achieving a complete colonization of the mind and body. And what better tool to colonize the mind than the education system?

It was also during my O' and A'Levels that I was introduced to post-colonialism as a prominent theoretical concept in the humanities and the social sciences. I studied English Literature at both the O' and A'Levels, and as I read authors such as V. S. Naipaul, Arundhati Roy, and Salman Rushdie alongside William Shakespeare, Charles Dickens, and Jane Austen, I unquestioningly accepted their position in the Western literary canon, even though these authors wrote about the South Asian experience. For my undergraduate education, I read Philosophy and English Literature at the University of Toronto. In reading Angod (2006), I thus felt that she was writing not about her own, but rather my, experiences:

> [My] thoughts wandered back to my undergraduate days pursuing an English literature degree. I was very good at critiquing "World Literature" or "Post-colonial Literature," using post-modern theory. For many years I looked forward to doing a Ph.D. in literature…As I think back on my literary studies, it becomes clear just how entrenched the University of Toronto English department is in post-colonial and post-modern thought. (Angod, 2006, p.160)

For indeed it was. It further cemented my thinking firmly in the post-colonial paradigm. At this juncture, however, I must also position myself as part of the privileged elite, and insofar as I have also benefited from colonial mimicry and investments and entitlements, especially in my education, I acknowledge *my* complicity in these projects of neo- and re-colonization.

From the Post-Colonial to the Anti-Colonial

As I thus came to this course as a post-colonialist, I was initially not aware that while there are many convergences between post-colonialism and anti-colonialism, these are in fact different discursive concepts; I assumed that they were, for the most part, interchangeable. Unlike Angod (2006), who began to transition away from post-colonialism because she felt it was too apolitical, my transition began as a result of the appeal of anti-colonialism as an action-oriented philosophy of praxis. At some intuitive level, I had always felt that post-colonialism was too passive; it is well enough to write a novel, or criticize it, for its colonial subject matter, but then what? This is not to say that post-colonialism did not make important contributions, for insofar as it raised important questions about identity, voice, authority, hybridity, "otherness," and the responsibilities of post-colonial intellectuals, it did. However, these contributions were largely intellectualizations and limited to the Western academy, even in the cases where the scholars were originating from post-colonial contexts. Furthermore, the theory itself, with its "referent of 'post' and its dependence on Western philosophies, frames of reference, [and] modes of thought" requires these "intellectuals seeking validation in Eurocentric standards…to refer to works in Western/Europe and America to validate and legitimize discourse" (Dei, 2006, p. 16). It demands that "resistance to and reformulation of colonialism be performed in particular ways that re-inscribe the veracity of and the need for a post-colonial scholarship" (Angod, 2006). Angod (2006) is then correct in suggesting that "post-colonialism is the colonization of anti-colonialism" (Angod, 2006, p.164).

It was essentially the exercise of juxtaposing post-colonialism with anti-colonialism that served to highlight, for me, the limitations of the former and the possibilities of the latter. The first, and perhaps biggest, limitation of post-colonialism is the suggestion, as implied by the prefix, that colonialism has come to an end, and now we, scholars (largely of the Western academy), may go back and analyze it as a discrete historical phenomenon. It reads colonization as "direct colonial occupation and rule, and the transition to 'post-colonial' is characterized by independence from direct colonial rule, [and] the formation of new nation states" (Hall, 1996, p. 248), which is the reading that I had also subscribed to. Second, it is antifoundational in that it is unable to adequately explain phenomena like capitalism and is often unwilling to engage in a discussion of capitalist globalization (Hall, 1996). It is similarly unable to adequately account for a broader world beyond the configurations of identity and subject. Third, it has universalizing and totalizing tendencies emerging from its post-modernist insistence on specificities, historicities, and particularities, which results in its inherent anti-essentialism itself becoming a form of essentialism, and a descent into a nihilistic and relativistic abyss. Fourth, it also does not adequately address the embeddedness of race and class in the colonial nation-state; and fifth—perhaps most significantly—by implicating all in the colonial project, it implicates none, thus absolving everyone from the responsibility of colonization and dissolving the politics of resistance (Hall, 1996). This in itself is perhaps what accounts for its espousal and privileging by the Western academy (Hall, 1996) at the expense of theories such as anti-colonialism, which is not afraid to clearly identify complicity, blame, and responsibility. Its very ubiquity has also led it to become "confusingly universalized: there is undoubtedly some careless homogenizing going on, as the phrase has caught on and become widely and sometimes inappropriately applied" (Hall, 1996, p. 246).

In contrast, the fact that anti-colonialism is both theoretically-informed as well as action-oriented appealed to me. I liked the anti-colonial focus on building communities of solidarities, comprised of bodies who are cognizant of difference, as part of imagining new futurities, which the project of colonialism, with its destruction of communities and Indigenous identities, interrupted. I liked its emphasis on returning to the past—reclaiming it, embracing it, learning from it—as part of looking toward the future. I liked its unending-ness, its resolve to always keep resisting and fighting until colonialism, in all its myriad forms of domination and control, is no more and a decolonized future is ours. I liked its inherent and raw anger, which even the concept of decolonization lacks in its frequent portrayal in a fetishized light—as a seductive historico-political fantasy. I liked its "calls for agency and resistance" against "subordination and domination" (Dei, 2006, p. 15). Above all, however, I liked the fact that it "challenges any form of economic, cultural, political and spiritual dominance. It is about identifying and countering all forms of colonial domination as manifested in everyday practice, including individual and collective social practices, as well as global interactions" (Dei, 2006, p. 7). In the case of a person with a fragmented identity such as myself, it provides the tools for analyzing the "experiences of Indigeneity, migration, post-migration, agency, resistance, and the reclamation of multiple identities and representations informing our understandings of the colonized subject" (Dei & Lordan, 2016, p.vii-viii).

Returning to My Native Land

As I gradually came to align myself with the anti-colonial discursive framework in my thinking and my work, I soon realized that anti-colonialism requires claiming one's identity in an Indigenous context, because unlike post-colonialism, it is rooted in difference and context; it is "an epistemology of the colonized, anchored in the Indigenous sense of collective and common colonial consciousness" (Dei & Asgharzadeh, 2000, p. 300). Dei and Asgharzadeh (2000) hold that

> such a consciousness emerges from an awareness of the intellectual agency of local subjects as well as from their capacity to articulate their condition in terms of their own geography, history, culture, language, and spirituality. The knowledge so produced can then be used to challenge, rupture, and resist colonial and imperial relations of domination. (p. 302)

It is thus in claiming one's identity as a colonized body that one can take the action that anti-colonialism demands of us. This reclaiming of identity necessitates a return to the native Land, in the words of the inimitable Aimé Césaire. It requires finding oneself amidst one's roots, culture, language, memories, history, and often, Land. It also requires finding what is missing, what one has lost in the process of colonization and alienation. It requires one to find one's authentic self.

As I embarked on this journey, my thoughts fled to my literal native Land, Pakistan, and my experiences growing up there. I began to ask questions of myself: Why did I never question the post-colonialism that I subscribed to? How did I so passively accept its assertion that our colonization had come to an end? I recognized the neocolonialism at play in Pakistan; why did I not connect the dots between colonialism and neocolonialism? Are there dots to connect? Are they a continuation of the same process with different actors? (Dei, 2006) Why was I never exposed to anti-colonialist movements, with their fierce and active resistance to continuing forms of domination, particularly in education?

Why was I not angry?

The focus of these questions expanded to Pakistan more broadly. I began to wonder at the absence of anti-colonial movements in the country, given its colonial history and its often troubled and deeply dependent relationship with the West. Is the country also stuck in the happy thought that its colonization ended in 1947? In recent years, there have been many movements to decolonize education in several post-colonial as well as settler states. Examples include the "Rhodes Must Fall" movement that began in South Africa in 2015 and spread around the world. Even India, which shared Pakistan's experience of colonization, saw movements to decolonize education, such as the move to teach English "the Indian way" in the state of Maharashtra (Lak, 2000). The marked absence of any such movement in Pakistan was then surprising. Did the people of Pakistan not see the marked and continued influence of their colonial past on their present-day education system, such as the privileging of English and Western pedagogies at the expense of Indigenous languages, cultures and religion? Did they not find these problematic? Did they not see the influence of the new colonizers, the bi- and multi-lateral donor agencies like the UN, the World Bank, the USAID and DFID and international non-profit organizations, who freely promote their own neoliberal education agenda in exchange for development aid? Why weren't the people angry?

Islamic Revival as Anti-Colonial Resistance

As I began searching for signs of anti-colonialism in Pakistan, I soon realized that there *was*, in fact, a very active and robust anti-colonial movement in place. Furthermore, this movement predates Pakistan's decolonization from British rule. This is the movement for Islamic revival, which opposes Western hegemony over the social, cultural, religious, politico-economic, and educational spheres, and agitates for a return to an Islamic way of life. The following is a brief history, and an overview of the current incarnations, of this movement.

The movement for Islamic revival in colonial India arose as a direct response to three key education policies with which the British sought to colonize their Indian subjects. British colonial rule in India can be divided into two periods, the first from 1767 to 1857 under the dominion of the East India Company, and the second under the direct rule of the British Crown until the partition of the Subcontinent into India and Pakistan in 1947. In a 1792 report, Charles Grant, the Chairman of the East India Company, advocated a policy of "downward filtration," which argued that the provision of English language instruction and Western education to local elites would eventually result in the civilizing message reaching the masses. His advocacy was successful, and the 1813 Charter of the Company placed responsibility for education in India on the Company and required the teaching of English alongside Indigenous languages. By 1835, there was a broader debate going on in Britain between the value of Western education and English as opposed to the value of traditional education and Indigenous languages. In 1835, Lord Thomas Macaulay, a prominent politician, produced his famous Minute on Education, which became the deciding voice in this debate, tipping the scale in favor of Western education, and leading to the passing of the Education Act of

1835. The Education Act of 1835 essentially allowed for a reallocation of the funds that the Company was required to spend on education in India according to new priorities. This policy resulted in funding being directed toward secular Western subjects, with English as the medium of instruction, and the immediate discontinuation of government support to *madrassas* (traditional Islamic schools) and other traditional educational institutions as well the publication of books in Indigenous languages like Sanskrit and Arabic. This Act became a watershed in the history of education in India and paved the way for policies such as the replacement of Persian by English in 1835 as the official language of India (Riaz, 2008, 2010; Qadir, 2013).

The second key policy was the 1854 dispatch sent by Sir Charles Wood, Chairman of the Board of the East India Company to the Governor-General of India. This was the result of an inquiry into the state of education in India conducted by the British Parliament as part of the renewal of the charter of the East India Company in 1853, which found the policy of downward filtration to have achieved only limited success. The dispatch instead proposed a new scheme for organizing education from the primary to the university level under the government's responsibility and proposed a transformation of Indigenous schools in India into Western-style institutions through funding and grants-in-aid. It also recommended the use of English-language instruction at higher education levels, although it allowed for Indigenous languages to still be used at primary levels. This dispatch essentially formalized and Westernized education in India. Government-sponsored education became secular, English-language instruction proliferated and the structure and organization of educational institutions changed permanently. After India came under the direct rule of the British Crown in 1857, the Western system of education became even more widespread. This paved the way for the third key policy intervention, which had also been recommended by Wood: the establishment of three universities in 1857 in Calcutta, Madras, and Bombay modeled on the University of London, which again served to formalize a secular, Western model of higher education in India (Qadir, 2013; Riaz, 2008, 2010).

As education in colonial India became increasingly secular and Westernized and traditional educational institutions such as *madrassas* began to be marginalized through the lack of government support and funding, Muslims began to establish their own institutions of higher education in response. In 1866, a group of religious scholars established a madrassa at Deoband, partly as a reaction to the growing interest of Muslims in European education and partly "as a center of Islamic revival in India in opposition to British imperialism" (Qadir, 2013, p. 132). It rejected Western education and pedagogy and advocated a return to traditional Islamic higher education as a form of colonial resistance. Although the Deoband madrassa was not the only such institution, it became an important center of Islamic revivalist thought, and its legacy can be traced to this day in the form of the powerful Deobandi sect of Islam in present-day Pakistan and Afghanistan, which counts many factions of the Taliban among its adherents.

It is beyond the scope of this paper to trace the descent of this Islamic revivalist movement to present-day Pakistan in detail. It will suffice for present purposes to identify the key figures and successor movements. One such key figure was Sir Mohammad Iqbal (1877–1938), an anti-colonial poet, philosopher, politician, barrister, and academic who is today widely revered as the "National Poet" of Pakistan for having inspired the Pakistan Movement and calling for an independent nation-state for Muslims (Raja, 2006). In 1930, he became the "first Muslim scholar and politician to delineate the physical boundaries of a future Muslim nation-state in India" (Raja, 2006, p. 149). Iqbal possessed "a deep knowledge of his own tradition and history along with a formidable knowledge of Western systems of thought, history and politics," and with this necessary arsenal he "offer[ed] the most formidable philosophical challenge to the dominant West" (Raja, 2006, pp. 135–36). In his poetry and other literary works, Iqbal takes it upon himself to complicate the benevolent view of the West, by highlighting its darker side [such as imperialism, secularism, materialism, and class system]. It is this challenge to West's claim to a civilizational and moral superiority that comes across as his complete distrust of the West [*sic*]. (Raja, 2006, p. 138)

One of Iqbal's most famous poems is the *Iblees Ki Majlis-e-Shura* (*The Parliament of Satan*), which is a "scathing criticism of the major socio-political and economic systems offered by the West" (Raja, 2006, p. 140). The poem is presented as a debate between Satan and his advisors, where Satan boasts of his achievements and his advisors remind him of the threats to his system, which are the various Western systems of governance and socio-economic ordering. Satan can refute all of these except one; he concedes that perhaps the one threat that can undo his entire empire is the resurgence of Islam. For this was Iqbal's key message: the future of Muslims depends upon a revival of their own Indigenous religion and knowledge systems; it "does not just depend on gaining Western knowledge but also by balancing this knowledge against their own tradition" (Raja, 2006, p. 139). This is to be achieved through embodying Islam's dynamic spirit.

After achieving independence in 1947, there have always been two competing forces at play in Pakistani society. One is a Westernizing force, and the other an Islamizing one. In recent decades, the latter in Pakistan has come to particular prominence as a result of the Western War on Terror and Pakistan's difficult involvement in this. Groups such as the various factions of the Taliban, Al-Qaeda, and the Islamic State that operate in Pakistan and employ particularly violent and terroristic tactics have come to represent the face of Islamic revival movements in the country. It is hardly ever questioned whether their use of violence is perhaps necessary because the colonial encounter it opposes is also inherently violent. This will be discussed in more detail below.

A non-violent but equally powerful social movement for Islamic revival is the Al-Huda movement. Established in 1994 by Dr. Farhat Hashmi, a Western-educated scholar, and her husband as a school of religious education for urban women, "Al-Huda's uniqueness lies in the fact that it has been able to make inroads into the middle and upper classes of the urban areas of Pakistan" (Ahmad, 2010, p. 299). Using the *Dars* (lecture/session) as a medium of instruction, the courses cover all aspects of Islamic education. The popularity of the program has been so great that starting with a dozen graduates in 1994, Al-Huda now has branches in all the major cities of Pakistan as well as in Canada, the U.S., and the U.K. It has become a prominent educational movement for Islamic revival among the educated urban middle and upper classes. Al-Huda is reflective of a larger trend in Pakistani society of the upwardly mobile middle classes adopting a more visibly religious identity and embracing Islamic culture and values (Maqsood, 2017).

The Recolonization of the Anti-Colonial

There thus appears, *prima facie*, to be a strong anti-colonial movement in Pakistan. However, to most Pakistanis, even those who are living through it, this does not appear as such. I found this to be initially puzzling: Why are these social movements not perceived to be movements of resistance? I soon realized, however, that this is because they are painted as rebellions against the greater good of the country. These anti-colonial movements have in fact been re-colonized by the local elites.

Because anti-colonialism uses a broad definition of coloniality to cover every form of domination and control, the issue of complicity also becomes complex. At some level, we all become a part of the problem insofar as we, consciously or unwittingly, reproduce the power structures and colonial hierarchies that perpetuate the domination and the multiple colonialisms. In the aftermath of the actual decolonization of a colonized state, however, there is often a power vacuum left behind by the colonizer. Oftentimes, this power vacuum is filled by local elites who take over the role vacated by the colonizer and become explicitly complicit in the ongoing colonization of their people. This is what happened in the case of Pakistan. The country's elite not only appropriated the ruling power but also began to re-colonize the country in support of its own agenda. One way in which this took place was through the immediate re-colonization of the anti-colonial movement of Islamic revival.

This recolonization was achieved in two ways. First, the national elite aligned themselves with the Western global elite and pushed an agenda of development derived from the concept of Western modernity and neoliberalism. Second, they developed an interpretation of nationalism, which subsequently shaped all their policies in the political, economic, and educational spheres, which was at odds with the Islamic revivalist conception of nationalism. Immediately after gaining independence, "[i]nspired by the economic progress of colonial rulers, the leaders of the newly independent [Pakistan] sought rapid economic prosperity and industrial growth…and any platform [in education] averse to modern scientific inquiry was considered suspect" (Bano, 2012, p. 5). The "native elites [thus] used the nation-state to link with the political [educational] and economic projects of Western Europeans [the United States] and private corporations" (Mignolo, 2007, p. 457). Perhaps this was due to the "seduction of achieving worthiness and belonging in the dominant strata of the global community," which fuels the "competition to leave the periphery and belong" but it is also an "integral motor in the reproduction of coloniality" (Shahjahan & Morgan, 2016, p. 94). At any rate, Indigenous forms of education were rejected and the public system of education was modeled on the Western, secular system to produce the workers that the modern economy supposedly required.

In thus interpreting development and modernization according to a European definition of modernity (Escobar, 2004) and pledging allegiance to the global capitalist system, Pakistan's elites essentially maintained and perpetuated the coloniality of power of European and White supremacist logics. The "correct" way to develop and modernize was the one defined by Western powers and their representative organizations such as the World Bank and the UN, which also funded this development. Because the country's education system was co-opted into this project of modernization as well, and stripped of its Indigenous knowledge production, it also came to reproduce the hegemony of geopolitical Western knowledge production, creating hybrid individuals such as myself who are steeped in Western culture but increasingly alienated from their own indigeneity. The underside of modernity is indeed coloniality (Escobar, 2004).

This alienation from one's own cultural knowledge and roots, and the unquestioning adoption of Western modernity and its accompanying epistemologies and Eurocentric curricula in education, also leads to the development of an inferiority complex in the colonized (Dei & Lordan, 2016). This is the psychic/psychological effect of colonization. Seduced by whiteness and the promised Land of modernity, the colonized begin to perceive their own culture, language, and Indigenous knowledges as inferior. I have witnessed this time and time again in Pakistan in my personal life and work in the education and development sectors. I was sent to an 'English medium' school, where the language of instruction was English, because it was perceived to be better. I did my O' and A'Levels because these are now increasingly common certifications in Pakistan, their very ubiquity reflecting "a desire to adopt tools and templates from enterprising, globally competitive [higher education institutions such as the University of Cambridge in the UK] that act as benchmarks, reproducing a competitive geopolitics of knowledge" (Shahjahan & Morgan, 2016, p. 95). I have met parents who insist on their children receiving 'English medium' education, even if it is not financially feasible or geographically possible and despite being presented with research evidence that children, in fact, learn better in their native tongue (Ball, 2014). They believe that learning English will be the key to upward social mobility for their children, and the sad truth is that they are partly correct in this assumption.

This allegiance to a capitalist modernity by the country's elite has resulted in a conflict within the society "between those groups and classes that are integrated into global capitalism and those who are increasingly marginalized by it" (Dirlik, 2006, p. 4). The Western, secular model of education that they have adopted has marginalized traditional and Indigenous Islamic knowledge. Movements such as Al-Huda and the Taliban, the latter often being associated with certain *madrassas*, have arisen in response to this coloniality; they advocate alternative modes of education. However, they have been re-colonized insofar as they are increasingly portrayed as "backward" and a rebellion against the forces of modernization and development. The media is one key tool that is employed to create this portrayal and influence public opinion against them. The constant negative media portrayal, both locally and globally, of movements such as the Taliban have successfully formed the idea in many quarters that these are fundamentalist ideologues who want nothing more than to revert to the dark ages of seventh-century Arabia. The shooting in San Bernardino, California, in December 2015 by one Tashfeen Malik and her husband brought Al-Huda under the media spotlight, as Tashfeen was allegedly linked to the institution, giving rise to media reports such as "Do Al-Huda schools' conservative teachings breed extremism?" (Sagan, 2015), critical and paternalistic analyses by thinktanks such as the Mackenzie Institute (Zahid, 2016), and the closure of an Al-Huda branch in Mississauga, Ontario. The point here is not to condone terror attacks, nor to deny that "[a]nti-colonial projects [also] need to be subjected to critical interrogation," especially those that are oppressive (Dei

& Lordan, 2016). The point is rather that perhaps we need to ask why these reactionaries need to resort to such extreme forms of violence to get their message of resistance across.

The local elites have also used nationalism as a tool to re-colonize anti-colonial resistance. Nowhere is this more evident than in the case of Iqbal. On the one hand, he is revered as the "spiritual father of the country"; his day of birth is celebrated as a national holiday. On the other hand, his very message of anti-colonial resistance has been re-colonized and de-fanged. Specifically, what has been re-colonized is his concept of the nation-state. It is true that Iqbal called for a separate nation-state for Muslims in 1930, and then outlined its geographical parameters in 1932. However, this call was a temporary, tactical measure. Iqbal realized that the need of the hour was a separate nation-state for Muslims. If one looks at his complete oeuvre, however, it is abundantly clear that Iqbal opposed the concept of Western territorial nationalism (Raja, 2006). Instead, he supported, in the longer term, the creation of the Muslim *Ummah*, a pan-nationalistic Islamic community, as a political system. This community of solidarity was to then define its own future for itself.

Iqbal was not just proposing rejection of Western modernity, however; instead, he desired the Muslim community to look within itself, its cultures and knowledges, and forge its own path and alternative worldview. He wanted the Muslims to write back: "[f]or Iqbal then, the Muslim literary production dismantles the house of masters ideas[*sic.*] and offers its own reinvigorated world-view" (Raja, 2006, p. 154). In doing so, the Muslim community will also place itself in a position to make its own contributions to the West, for indeed, Iqbal desired the "East-West exchange [to be] a reciprocal one in which both can share their core values to create a better world" (Raja, 2006, p. 139). He criticized not only the "surface realities of colonialism" but also the "inherent brutalities of western power and knowledge paradigm"; he wanted to move the "native-master relationship" from "apologetic loyalism to philosophical challenge and criticism" (Raja, 2006, pp. 140–41). For Iqbal, then, the alternative to the dominance of the West is a global Islamic system, trans-historical and supranational. Iqbal was, in fact, "militantly opposed" to the form of Western territorial nation-state model that the Pakistani elites have espoused (Raja, 2006, p. 151). This model of nationalism impedes the creation of a global Muslim community and limits the potential of Islamic revival to create an alternative worldview for the Muslims. However, this is the nationalism that the Pakistani elites now promote, in support of their own agendas and goals, and celebrate each year in the name of Iqbal on Iqbal Day. This is the view that shapes the country's policies as well as its history and other textbooks (Sokefeld & Moss, 1996; Chughtai, 2015).

Conclusion

Both my decolonial journey, as well as that of my country, are ongoing. They will remain ongoing as long as there is domination and control. They will require, first, the adoption of a conscious, action-oriented philosophy of praxis that understands the complexity, nature, and mechanics of our oppression. Second, the resistance will have to come from within us: *we* have to empower ourselves. No one is going to give us our freedom; we have to take it ourselves, for ourselves. In the case of Pakistan, the subaltern has to empower itself. It has to reclaim the identity, the indigeneity, that we, as a nation, have lost along the way. We need to turn back to our past, reconcile ourselves with it, learn from it, and reclaim it; only then can we look towards the future. We cannot rely on the local elites or the ruling classes for they have thrown in their allegiances with the Western global elites. They are complicit in the ongoing coloniality of the nation. We need to build our own communities of solidarity so that we can collectively imagine new futurities.

Most importantly, we need to develop our own vision of the future, a new path forward informed by our personal histories and acknowledging the effects on us of our colonial histories. We need to develop a new analytical framework that is rooted in our own Indigenous knowledges, truths, and perspectives, to counter the hegemony of Western epistemological frameworks, as Iqbal inspired us to do. We need to carve out a space for this framework in a world that privileges only certain epistemologies. Only then can we achieve epistemic decolonization. We need to decolonize our education systems, which, like other "institutional structures are sanctioned by the state to serve the material, political and ideological interests of the state and the economic/social formation" because we, the "colonized [have] also the power to question, challenge, and subsequently subvert the oppressive structures of power and privilege" (Dei & Asgharzadeh, 2000, p. 300). We need to write back and tell our own stories, for this is a necessary part of our own decolonization.

We need to define and validate our own modernity and "delink from the dream that if you are not modern you are out of history. Alternative or subaltern modernities claiming their right to exist reaffirm the imperiality of Western modernity disguised as universal modernity" (Mignolo, 2011, p. 279). Islamic revival, as its long history shows us, has the potential to be a viable alternative/subaltern modernity. It has been a direct engagement with Western modernity (Lapidus, 1997), as well as a critique of it, and revivalists have made "significant contributions to both modernity and Islamic thought" by positing multiple modernities and Islamic discourses on development (Sinanovic, 2012, pp. 3–4). We need to explore this further. In his poetry, Iqbal often described the East as the world of *mann* (heart) with *Ishq* (love) as its driving force, and the West as the world of *tann* (body), with *aql* (intellect) as its driving force. In the modern world, we need all four: *mann, Ishq, tann*, and *aql*.

References

Ahmad, S. (2010). Al-Huda: Of Allah and the power-point. In M. Marsden (Ed.), *Islam and society in Pakistan* (pp. 299–326). Karachi: Oxford University Press.

Angod, L. (2006). From post-colonial to anti-colonial politics: Difference, knowledge and R v R.D.S. In G. Dei, & A. Kempf (Eds.), *Anti-colonialism and education: The politics of resistance* (pp. 159–174). Rotterdam (Netherlands): Sense Publishers.

Ball, J. (2014, February 21). *Children learn better in their mother tongue*. Retrieved from Global Partnership for Education: https://www.globalpartnership.org/blog/children-learn-better-their-mother-tongue

Bano, M. (2012). *The rational believer.* Ithaca and London: Cornell University Press.

Chughtai, M. (2015). *What produces a history textbook?* Retrieved from ERIC: https://eric.ed.gov /?id=ED576851

Dei, G. J. (2006). Introduction: Mapping the terrain - towards a new politics of resistance. In G. Dei, & A. Kempf (Eds.), *Anti-colonialism and education: The politics of resistance* (pp. 1–24). Rotterdam (Netherlands): Sense Publishers.

Dei, G., & Asgharzadeh, A. (2000). The power of social theory: Towards an anti-colonial discursive framework. *Journal of Educational Thought,* 297–323.

Dei, G., & Lordan, M. (2016). Introduction: Envisioning new meanings, new memories and actions for anti-colonial theory and decolonial praxis. In G. Dei, & M. Lordan (Eds.), *Anti-Colonial Theory and Decolonial Praxis* (pp. vii–xxi). New York: Peter Lang.

Dirlik, A. (2006). Our ways of knowing--and what to do about them. In A. Dirlik (Ed.), *Pedagogies of the global: Knowledge in the human interest* (pp. 3–18). Boulder (CO): Paradigm Publishers.

Escobar, A. (2004). Beyond the third world: Imperial globality, global coloniality and anti-globalisation social movements. *Third World Quarterly, 25*(1), 207–230. DOI: 10.1080/0143659042000185417

Hall, S. (1996). When was the post-colonial? --Thinking at the limit. In I. Chambers, & L. C. (Eds.), *The post-colonial question* (pp. 242–259). London: Routledge.

Lak, D. (2000, May 17). *Teaching English the Indian way.* Retrieved from BBC News: http://news. bbc.co.uk/2/hi/south_asia/752124.stm

Lapidus, I. M. (1997). Islamic revival and modernity: The contemporary movements and the historical paradigms. *Journal of Economic and Social History of the Orient, 40*(4), 444–460. DOI: https://doi.org/10.1163/1568520972601486

Maqsood, A. (2017). *The new Pakistani middle class.* Cambridge (MA): Harvard University Press.

Mignolo, W. (2007). De-linking: The rhetoric of modernity, the logic of coloniality and the grammar of de-coloniality. *Cultural Studies, 21*(2–3), 449–514. DOI:10.1080/09502380601162647

Mignolo, W. D. (2011). The geopolitics of sensing and knowing: On (de)coloniality, border thinking, and epistemic disobedience. *Postcolonial Studies, 14*(3), 273–283. https://doi.org/10.1080/13 688790.2011.613105

Qadir, A. (2013). Between Secularism/s: Islam and the institutionalization of modern higher education in mid-nineteenth century British India. *British Journal of Religious Education, 35*(2), 125-139. DOI: 10.1080/01416200.2012.717065

Raja, M. A. (2006). *Texts of a nation: The literary, political and religious imaginary of Pakistan.* Retrieved from Florida State University Libraries: https://fsu.digital.flvc.org/islandora/object/ fsu:180380/datastream/PDF/view

Riaz, A. (2010). Madrassah Education in Pre-colonial and Colonial South Asia. *Journal of Asian and African Studies, 46*(1), 69-86. https://doi.org/10.1177/0021909610387758

Riaz, A. (2008). *Faithful education.* New Jersey: Rutgers University Press.

Sagan, A. (2015, December 10). *Do Al-huda schools' conservative teachings breed extremism?* Retrieved from CBC News: https://www.cbc.ca/news/world/san-bernardino-tashfeen-malik-al-huda-school-1.3353888

Shahjahan, R., & Morgan, C. (2016). Global competition, coloniality, and the geopolitics of knowledge in higher education. *British Journal of Sociology of Education, 37*(1), 92–109. https://doi. org/10.1080/01425692.2015.1095635

Sinanovic, E. (2012). Islamic revival as development: Discourses on Islam, modernity, and democracy since the 1950s. *Politics, Religion & Ideology, 13*(1), 3–24. https://doi.org/10.1080/2156 7689.2012.659500

Sokefeld, M., & Moss, C. (1996). Teaching the values of nation and Islam in Pakistani textbooks. *Internationale Schulbuchforschung, 18*(3), 289–306. https://www.jstor.org/stable/43057034

Zahid, F. (2016, May 24). *Understanding the Al-huda ideology.* Retrieved from MacKenzie Institute: http://mackenzieinstitute.com/4852-2/

Chapter Three

Interrogating and Reframing Science Education under the Anti-Colonial Discursive Framework

Zainab Zafar

Introduction

Science played a major role in sustaining hegemonic practices that dehumanize the experience of any race other than white. In 1859, Darwin published his book, *On the Origin of Species,* in which he discussed his belief about the natural order of species. He discussed how the weak die off and the strong will always survive. This concept of evolutionary theory led social scientists to justify racism and genocide of nations (Western States Center, 2003). Winwood Reade, in 1864, published a book *Savage Africa,* in which he proclaimed African people were of weaker race and would be ruled by the Europeans forever (Western States Center, 2003). In 1866, Frederick Farrar, a social scientist, use a way to classify people of savages (Black, Indigenous, and other racialized people, with the exception of the Chinese), semi-civilized (Chinese), and civilized (European, Aryan, and Semitic peoples) (Western States Center, 2003). In 1850, Robert Knox, a famous anatomist, in his book *Races of Man,* stated that race and intelligence were linked, where he classified people of color to be intellectually inferior because of differences in the formation of the brain. It was found later that his conclusion was based on the autopsy of only one man of color (Western States Center, 2003).

The emergence of the Eugenics pseudoscience was used as an effort to breed better human beings by encouraging the reproduction of people with "good" genes and discouraging the "bad" genes (Western States Center, 2003). This pseudoscience and theories led to further dehumanizing of Black, Indigenous people and people of color, leading to the formation of immigration laws, criminalizing of interracial marriage, and brutal implications in the other areas such as the justice system, education system, and daily encounters with people of color (Ihenetu, 2019). The brutal impacts of these concepts and theories still remain relevant today as racism continues to rise and impact the lives of Indigenous, Black, and racialized people, the impact can be seen in the schooling system as well.

Schooling and the educational system have played a significant role in sustaining the hegemonic social, economic, and political interests of the state and the capital (Dei, 2018). The sustaining of hegemonic practices is reflected in the schooling system through the curriculum, textbooks, assessments, and evaluation practices. This is evident in the scientific knowledge taught in schools today. Science education plays a major role in sustaining that oppression by alienating experiences for Indigenous and Black students (Aikenhead & Elliott, 2010; Bauer-Wolf, 2019). The constant silencing of racialized bodies results in the spiritual, emotional and psychological wounding (Dei, 2018). According to Thésée (2006), scientific knowledge taught in schools become an epistemological tool or weapon used to develop, dominate, and shape minds of our students, ensuring success only for a few. As a concerned educator, many questions arise by listening to racialized students and their concerns. Some of the following include:

- Why do schools tend to leave out the historical implications of science that benefited certain bodies?

- Why does school science not recognize contributions, knowledge production, and cultural significance of diverse groups of people?

- Which bodies can validate knowledge produced under the scientific scope?

- Whose knowledge is more valuable? Whose voices are silenced in science?

- Are there multiple sciences, and how do they get manifested?

The Ontario Curriculum of Science and Technology describes Science Education as the following:

> The primary goal of science is to understand the natural and human-designed worlds. Science refers to certain processes used by humans for obtaining knowledge about nature, and to an organized body of knowledge about nature obtained by these processes. Science is a dynamic and creative activity with a long and interesting history. Many societies have contributed to the development of scientific knowledge and understanding. (Ontario Science and Technology Curriculum, 2008, p. 4)

The Science and Technology curriculum clearly states that science is a way of understanding nature and human-designed worlds. It comes from various bodies of knowledge, it has a long and exciting history; its contributions have been from various societies. This definition fails to stand true in current science practices in our schooling systems. It is not enough to have images of developing countries or to have certain racialized scientists to be depicted in science textbooks for inclusivity. If science is a way of knowing nature, then there is a need to include how various cultures have their relationship with nature and how they have survived for centuries without the assistance of Eurocentric scientific development and advancement. Not only will incorporating other ways of knowing science help us towards inclusive education, but it will also help us to investigate how scientific advancements may assist developing nations or oppressed people to fulfill their needs and accessibility to services they deserve. In this chapter, let us explore the following:

- Current Science Education and Challenges Associated with It.

- Interrogating Globalized Science—A Tool of Development or Domination?

- Interrogating Science Curriculum—Eurocentric Knowledge: Where Is the Credit Due?

- Reframing Science Curriculum—Anti-Colonial and Discursive Framework

- Futurities of Science Education—Incorporating Indigenous Ways of Knowing

Positionality

As I write, I'm trying to find my voice. It's not like it's lost or silenced; it's as if I have been mute all my life. (Boisselle, 2016, p. 3)

As a visibly identified Muslim woman of South Asian descent, the above quote resonated with me throughout my life. I came to Canada from Pakistan in my early years of elementary school. Since then, I have been in the education system as a student and now as an educator. It has been quite a journey for me as I moved up in the Western educational institutions while longing to find myself and my inner voice. While growing up, my family stressed the importance of science education. My parents wanted us to survive by attaining education that would bring economic stability. As I enrolled in science courses, my experience of alienation and isolation increased. My high school years were during the time of 9-11, which heightened my experience of alienation due to anti-Muslim racism. These experiences were not only by the encounter of the teacher through a Western gaze but also by how the curriculum, textbooks, and classrooms never reflected my identity. Science courses became a sense of alienation, and I inclined towards my religion as a source of an anchor and resistance.

Zine (2001) states that her research has shown that Muslim students use their religious identities as a means of resistance to counteract their marginality within secular Eurocentric schools. As a result of isolation and alienation, I would turn towards reading spiritual books of Islamic teachings to gain a sense of strength. I remember one saying of Imam Ghazali that got me through my experience "to get what you love, you must first be patient with what you hate" (Meah, 2018).

The year of 2019 has been transformative for me, especially taking Professor Dei's class on Anticolonial Thought and Pedagogical Implication. As I went to each class, I felt a voice was given back to me, a voice of reason that was heard and not silenced, which was respected but not pitied, which was a source of strength and not weakness. I felt my experiences became visible while my soul has injuries that are yet to be healed. But the process has begun. An anti-colonial discursive framework is about starting the process of healing. Giving voice to the silent and visibility to the invisible, an anti-colonial framework is the validation and recognition of knowledge of and by the colonized, which implies being respected and recognized for our strengths.

Science Education and the Challenges

Science Education in our current schooling system does not serve the interest of the Indigenous, Black, and racialized youth for various unfortunate reasons. Students of minority backgrounds feel isolated, excluded, and alienated from science courses. According to the Pew Research Centre, the statistics also show that there is a considerable decline in minority groups in science and engineering, particularly for Black men and women, who make up 9% of STEM workers in the US; and Hispanics, who make up 7%; compared to Asian (13%) and white who make up 69% of the STEM workers (Pew Research Centre, 2018). Some are shocked at these statistics and wonder why we continuously see a lack of minority representation in STEM-related workforce. To varying degrees, most minority students tend to experience school science as a foreign culture (Aikenhead & Elliott, 2010), and as a result, do not see themselves inclined towards continuing science courses.

Aikenhead, as cited in Aikenhead and Elliott (2010) discussed five significant problems associated with the current schooling of scientific knowledge:

a) Students generally continue to devalue Eurocentric science in their world out of school, as there is an alarming decline in enrollment into science courses.
b) School science alienates students from diverse backgrounds whose culture does not represent the Eurocentric background.
c) Students lack a meaningful way of learning science in schools, which is unrelated to their everyday experiences.
d) School science encourages students to pass courses and is geared towards a STEM-related career more than the emphasis on understanding nature.
e) School science is a misleading representation of scientific knowledge production and scientific processes of obtaining scientific knowledge (i.e., scientific method).

If we want success for all students in the STEM field, it must serve as a relevant knowledge in which they see fruits benefiting their people and communities. The STEM education must be geared towards finding solutions for the oppressed, giving voice to them, and allowing them to be active members of the scientific communities. Students will not remain in classes where science is not relevant for themselves or their communities. Let us interrogate the current scientific advancement for the colonized nations and the validity of the Eurocentric sciences.

Interrogating Globalized Science—A Tool of Development or Domination?

Is science a tool of domination, or is it a tool for helping developing nations move toward their advancement? Globalization of science education does a disservice to the colonized nation as it controls their knowledge production and economic growth (Boisselle, 2016). It excludes Indigenous and African sciences that represent a diverse view from the Eurocentric curriculum. It does not investigate advancement or best interests for the oppressed; rather, it furthers and sustains the colonial project by maintaining the hierarchy of Eurocentric knowledge and advancements.

Globalization of science knowledge is viewed as an advancement of the developing world, where the reality is that most of the developing world will continue to suffer from poverty, diseases, and lower literacy rates as the globalized education or Education for All (EFA) initiatives are not geared toward advancing the developed nations. Boisselle (2016, p. 3) puts it

> For instance, even global initiatives such as Education for All (EFA) that focus on developmental goals can be disadvantageous to developing nations. Investigation of the EFA goals reveals a focus on lower levels of education ("Education for All Goals") and a lack of focus on the higher and tertiary level education crucial to the progress of a nation.

The primary focus of the globalization of education is on developmental goals rather than on beneficiary goals for the developing world. It creates competition to ensure that the developing world has equal chances of improving if they work toward the advancement of their science education, which further sustains colonial thinking. Hickling-Hudson (2002, p. 11) observes the fallacy of thinking that "we can magically ensure outcomes such as material sufficiency, harmony, and social cohesion," if only the colonial systems of education are strengthened.

When American and UK-based curriculums are frequently used in schools to allow advancement of colonized society; when colonized nations are used as bodies to be tested on for scientific research; when the future of the colonized nations remains at stake; the question becomes, who is benefiting from these advancements? And what must be done to ensure there is equity in scientific advancement?

In his book *Discourse on Colonialism*, Césaire (1972, p. 8) criticizes the tendency of the colonizer to stand in the way of educational demands of the colonized:

> The proof is that at present it is the Indigenous people of Africa and Asia who are demanding schools, and colonialist Europe refuses them; that it is the African who is asking for ports and roads, and colonialist Europe which is niggardly on this score; that it is the colonized man who wants to move forward, and the colonizer who holds things back.

Where is the advancement and development of the country when it comes to learning science education? Whom does the system of science education end up benefiting? Globalization of science education is questionable; it ensures that colonial systems continue and profit from the labor of people of color. Standardized science testing such as TIMSS, PISA, or PIRLS does not include low-income countries (DeBoer, 2011). How can developing nations compete to test for scientific knowledge when not on equal footing? What does standardized science testing measure? Whose future are we concerned about here? Can standardized testing be measuring the relevance and advancement of colonized nations? All these questions should be asked about when considering how science knowledge and scientific advancement benefit the developing countries. As we work toward advancing scientific knowledge, one must consider the following quote: "No pedagogy which is truly liberating can remain distant from the oppressed by treating them as unfortunates and by presenting for their emulation models from among the oppressors. The oppressed must be their example in the struggle for their redemption" (Freire, 1970, p. 54).

Freire stresses the importance of including the voices of the oppressed in knowledge production. No pedagogy will be genuinely liberating if we repeat the same colonial thinking, reproducing the same structures that exist today. It is knowledge production by the dominant voice, excluding the voices of those that exist as inferior, non-worthy, or the colonized. It is time for us to interrogate the teaching of Eurocentric knowledge.

Interrogating Eurocentric Sciences—Eurocentric Knowledge: Where Is the Credit Due?

Eurocentric knowledge is not the product of Europe alone. Although Europe has made advancements in science, the advancements are not only made by the European or the Western nation (DebRoy, 2018). In an anti-colonial discursive framework, we must move toward giving recognition and validation to the appropriate people who have made significant advancements in the field of knowledge production. For instance, Abu Musa Jabir Ibn Hayyam, (720 – 812 A.C.) introduced an experimental investigation into alchemy, which created modern chemistry today (Salloum, 2016). I do not recall learning Abu Musa Jabir's name in any of my science classes. I did not see any recognition given to scientists who are of diverse backgrounds. If anyone is to question that, ask a high school student, Who does a scientist look like? You will not be surprised if the answers tend to be: "A White male from a European background."

Loss of language is another significant result of colonialism. Many of the European scientists such as Adelard of Bath, Daniel of Morley, Gerard of Cremona, Johannes Campanus, Michael Scott, Philip of Tripoli, Rober of Chester, Stephenson of Saragossa and William of Lunis, would learn Arabic to translate the work of Arab scientists (Salloum, 2016). In fact, all scientific researches were in the Arabic language, which became the universal language of science (Salloum, 2016). During the 12th and 13th centuries, Arabic studies were translated into Latin, which is commonly used in scientific terms today (Salloum, 2016). Nonetheless, British politician Thomas Macaulay denounced Arabic and Indian languages, calling them "barren of useful knowledge" as they lacked scientific terms; he claimed they were known to be "fruitful of monstrous superstitions" and contained false history, false astronomy, and false medicine (DebRoy, 2018).

Through the lens of an anti-colonial discursive framework, one can understand how colonialism is ongoing and continuing with the same mentality that sees the colonized as barbaric, inferior, and worthless. As Charles Darwin implied, "'savage races' such as the Negro and Australian were closer to gorillas than were white Caucasians" (DebRoy, 2018). Yet the interesting part is that Charles Darwin's collection of evidence was from the countries that were colonized, as he rode on the voyages of British exploration and conquest that enabled imperialism

(DebRoy, 2018). Modern science was effectively built on a system of millions of exploited people. At the same time, it helped to justify and sustain that exploitation in ways that hugely influenced how Europeans saw other races and countries (DebRoy, 2018).

How can we move toward the decolonization of science education when we don't see representatives from diverse backgrounds, their contribution to science, and their relationship with nature, plus their Indigenous ways of living? How do we assume that we were not free and knowledgeable and lived peaceful lifestyles before colonialism? One should not forget that these were not only practices of the past and must be forgotten as science has progressed further, but we must also look at the examples of today and how colonialism in science is on a continuous spectrum. The ongoing impact of colonialism in science continues today as most of Asia, Africa, and the Caribbean are still seen as playing catch-up with the developed world, depending on its scientific expertise and financial aid (DebRoy, 2018). The "intellectual domination of the West" continues while seeing other nations as inferior, un-intellectual, and lacking bodies of sound knowledge (DebRoy, 2018). Thus, legitimization, validation, and recognition of knowledge production and dissemination continue to be monopolized by the colonizer.

A study done in 2009 showed that 80% of central Africa's scientific research papers were produced with collaborators based outside the region. Each of these African countries principally collaborated with its former colonizer (DebRoy, 2018). As a result, the knowledge production was in the hands of the colonizer and the dominant collaborated in shaping the scientific work in the region, with credits and acknowledgment going to the dominant collaborator. Even the focus of research depended on the colonizer rather than the local people in the area. Consequently, the need to decolonize science education is further established. The anti-colonial framework would imply recognizing these injustices, giving voice to the colonized and involving them fully in knowledge production and dissemination. It is essential that in our effort to decolonize education, knowledge production be a necessary part of the process. We must recognize its impact.

Anti-Colonial Framework

The anti-colonial framework interrogates the production, validation, and use of knowledge in relation to culture and histories (Dei & Asgharzadeh, 2001). It focuses on the pursuit of agency and community building. One of the critical aspects of the anti-colonial framework is focusing on Indigenous knowledge of the colonized groups. An anti-colonial discursive framework challenges the hierarchical claims of a dominating colonial knowledge. As Dei and Asgharzadeh (2001) point out, the anti-colonial approach recognizes the importance of locally produced knowledge that is generated from cultural history, daily human experiences, and social interactions. They further state that the goal of the anti-colonial framework is to question, interrogate, and challenge the foundation of institutionalized power and privilege and how these benefit the dominant culture (Dei & Asgharzadeh, 2001).

Anti-colonial work gives agency to the colonized, insisting that they, too, have the power to question, interrogate and challenge the status quo. It focuses on creating multiple communities and multicentric knowledge produced by multiple perspectives. Knowledge production is ongoing in an anti-colonial framework

(Dei, 2018). The anti-colonial framework also focuses on the fact that colonialism is not the problem of the past, but an ongoing problem that impacts our society today. The anti-colonial framework emphasizes the importance of colonialism and imperialism plus their continuing effects on marginalized communities in terms of economics, poverty, development, hierarchy in knowledge, and so forth (Dei & Asgharzadeh, 2001). An anti-colonial discursive framework is about creating individuality and communities; part of colonialism is to break down communities. Anti-colonialism is about creating an agency; it is about working together as an ongoing process to create a de-colonial structure. The anti-colonialism framework does not depend on western knowledge and extensions of it but allows communities of colonized groups to form their own knowledge and sustain their intellectual life (Dei, 2018). Anti-colonial praxis is about claiming our identities, which are not reduced to the gaze of a dominant lens. Let us explore the Indigenous teaching of science and ways to incorporate other sciences into the current science curriculum.

Futurities of Science Education—Incorporating Indigenous Ways of Knowing

In her book *Decolonizing Education* Marie Battiste says,

> Imagine how uncertain a person whose success is only achieved by a complete makeover of themselves, by their need to learn English and the polished rules and habits that go with that identity. They are thrust into a society that does not want them to show too much success or too much Indian identity, losing their connections to their land, family, and community when they have to move away as there is no work in their homeland. Assimilation. (Battiste, 2013, p. 23)

The question arises as we reside on the land of Aboriginal people, how do we justify learning only one form of knowledge without meaningful inclusion of Indigenous knowledge? We live in a country where there is a history of colonial oppression upon the colonized. It is incumbent upon educators to bring forth practices from Indigenous teaching; these inclusions must be meaningful and seen as equally important as Eurocentric science. School science overtly and covertly marginalizes Indigenous students by its ideology of neo-colonialism (Ryan, 2008).

Indigenous knowledge "refers to traditional norms and social values, as well as to mental constructs that guide, organize and regulate the people's way of living and making sense of their world" (Dei, Hall, & Rosenberg, 2000, p. 6). School teachers must become aware of the Indigenous science teaching of *coming to know*, a term used to describe the process of developing understanding in Indigenous science (Cajete, 2000). Aikenhead and Elliott (2010) describes the concept of coming to know:

> The Eurocentric meaning of "to learn" becomes "coming to know" in most Indigenous contexts, a meaning which signifies a personal, participatory, holistic journey towards gaining wisdom-in-action. The verb "to learn" fits a Eurocentric framework, while the action "coming to know" assumes an Indigenous perspective. (p. 3)

Indigenous ways of learning fall under the anti-colonial framework of involving multiple knowledges, uncompetitive ways of learning, collaboration among communities, living harmoniously, and making sure the relationship with the land is valued. What follows are the current approaches that have been used in integrating the Indigenous knowledge within Eurocentric science.

Cross-Cultural School Science

Cross-cultural school sciences have been used to make meaningful integration of Indigenous knowledge. Cross-cultural school science takes a hybrid approach to school sciences. This approach combines Indigenous knowledge with Eurocentric knowledge. It creates a third space, without a tokenistic approach that serves neo-colonialism. Four themes are derived in cross-cultural school science: elders, culture, language, and experimental learning (Aikenhead & Jegede, 1999). Successful cross-cultural science avoids tokenism and neo-colonialism. The main aim is to nurture Indigenous student's scientific literacy, so they can successfully participate in their local community's Indigenous culture as well as the Eurocentric science (Aikenhead & Jegede, 1999).

Cross-cultural science has shown success in student's performance in various regions such as Alaska and Saskatchewan, where students have demonstrated improved results in standardized science test scores uniformly improving four years to meet national averages (Barnhardt, Kawagley & Hill, 2000). Increased success of students is seen when Indigenous sciences are combined with African community collaboration. South Africa has established a goal of integrating Indigenous African knowledges in science classrooms, which has led to an increase involvement of students in agriculture practices locally (Keane, 2008).

Humanistic Approach

A humanistic approach is another possible way to start the work of decolonizing science education. This approach focuses on various factors such as gender equality, student identities, a student-centered approach, and teaching with the lens of Science, Technology, Societal, and Environmental issues (STSE) (Aikenhead, 2006). The humanistic perspective allows students to become aware of societal issues by researching, analyzing, making decisions, and carrying out actions when necessary. It is about taking a proactive step towards societal, environmental, and socio-economic issues that affect their society (Aikenhead, 2006). Humanistic approaches to science teaching have been known worldwide, as Aikenhead shows. It is known as science technology citizenship, citizen science, functional scientific literacy, and cross-cultural school science. Aikenhead sees humanistic science as an approach for achieving goals such as science for all, scientific literacy, and improving minority or marginalized students' participation and achievement (Aikenhead, 2006).

Although approaches such as cross-cultural science and the humanistic approach are useful in the beginning process of decolonization, such approaches must be integrated in a meaningful way and include the voices of those who are oppressed. The process of decolonization involves a critical gaze on the practices we attempt to integrate. We need to begin somewhere, however complicit we are in the systems. We must begin somewhere, even if the process is complicated, but it must be an ongoing process.

Conclusion

Writing this piece of work was not an easy task for me. It allowed me to understand how complicit we are in the systems, and how we must claim our responsibility. When we see how disadvantaged Indigenous, Black and racialized youth are in the system, we must begin somewhere. In the quest of social justice and claiming the humanity of oppressed and silenced nations, we must need what Dei (2018) would refer to as "New humans" who will resist complacency, question power, domination, oppression and injustice. The anti-colonial discursive framework allows us to interrogate current practices of science education. It requires us to question the validity of Eurocentric knowledge and its origins. Lastly, an anti-colonial framework is "action-oriented," and it must allow us to make meaningful integration of Indigenous knowledge (Dei, 2018).

References

Aikenhead, G. S. (2006). *Science education for everyday life: Evidence-based practice*. New York: Teachers College Press.

Aikenhead, G. S., & Jegede, O. J. (1999). Cross-cultural science education: A cognitive explanation of cultural phenomena. *Journal of Research in Science Teaching, 36*(3), 269–287. https://doi.org/10.1002/(SICI)1098-2736(199903)36:3<269::AID-TEA3>3.0.CO;2-T

Aikenhead, G. S & Elliott, D. (2010). An emerging decolonizing science education in Canada. *Canadian Journal of Science, Mathematics and Technology Education, 10*(4), 321–338. DOI: 10.1080/14926156.2010.524967

Barnhardt, R., Kawagley, A. O., & Hill, F. (2000). Cultural standards and test scores. *Sharing Our Pathways, 5*(4), 1–4.

Battiste, M. (2013). *Decolonizing education: Nourishing the learning spirit*. Saskatoon: Purich Publishing.

Bauer-Wolf, J. (2019, February 26). Early Departures, A new study shows that Latinx and black students leave STEM majors at far higher rates than their white peers. *Inside Higher Ed*. Retrieved online from https://www.insidehighered.com/news/2019/02/26/latinx-black-college-students-leave-stem-majors more-white-students

Boisselle, L. N. (2016). Decolonizing science and science education in a postcolonial space. (Trinidad, a Developing Caribbean Nation, Illustrates). *Sage Open 6*(1), 1–11. https://doi.org/10.1177/2158244016635257

Cajete, G. (2000). *Native science: Natural Laws of Interdependence*. Santa Fe, NM: Clear Light Publishers.

Césaire, A. (1972). *Discourse on colonialism*. New York: MR.

DeBoer, G. E. (2011). The globalization of science education. *Journal of Research in Science Teaching, 48*(6), 567–591. doi:10.1002/tea.20421

DebRoy, R. (2018, April 9th). Science bears fingerprints colonialism. [Weblog]. Retrieved 19 December 2018, from https://www.smithsonianmag.com/science-nature/science-bears-fingerprints-colonialism-180968709/

Dei, G. J. S, Hall, B. L., & Rosenberg, G. D. (eds.) (2000). *Indigenous knowledges in global contexts: Multiple readings of our world.* Toronto: University of Toronto Press.

Dei, G. J. S. (2018). Reframing education through indigenous, anti-colonial and decolonial prisms. In P. McLaren & S. Soohoo (eds.), *The Radical Imagine-Nation* (pp. 214–235). New York: Peter Lang.

Dei, G., & Asgharzadeh, A. (2001). The power of social theory: The anti-colonial discursive framework. *The Journal of Educational Thought (JET) / Revue De La Pensée Éducative, 35*(3), 297–323.

Freire, P. (1972). *Pedagogy of the oppressed.* New York: Herder and Herder.

Hickling-Hudson, A. (2002). Re-visioning from the inside: Getting under the skin of the World Bank's education sector strategy. *International Journal of Educational Development, 22*(6), 565–577. https://doi.org/10.1016/S0738-0593(02)00004-4

Ihenetu, E. (2019, Aug 5). Race is fake and racism is real: Analyzing the race construct. Retrieved online from https://medium.com/swlh/race-is-fake-and-racism-is-real-analyzing-the-race-construct-58143aecee3b

Keane, M. (2008). Science education and worldview. *Cultural Studies of Science Education, 3,* 587–621. DOI: 10.1007/s11422-007-9086-5

Meah, A. (2018). Awaken the greatness within. Retrieved 21 December, 2018, from https://awakenthegreatnesswithin.com/35-inspirational-imam-al-ghazali-quotes-on-success/

Ontario Ministry of Education (2008). The Ontario Science and Technology Curriculum 11–12: Science Education. Retrieved from http://www.edu.gov.on.ca/eng/curriculum/secondary/2009science11_12.pdf

Pew Research Center (January 2018). "Women and Men in STEM Often at Odds Over Workplace Equity". Retrieved online from https://www.pewsocialtrends.org/wpcontent/uploads/sites/3/2018/01/PS_2018.01.09_STEM_FINAL.pdf

Ryan, A. (2008). Indigenous knowledge in the science curriculum: Avoiding neo-colonialism. *Cultural Studies of Science Education, 3,* 663–683. DOI: 10.1007/s11422-007-9087-4

Salloum, H. (2016, NOV 9,). Arab contributions to the sciences. [Weblog]. Retrieved 19 December 2018, from https://www.arabamerica.com/arab-contributions-to-the-sciences/

Thésée, G. (2006). A tool of massive erosion: Scientific knowledge in the neo-colonial enterprise. In G. S. Dei & A. Kempf (eds.), *Anti-colonialism and education: The politics of resistance* (pp. 25–42). Rotterdam, The Netherlands: Sense Publishers.

Western States Center (2003). *A history: The construction of race and racism dismantling racism project.* Portland, OR, USA. Western State Center. Retrieved from: https://www.racialequitytools.org/resourcefiles/Western%20States%20-%20Construction%20of%20Race.pdf

Zine, J. (2001). Muslim youth in Canadian schools: Education and the politics of religious identity. *Anthropology & Education Quarterly, 32*(4), 399–423. DOI: 10.1525/aeq.2001.32.4.399

Chapter Four

The Rhetoric of "Culturally Competent Care" in Colonized Healthcare Spaces

Hellen Chepkoech Komen - Taabu

Introduction

Colonialism is known to perpetuate the dominance of the Western Eurocentric culture, language, health models, and research methodologies that increasingly displace Indigenous knowledge systems (Dei & Kempf, 2006; Kuokkanen, 2008). This chapter seeks to find ways of contesting this dominance and creating methods to enhance paradigm shifts in ways of knowing that will inform nursing practices in the Canadian context. The anti-colonial lens is used to interrogate the contemporary biomedical approach as used in nursing practice, education, leadership, and ethics. The ultimate aim is to make contributions to knowledge by creating a path towards the labourious task of decolonizing nursing. This chapter critiques the much-touted Eurocentric concept of "Culturally Competent Care" as an exemplar of the extent to which nursing is colonized and in desperate need of decolonizing from multiple angles. The chapter interrogates racism in nursing, its impact on racialized bodies, and how it undermines the efforts to decolonize nursing. It attempts to examine how we can foster resistance and reimagine collective futures in the nursing profession. In my exploration of this topic, I encountered more questions than answers. I realized that there are no definite answers or formulas that can be used in decolonizing nursing and forming resistance. Therefore, I postulate that each of us should find our vantage points that we can use to form resistances as individuals and in our communities. We need to come together using our varied strengths and strategies to start chipping away at the block of colonialism, and sooner or later, we might make some progress in this extremely challenging endeavor of decolonizing the nursing profession.

Subject Location

This chapter is a reflection on my journey as a Black female body trying to navigate and find my voice in a racialized space that is the contemporary canadian healthcare setting. My awareness and sensitivity towards this topic have and continue to be fueled by my daily struggles and those of other immigrant nurses as we try to negotiate and navigate our foreignness and its attendant liabilities within varied spaces in the canadian healthcare setting. While attending Dr. Dei's class, I have gained a lot of knowledge and insights on decolonization and the anti-colonial thought and what a daunting task it is! The numerous classroom discussions on decolonization and the anti-colonial thought illuminate its nuances and complications. These discussions call for openness and vulnerability if we are to be able to disrupt persistent colonialism within society. In this class, I was able to re-affirm the importance of telling our stories and ensuring that they are as pure and authentic as can be to counter the narrative of the oppressor with his "expert" knowledge. As Chimamanda Ngozi Adichie (2009) states, "Stories matter. Many stories matter. Stories have been used to dispossess and to malign, but stories can also be used to empower and to humanize. Stories can break the dignity of a people, but stories can also repair that broken dignity." I use this as a clarion call for us as scholars to seek diverse perspectives and be able to tell our stories as a counter-narrative. By telling the stories that are particular to us, we will be ready to start the journey of resilience and writing back in our attempt at decolonization of the nursing profession. As wounded storytellers in the canadian healthcare setting, we need to share our stories with the hopes that something positive will germinate from the wounding and that the experiences of those who come after us will be better.

Discursive Framework

I will interrogate this discourse using an anti-colonial lens and Critical Race Theory. The anti-colonial lens will allow for theorizing, re-articulation, and challenging colonial relationships in nursing (Dei, Hall & Rosenberg, 2000). The anti-colonial perspective is relevant because it recognizes that colonialism is ongoing and its machinations continue to be actively at work in hospitals and other healthcare settings (Dei & Kempf, 2006). It acknowledges that as Indigenous Black African women, we have always resisted colonialism and encourages us to continue to foster this spirit of resistance by creating spaces with multicentricity of knowledge where Indigenous ways of knowing can be accommodated (Wane, 2013; Wangoola, 2000). The anti-colonial thought calls on us to remember, recognize, and address colonial systems of oppression as we actively contest power and privilege (Angod, 2006; Dei & Asgharzadeh, 2001) in healthcare spaces. It empowers us to challenge the prevailing unjust social structures and processes that cause colonized people always to have poor health outcomes as a consequence of being poorly positioned in the social determinants of health.

I choose to use the anti-colonial lens because, unlike the post-colonial lens, it is political from the onset (Angod, 2006; Dei & Asgharzadeh, 2001) and will allow me to argue my stance from an oppositional perspective in order to resist colonial oppression and and pave a new path in the nursing profession. As Dei and Asgharzadeh (2001) contend, the anti-colonial theory as a discursive framework gives us an avenue as subalterns to voice our experiences of oppression and marginalization. The anti-colonial paradigm allows for the envisioning of knowledge as a powerful tool for resistance that will make the arduous project of decolonizing the nursing profession possible. It will enable us to look back at our histories, which have important bodies of knowledge that can be used to build new identities that are instrumental in challenging and resisting the subordination and negation of our experiences and our Indigenous knowledges (Dei & Asgharzadeh, 2001). The anti-colonial lens will allow us to understand the burden of colonization and how it shapes our experiences and forms new forms of injustices. It will enable us to understand unequal power relations and how dominant groups have created and redefined our world view and dictated social structures such as the healthcare delivery systems.

In this chapter the framework of Critical Race Theory (CRT) is used to interrogate the effect of race and racism on social structures, practices, and discourses in the nursing profession. CRT, which emerged in legal scholarship in the 1980s, aims at unraveling the troubling paradox of the universal persistence of racism despite condemnation by state policies and the norms of polite society (Crenshaw, Gotanda, Peller, & Thomas, 1995). CRT exposes race as a social construct entrenched in institutions such as healthcare that prohibits people of color from accessing essential services (Bhui, Ascoli, & Naumh, 2012; Calliste, 1996; Carpenter-Song et al., 2007). It shows how race has become more subtle, but no less pervasive in healthcare institutions today. It reminds us of the persistence of race and the importance of listening to the perspective of the silenced voices in healthcare settings.

CRT uses stories as a powerful tool for creating a counter-narrative that rejects mainstream political and intellectual views, denounces capitalism, promotes human liberation and exposes the many forms of domination and oppression (Crenshaw et al., 1995). CRT reveals how science and technology, as used in nursing, are privileged Eurocentric epistemology that propagates domination and oppression (McGibbon et al., 2014). It highlights the importance of including the perspective of the racially subordinated voice of color when making laws, policies, and programs since they have some knowledge that the privilege lack (Crenshaw, 1995; McGibbon et al., 2014). It calls us to challenge the dominant discourse through telling of personal anecdotes or fables using our Black epistemology to convey ideas that cannot be expressed in the traditional Eurocentric scholarly language (Wane, 2013). It critiques the false assumption that Eurocentric epistemology is always objective and unbiased by deconstructing dominant ideologies that propagate and justify the interests of those in power (Ford & Airhihenbuwa, 2010). It shows how the Eurocentric epistemology is aligned with white privilege, which continues to be replicated in public policies and practices (McGibbon et al., 2014).

CRT will be used in this context to demand nursing practice that is safe and that does not alienate patients and prevent them from accessing the necessary care that they need and deserve. It acknowledges that cultural safety is not about cultural practices, but it involves examining the socio-economic and political advantages that some groups have over others (McGibbon et al., 2014). Using CRT as a nurse reminds me always to be cognizant of healthcare disparities and work to improve healthcare access. It challenges me to acknowledge and appreciate all cultures and expose the repressive socio-political and historical context inherent in healthcare in a bid to disrupt unequal power relations. CRT reminds us as nurses to look beyond the cultural characteristics of others to be able to visualize and critique institutional racism and discrimination that is pervasive in the healthcare system. It provides anti-racists with a framework to challenge narrow perceptions of race and the silence surrounding race in nursing in order to facilitate and strengthen its recognition, interrogation and disruption (Crenshaw et al., 1995).

The Concept of Cultural Competent Care in Healthcare

Although a lot has been written about the need for nurses and other healthcare professionals to provide safe and optimal care to patients of diverse groups, little has been said about delivering culturally competent care in lieu of an increasingly toxic racist healthcare environment. Narratives of cultural competence and race equality are not palatable as they provoke some tensions for policymakers and clinicians in healthcare environments (Bourque-Bearskin, 2011; McGibbon et al., 2013). It is interesting to note that many institutions and specialties have different definitions and understandings of the concept of cultural competence. Still, its up-take largely depends on location, people's interest, and preparedness for change as well as their political position on diversity and immigrants (Bhui et al., 2012).

The Canadian Nurses Association (CNA) states that Cultural Competence is a set of behaviors, attitudes, and policies that converge in a system, agency, or among professionals that make them work harmoniously and productively in cross-cultural situations (Canadian Nursing Association, [CAN] 2010). It is thus an expectation that all nurses in Canada be culturally competent as measured by their ability to possess and exude values such as inclusivity, respect, valuing differences and commitment (CNA, 2010). The ideal end product of Culturally Competent Care is to create a healthcare system and workforce capable of providing the highest quality of care to every patient regardless of their race, ethnicity, culture or language proficiency (Carpenter, Schwallie, & Longhofer, 2007). I have worked as a nurse and a Personal Support Worker for the last fifteen years. I still struggle with the notion of the provision of culturally competent care under the prevailing circumstances where our Black bodies are continuously scripted as we are on the receiving end of extreme racism. There is a nagging question I am always asking myself: Is it feasible to achieve or provide culturally competent care in a system that is rife with racism and white privilege as the Canadian healthcare?

We share the healthcare space with settler colonialists, where immigrants are always viewed in negative ways. Our voices are constantly being silenced during discussions, and we still find ourselves in paradoxical situations where we are the invited but unwanted guest who is invading spaces where on many occasions we feel and look like misplaced bodies. It is sad to note how many healthcare workers and patients internalize the institutionalized racism and embody feelings of resignation, helplessness, and hopelessness as a consequence of their experiences of oppression. One of my Black nurse colleagues confided in me that she copes by adopting a different persona every time she walks in the hospital. She talks in a subdued, low tone and engages minimally for fear of being branded as angry, aggressive, loud, and uncouth, or a poor team player, as is the norm when Black women speak up. This revelation shocked, enraged, and saddened me as I pondered how this impacts her health. Paradoxically, she has adopted a split personality, a mental health disorder to survive at a work space where healing is our philosophy. This tragedy is replicated in multiple locations in the healthcare field, which is ironic since these are the healthcare workers who are entrusted with the provision of culturally competent care.

The Fallacy and Nuances of Cultural Competence Care in Healthcare

The whole idea of cultural competence in healthcare is gaining a lot of currency and is propelled by ongoing concerns about social justice and attendant health disparities. There is a recognition that the ethnic landscape of the Canadian population has changed significantly, challenging a healthcare system dominated by a white, male, middle-class biomedical model that is not keeping pace (Carpenter-Song et al., 2007; CNA, 2010). Therefore, as Canada continues to evolve as a multi-ethnic, culturally diverse society, there is a demand for a standard of cultural competence that aligns with the democratic principles that we purport to uphold as a multicultural nation (Bourque-Bearskin, 2011). It is therefore an expectation that all nurses and other clinicians provide culturally competent care both in the content and structure of their clinical encounter with patients (CNA, 2010). What this implies is that to be culturally competent, all nurses are to be aware of the differences in the way patients and families from different cultures respond to illness and treatment.

Cultural competence means having a good understanding of culturally sensitive issues such as dietary practices, modesty, patients' response to pain, death, and dying, taboos all which are to be respected, acknowledged, and incorporated in their care plan to anticipate possible barriers to healthcare access or compliance. The main goal is to reduce cultural dissonance, improve communication, reduce opportunities for errors, and increase healthcare uptake (CNA, 2010). This idea troubles me for although the intentions might be good, are these expectations practical or viable? Is it possible for one person to be a "guru" of all cultures by virtue of their status as a nurse? In my opinion, all these expectations sound good on paper but are based on a very flawed understanding of what culture truly entails. It is critical that we re-examine the assumptions that underpin the concept of culture and cultural competence in nursing. This skewed notion of culture fails to appreciate the complex relationship that individuals have with their culture.

Culture is a socially-constructed, learned pattern of behavior and beliefs attributed to a specific group (Bourque-Bearskin, 2011). As individuals, many of us have a minimal impact on our culture, which is dynamic and has a life of its own (Bourque-Bearskin, 2011). As such, many generations of families and communities have varying levels of conformity to traditional cultural norms. Although individuals belong to the same culture, it is erroneous to assume that they are the same. Generalizations can lead to very embarrassing assumptions and misconceptions. In the pursuit of culturally sensitive care, we have based our knowledge on very few cultural carriers by assuming that culture is a monolithic collection of traditional behaviors that are static or frozen in time (Bourque Bearskin, 2011). We have forgotten that culture is dynamic and changes with new environments, whether physical, socio-economic, or political. No wonder we encounter nurses and other healthcare providers that are worn out, frustrated, and discouraged by the burden and pressures of the unattainable expectations of providing culturally competent care. Rather than aspire for this misconstrued notion of cultural competence, I think we should have alternate ideas such as cultural humility. Unlike cultural competence, which implies a set of skills that a nurse needs to master, like

45

taking a patient's vital signs, cultural humility acknowledges that the nurse is open and willing to learn, collaborate, listen, and negotiate with the patient and his/her family.

Cultural humility is about acknowledging our naiveté with regards to other people's cultures and looking up to them as experts to educate us. I witness sad incidences replicated on an ongoing basis in healthcare settings where nurses whose purview is cultural competence behave in very appalling ways, especially when dealing with immigrants. A case in mind was that of Obi (pseudonym), a middle-aged Nigerian gentleman who was under our care for two months then started deteriorating rapidly. Within a short duration, Obi was ventilator-dependent, bedbound and with a tracheostomy, tube feeds, and a cascade of complications following a severe stroke. Nurses could be heard saying, "This is torture and a complete waste of hospital resources. The family should come to their senses and withdraw the vent. It is hopeless; he will never recover!" Obi's family, on the other hand, was very spiritual and kept hoping and praying for a miracle; hence they continued to demand everything to be done to save his life. Confronted by many different physicians and nurses telling them that Obi's ventilator support should be withdrawn, the family had rejected the involvement of most of these staff with his care.

One nurse, Anna, was the only healthcare professional they would talk with about decisions regarding Obi's care because she was humble, non-judgmental, empathized, and readily listened to them. She understood that based on Obi's family's history of being disenfranchised and having poor access to healthcare, they wanted everything done. Anna understood the family's strong spiritual beliefs and how they hoped for miracles, even in seemingly futile circumstances. It is important to note that while the other team members were deemed culturally competent based on their knowledge and skills, their attitudes were based on assumptions and stereotypes. They displayed their superiority complex and flexed their muscles as "experts" while dismissing the knowledge and beliefs of Obi and his family. This created great distrust and conflict between Obi's family and the nurses on the unit. To the healthcare team's surprise and Obi's family's delight, Obi rallied back and was discharged home with his family. This increased the familys' suspicion of the healthcare professionals, for they found them very disrespectful, racist, and lacking compassion in their time of need.

It is also worth noting that even though the nursing institution is committed to addressing healthcare disparities using cultural competence care, these seemingly good intentions cannot compete with the already existing structures of power imbalances that perpetuate inequities in healthcare access (Bhui et al., 2012; Carpenter-Song, 2007). It is ridiculous to expect nurses to be culturally competent when the philosophies and theories that underlie their knowledge base exclusively emanate from a Eurocentric context (McGibbon et al., 2014). There is a need to recognize and acknowledge that Eurocentric theoretical models and research methods will not satisfy the needs of multiculturally diverse groups. We should accept the fact that there are other ways of knowing and that scientific and empirically-derived knowledge developed within a Eurocentric paradigm might not be responsive to the needs of diverse groups. Therefore, this paradigm needs to be re-evaluated and critiqued (McGibbon et al., 2014).

For instance, I recently had an encounter that was truly heart-rending with the death of an Indigenous youth Tau (pseudonym). Tau was brought to the hospital in a coma induced by a drug overdose. On learning that Tau might not recover from the coma, the family approached me requesting to perform a dying ceremony for Tau. They had invited an elder to come and perform the ceremony, which involved some prayers, pouring libations, burning of sages and/or tobacco, and chanting to guide Tau's spirit back to the spirit world. This request did not surprise me since I am familiar with similar rites of passage in my Kalenjin culture. I knew it was the right thing to do. I therefore, approached my manager to facilitate an opportunity and private space for the ceremony. To my utmost surprise, my manager was appalled and even somewhat disgusted by the idea. She retorted, "Is there even any scientific evidence to back that? I cannot believe that you considered consenting to such a bizarre request. This hospital is scent-free, and burning of any sages is not allowed. Look at our smoking policy! What about the privacy of the other patients in the room?" I went back and forth, attempting to advocate for Tau but was not successful.

The family pleaded with the hospital management, but they would not hear of it because, to them, it made no sense. The family demanded to take Tau home but were not allowed since he was on a ventilator. Tau's family asked if they could be allowed to apply some special oils and ashes to his body as an alternative, but the management refused, citing infection control policies and issues. Tau eventually died without having his death rites performed. The family was enraged, stating that Tau's cycle of life was incomplete, and his spirit would not rest. They vowed never to come back to the hospital, stating that it is better to die with respect at home! I felt so angry, ashamed, and conflicted with the hospital that prides itself on providing culturally competent care, yet they could not make very simple fundamental cultural accommodations. Why would we allow catholic priests, sheikhs and other religious leaders to offer death rites in hospitals yet discriminate against Tau's family? Was Tau not worthy of a proper send-off? Why did the manager choose to pathologize Tau and his family's culture? Was it because of his socio-economic status or his indigeneity? What about when nurses use intuition or the sixth sense, is their empirical evidence for this? I felt distraught and equally implicated and complicit in a hospital culture that fosters racism and discrimination! This incident challenged me to find ways of disrupting these Eurocentric beliefs that have shaped our dominant knowledges as nurses, hence silencing others like Tau's and his family, which are equally valuable and relevant. Because of our tunnel vision, we missed opportunities to learn precious lessons from this experience.

Racism in Nursing and How It Impedes Providing Culturally Competent Care

Many scholars have studied racism and White privilege, but discussion of these concepts continue to be silenced in nursing discourse and practice (McGibbon et al., 2014). Essed (1991) described racism as any structure where dominance and discrimination exist and are reproduced through the control of access to and allocation of resources. Institutional racism is embedded in places such as healthcare, education, and legal systems, where it is formalized and legitimized (Essed, 1991). In nursing practice, racism takes forms such as discrimination in hiring practices and promotion; it also takes the form of discrimination in actual nursing practice through being degraded or insulted by virtue of race, ethnicity, or color (McGibbon et al., 2014). It is puzzling that racialized nurses face racism on an ongoing basis, yet they are hardly represented in the realms of governance or policy-making (McGibbon et al., 2014). The other hidden side of the racism equation is white privilege, which is the backbone of racism in nursing, as seen in individual acts such as treating Black families unethically or systemic practices such as limiting the enrollment of Black students in nursing school (McGibbon et al., 2014). In nursing knowledge development, western science dominates nursing education and, as such, accounts for nursing evolution as a profession. Cosequently, this narratives silence and renders invisible Black and Indigenous nurses such as Jamaican-born Mary Seacole, who served as a nurse as well as a financial benefactress in the Crimean war of 1853–1856. Instead, we are flooded with heroic stories of Florence Nightingale, who was white and wealthy (McGibbon et al., 2014).

The dominant discussions in healthcare settings on Black migrant nurses center on the assumption that these nurses have compromised as opposed to enriching the historical, cultural, and social fabric of nursing (Masamha, 2018). Our experiences as migrant nurses are often ignored and discounted, and the legitimacy of our skills and knowledge often contested and situated in the realms of foreignness (Masamha, 2018). People fail to see beyond our foreignness and accept our contributions as competent and valid. For instance, as an African immigrant nurse, identity has always dictated the realms of my knowledge in such a way that I am expected to be the guru on all matters concerning race and culture. However, when it comes to science and technology, I am supposed to be a buffoon bereft of any knowledge. This, to me, is a perpetuation of colonial indignities. This epistemic ignorance is a form of subtle violence (Kuokkanen, 2008). Little do they know that in addition to mainstream nursing knowledge, many of us embody other Indigenous ways of knowing that might be beneficial to nursing practice and patient experiences!

However, because we are positioned within a different Eurocentric episteme, we are forced to always question ourselves on whether our Indigenous knowledges will be welcome, misunderstood, or labelled as primitive or backward. In her essay Can the Subaltern Speak?, Spivak (1988) clearly illustrates the fact that it is nearly impossible for the subaltern to be heard or read since they are either ignored, forgotten, or simply made to disappear; thus, their intended message is either silenced or totally misrepresented. I choose to challenge this notion and insist on pushing boundaries and allowing myself to speak and be heard in my own terms and relevant contexts. As Wane (2013) contends, we need to reclaim the central tenets of our Indigenous culture and apply them to our contemporary contexts for, as with any cultural project, this decision to reclaim our Indigenous knowledges can begin with a single moment, a thought or a social challenge. For instance, on many occasions, in my interactions with African patients whom I naturally tend to gravitate to, I have grasped opportunities to use Indigenous African epistemology to accomplish healthcare teachings successfully. When teaching difficult topics like sexuality, instead of using taboo words and terminologies that at times tend to be culturally offensive and repulsive, I find the use of proverbs, riddles, and storytelling effective in relaying my messages and accomplishing very crucial healthcare lessons. My favorite is when teaching youth about the prevention of sexually transmitted diseases; I encourage them to "stick to their wells and avoid fetching water from other people's wells for it might be riddled with snakes!" Though simple, this message is always clear and concise and rarely requires any further elaboration.

In nursing, social performance is a professional activity (Willets & Clarke, 2014). The construction of the professional identities of nurses is seen in their performance of their professional and daily activities within their social working groups. To have a sense of belonging in the workplace is crucial for all nurses and as such, social identity is displayed through group membership. The lack of socialization in the local culture increases the feelings of incompetence and poor social performance by immigrant nurses. Therefore, our Africanness becomes a liability of being foreign. As a consequence, many immigrant African nurses purpose to understand Canadians' cultural and social regulations that have an impact on their daily interactions. Depending on how they navigate through this, it can lead to an inferiority complex whereby they immerse themselves in and are swallowed by the dominant culture. The tragedy is that such nurses are caught up in muddy situations where to gain acceptance, they totally overhaul their character, ape the white man, and detest their very own people and culture. They perpetuate colonization through instilling in themselves an inferiority complex, and as they get embroiled in this act, their very own authentic culture is buried (Fanon, 2008). As Fanon (2008) opines, they use a certain syntax and adopt the morphology of the civilizing language and eventually end up assuming a culture and bearing the weight of its skewed civilization. The tragedy is that such nurses end up being imposters who shout louder than the bereaved. They do not serve the interests of their colonial master, who will never embrace them, or of their fellow community members, who would have benefited from their insider status. As the Swahili saying goes, *Mkosa Kabila ni Mtumwa* - He who is devoid of culture/rootedness is genuinely a slave!

Fostering Resistance in the Nursing Profession

As a form of resistance, nursing knowledge development needs to be revamped, allowing its values, theories, assumptions, and practices to be scrutinized cross-culturally if we are to provide culturally sensitive care with humility (Dreher & MacNaughton, 2002; McGibbon et al., 2013). For instance, all patients deserve individualized care that is open to biomedical alternatives such as the use of herbs and evoking faith and spirituality to prevent and treat illnesses. As nurses, we should not underestimate the capacity of our patient's to realize that the biomedical models we represent do not meet all their healthcare needs and that all the healthcare providers may not share their beliefs and traditions. All they ask for is to be cared for with dignity, respect, compassion, and sincerity as opposed to all of these cultural competence shenanigans. By falsely representing problems as cultural barriers that nurses can overcome through taking courses on cultural competence, meeting regulatory mandates, and being more informed about various cultures, we ignore the elephant in the room, which is institutional racism. Healthcare professions must understand that in any clinical encounter, two systems of knowledge interact. The nurses might be experts in biomedicine, a cultural system of its own, whereas the patients are experts in their own experiences of distress as informed by their culture. Therefore, the clinical encounter has to involve a two-way traffic, which calls on nurses to be open and willing to seek clarification when faced with unfamiliar or unusual situations. An appreciation of the complexity and indeterminate nature of culture (Kuokkanen, 2008; McGibbon et al., 2014) would foster clinical encounters that are characterized by openness and willingness on both ends to seek clarity when faced with unusual situations, as illustrated by Tau's and Obi's cases above.

Nurses should make a conscious effort of making connections between structural, historical, and political dimensions by viewing healthcare through an anti-colonial lens and asking pertinent moral questions to unearth and tackle current healthcare disparities (Dreher & MacNaughton, 2002; Kuokkanen, 2008). Rather than struggle with the unattainable concept of cultural competency in healthcare, we should look beyond the cultural characteristics of others and critique the issues of institutional racism and discrimination in the healthcare system. We should be self-conscious and aware of the power dynamics in healthcare, especially, and begin to ask critical and ethical questions. This new level of knowledge will equip nurses with tools to make decisions that are culturally appropriate for patients and their families. As healthcare workers, we should create spaces for nurturing and valuing the embodied experience of our patients and their families (Dei, 2012; Wane, 2013).

As Dei (2012) contends, while using the 'trialectic thinking,' nurses should be cognisant of their embodied experiences and those of others which forms their multiple identities through space, time and colonial geographies and consequently how all these are intertwined and interconnected as opposed to being segregated and demarcated bodies of knowledge. Hence, it is imperative that we all understand that cultural competency does not mandate our need to know everything about every culture or to abandon our own cultural identity. Instead, it implies that we respect differences and be open to the idea that there are many ways to view the world. The sad reality of the cultural competence movement is that it puts a lot of pressure on the nurse and other healthcare providers to achieve while ignoring the role of the patient and their family. Since colonization imposed on us only one superior way of knowing (Dei & Asgharzadeh, 2001; Dei & Kempf, 2006), as evidenced in nursing and its ethos, we need to decolonize by creating new spaces in healthcare that would accommodate alternative ways of knowing. This will allow us to be respectful as we acknowledge differences in persons, their knowledge, cultural values, attitudes, their spirituality and its influence on their perception of health and illness. However, it is important to understand that opening up new spaces does not imply undoing colonial knowledge but challenging its position, dominance, and legitimacy as the epitome of knowledge (Fanon, 1963; Wa Thiong'o, 1986).

Nurses can fight back by challenging the hegemony of power vested in the biomedical model of nursing practice, research, ethics, and leadership to decolonize nursing scholarship (McGibbon et al., 2013). As nurses, we must advocate for social justice wherever we are situated. We should form partnerships with our community members where we can empower and advocate for ourselves, especially during vulnerable times. As Nana Dei persistently reinforced in our classroom discussions, our presence in academia or professional workplaces makes us suspect in the eyes of our community members; therefore, we should always strive to be credible and accountable. We should interrogate our complicities and privileged positions and use them to make a positive impact within our communities. As such, we must work with our communities to pioneer new pathways of resistance. An example would be partnering with our communities to form community-based health promotion and disease-prevention initiatives where we can share our spirituality and Indigenous health practices to create alternatives centers of health knowledge. When dealing with members of different cultures, we have to be humble and position ourselves at their behest to inform, facilitate, and advocate for them while enabling them to make their own decisions. We need to be open and willing to engage with them and reflect on our own biases.

As nurses from Africa, we should refrain from being passive and silent, for this might lead to embracing a trespasser identity, which, if unchecked, will lead to the perpetuation of internalized inferiority complexes (Calliste, 1996; Fanon, 2008). As Adichie (2009) states, we need to guard against patronising well-meaning pity, the uncritical consumption of the corrupted narrative where we as African women, regardless of our experiences and position in society, are seen as destitute refugees, fleeing poverty and various catastrophes. We have to tell our stories to avoid being seen as if we have nothing to give, pests who are dependent, subservient, and lacking valuable knowledge as compared to other women globally. We need to decolonize how we are perceived, for as Mbembe (2015) says, we need to eliminate the gap between image and essence, placing emphasis on the restoration of the image, allowing it to exist in itself and not in something other than itself, which is usually distorted, clumsy, debased and unworthy. We thus need to counter the stereotypes and negative assumptions by proving our competence in all spheres of nursing and above all else by not being afraid to use our Indigenous knowledges to effect positive change. We should be ready and willing to name and shame racism when we encounter it. We should create a self-reflection and awareness of stereotypes and power relationships, however subtle. For instance, when a patient or co-worker refers to us as exotic, we should question the underlying assumptions and racist undertones. Do we look wild?

As for those nurses among us who suffer inferiority complexes, they need to be guided and enlightened to understand its genesis - the intersections of oppression, immigrant status, and being a colonized subject (Essed, 1991). This layered sense of inferiority will need to be unpacked before we make attempts at decolonizing the nursing profession; especially for the poor nurses who according to Wa Thiong'o (1986) are victims of a 'Cultural bomb' that has succeeded in annihilating their belief in their names, language, heritage, their struggles, unity, environment, capacities and ultimately themselves. This is a hegemonic weapon used by the dominant culture to control, manipulate, and subjugate the identities and sense of self of groups perceived to be less articulate (Wa Thiong'o, 1986), such as Black African nurses. They see themselves, their communities, and their past as unworthy. Such nurses need a true awareness of their identity, their roots, and their heritage. They have opted to identify with a culture that is too far removed from them. As was the case with Fanon, they need a return to their homeland, whether real or symbolic, by countering the denigration, dehumanizing experiences they have encountered and internalized as a consequence of racism in healthcare. They need to be able to understand and appreciate their Blackness or Africanness before coming to terms with other cultures.

Reimagining Collective Futures in Nursing

To reimagine our collective futures in nursing, we have to look back at our history to map out future directions. As per our classroom discussions, the past has a lot to offer us in the form of lessons, experiences, and even at times nostalgia. We have to recognize our history and what or who made it possible for us to be here. Therefore, we have to honor that and use our somewhat priviledged positions to advocate for others. We should use our insider positions in the Eurocentric episteme to find ways of disrupting it by countering their narrative with our Indigenous episteme. We have to find ways of creating multiple centers of knowledge in nursing. We all have to work together as a community to regain our humanity. We need to understand our Blackness or Africanness and understand how race has and continues to center our realities, especially in the nursing profession.

In reimagining humanity, we have to open up spaces in the nursing profession to talk about racism and white privilege, however complicated and uncomfortable it is. By centering race, we will be able to acknowledge that the perceptions of racial differences are the basis of one of the key divides in social life that has led to deep-rooted discrimination that minorities continue to face (Carpenter-Song et al., 2007) and that greatly impacts their health. Therefore, as colonized bodies, we should be able to exercise self-determination and autonomy and create opportunities for our voices to be heard wherever we are situated, be it in nursing practice, research, education, or in the academy. We must strive to return to our native lands, whatever we perceive them to be, whether real or metaphorical, to reclaim our culture and our humanity. As part of marginalized cultures, we cannot afford to be bystanders as we wait for our obliteration and extinction. We should use our Indigenous cultures and knowledge to trouble Eurocentric knowledges and inform the discipline of nursing. We must realize that it is within our power to challenge the colonization of the discipline of nursing and engage in decolonizing actions. We have to be aware that focusing on our cultural identity and Indigenous ways of knowing is also deemed as a political act. As anti-racists, we must use introspection, dialogue, and action to interrogate preconceived ideas about nursing and recognize racism and white privilege embedded in Eurocentric worldviews as significant influences in nursing. We need to widen the net and participate both locally and globally in social justice issues that pertain to nursing, ensuring that multiple voices are included in the dialogue on decolonizing nursing.

Conclusion

The work of decolonizing nursing calls for a commitment to exposing ideologies values and structures of racism and discrimination embedded in all facets of the nursing profession. As nurses, we need to be more critical by looking beyond culture and its attendant politics such as cultural competence to confront the structural, historical and political machinations that lead to discrimination and racism contributing to significant health disparities. The critical Race Theory and the anti-racist framework can guide us in recognising and identifying systemic power structures that emanate from colonialism, which perpetuate racism and discrimination. We need to work towards social justice by fostering and engaging in anti-oppressive culture and practice in nursing. Minority nurses should be adept at recognizing racism and be willing to confront it by dialoguing about it as opposed to being silent. Engaging in the ominous task of decolonizing the nursing profession demands our commitment to exposing colonizing ideologies, values and structures in the nursing discipline. We must find ways of integrating our Indigenous epistemology into the nursing discipline as a way of rekindling and reinstating our own cultures and traditions.

References

Adichie, C. (2009). The danger of a single story. TED talk. Retrieved [Online], October 2009.

Angod, L. (2006). From post-colonial thought to anti-colonial politics: Difference, knowledge and RVRDS. In G.J.S. Dei and A. Kempt (eds.), *Anti-colonialism and education: The politics of resistance* (pp. 159–173). Rotterdam, Netherland: Sense Publishers.

Bhui, K., Ascoli, M., & Nuamh, O. (2012). The place of race and racism in cultural competence: What can we learn from the English experience about the narratives of evidence and argument? *Transcultural psychiatry, 49*(2), 185–205.doi: 10.1177/1363461512437589

Bourque-Bearskin, R. L. (2011). A critical lens on culture in nursing practice. *Nursing Ethics, 18*(4), 548–559. https://doi.org/10.1177/0969733011408048

Calliste, A. (1996). Antiracism organizing and resistance in nursing: African Canadian women. *Canadian Review of Sociology/Revue Canadienne de Sociologie, 33*(3), 361–390. https://doi.org/10.1111/j.1755-618X.1996.tb02457.x

Canadian Nurses Association (CNA). (2010). Promoting cultural competence in nursing. Ottawa, ON: CNA.

Carpenter-Song, E., Schwallie, M. N., & Longhofer, J. (2007). Cultural competence re-examined: Critique and directions for the future. *Psychiatric Services, 58*(10), 1362–1365. DOI: 10.1176/ps.2007.58.10.1362

Crenshaw, K., Gotanda, N., Peller, G. & Thomas, K. (1995). *Critical race theory: The key writing that formed the movement.* New York, NY: The New York Press.

Dei, G. J. S. (2012). "Suahunu," the trialectic space. *Journal of Black Studies, 43*(8), 823–846. https://doi.org/10.1177/0021934712463065

Dei, G. J. S., & Asgharzadeh, A. (2001). The power of social theory: Towards an anti-colonial discursive framework. *Journal of Educational Thought, 35*(3), 297–323. https://www.jstor.org/stable/23767242

Dei, G. J. S., Hall, B, & Golden Rosenberg, D (2000). *Indigenous knowledges in global contexts: Multiple readings of our world* . Toronto: University of Toronto Press.

Dei, G. J. S., & Kempf, A. (2006). *Anti-colonialism and education: The politics of resistance.* Amsterdam, Netherlands: Sense.

Dreher, M., & MacNaughton, N. (2002). Cultural competence in nursing: Foundation or fallacy? *Nursing Outlook, 50*(5), 181–186. doi:https://doi.org/10.1067/mno.2002.125800

Essed, P. (1991). *Understanding everyday racism: An interdisciplinary theory* (Vol. 2). Sage.

Fanon, F. (2008). *Black skin, white masks.* Grove Press.

Fanon, F. (1963). *The wretched of the earth.* New York: Grove Press.

Ford, C. L., & Airhihenbuwa, C. O. (2010). Critical race theory, race equity, and public health:toward antiracism praxis. *American journal of public health, 100*(S1), S30-S35.doi: 10.2105/AJPH.2009.171058

Kuokkanen, R. (2008). What is hospitality in the academy? Epistemic ignorance and the (im)possible gift. *The review of education, pedagogy, and cultural studies, 30*(1), 60–82. https://doi.org/10.1080/10714410701821297

Masamha, R. (2018). The liability of foreignness: Decolonial struggles of migrants negotiating African identity within UK nurse education. In *Decolonization and Feminisms in Global Teaching and Learning* (pp. 109–124). Routledge.

Mbembe, A. (2015). Decolonizing knowledge and the question of the archive. *Aula magistral proferida*.Retrieved from https://wiser.wits.ac.za/sites/default/files/private/Achille%20Mbembe%20-%20Decolonizing%20Knowledge%20and%20the%20Question%20of%20the%20Archive.pdf

McGibbon, E., Mulaudzi, F. M., Didham, P., Barton, S., & Sochan, A. (2014). Toward decolonizing nursing: The colonization of nursing and strategies for increasing the counter narrative. *Nursing Inquiry, 21*(3), 179–191. doi: 10.1111/nin.12042

Spivak, G. C. (1988). Can the subaltern speak? In R. Morris (ed.), *Can the subaltern speak? Reflections on the history of an idea* (pp. 21–78). Columbia University Press.

Wa Thiong'o, N. (1992). *Decolonising the mind: The politics of language in African literature*. East African Publishers.

Wane, N. N. (2013). (Re)claiming Indigenous Knowledge: Challenges, resistance, and opportunities. *Decolonization: Indigeneity, Education & Society, 2*(1), 93–107. https://www.jstor.org/stable/42589823

Wangoola, P. M. (2000). The African multiversity: A philosophy to rekindle the African spirit. In G. Dei, B. Hall, D. Rosenberg (eds.). *Indigenous knowledges in global contexts: Multiple readings of our world* (pp. 265–277). Toronto: University of Toronto Press.

Willetts, G., & Clarke, D. (2014). Constructing nurses' professional identity through social identity theory. *International Journal of Nursing Practice, 20*(2), 164–169. doi: 10.1111/ijn.12108

Chapter Five

Human Colonial Projects and Capitalism

Shamugapriya Thanuja Thananayagam

Capitalism does not permit an even flow of economic resources. With this system, a small privileged few are rich beyond conscience, and almost all others are doomed to be poor at some level. That's the way the system works. And since we know that the system will not change the rules, we are going to have to change the system.

—Martin Luther King, Jr.

Introduction

Capitalism is the modern-day colonialism rooted in settler-colonial history. Whether willingly or unwillingly, we are being colonized every day through a neoliberal ideology of a capitalistic society that translates to the corporate world in the form of policies, procedures, and practices that are geared to benefit modern-day colonizers. Our dependence on both consumption and modernity contributes towards free-market capitalism. While we humans see this as a development towards human evolution, I am not convinced that it is truly a human evolution. So, in this chapter, I am going to explore how capitalism perpetrates coloniality practices in the corporate world through its various everyday practices and corporate strategy. While I am not going to focus on a specific industry, I am going to base my analysis on my experience of having worked in various corporate sectors in Canada and elsewhere and bring in a general argument. In this argument, it is crucial to look at settler colonialism as the beginning of capitalism. Tuck and Young (2012, p. 5) argue that in settler colonialism, the most important concern is land/ water/ air/ subterranean earth, which are natural resources. They go on to say that settlers make Indigenous land their new home and *source of capital*, and also because disruption of the Indigenous relationship to land represents a profound epistemic, ontological, and cosmological violence. Violence is affirmed each day of occupation of the land that was stolen from Indigenous peoples. The important aspect of this argument is that this land connection, which is sacred to Indigenous peoples, becomes the source of capital for settlers. Hence, the principle of capitalism is historical and rooted in settler colonization and land dispossession.

Moreover, at a macro level, the impact on the environment as a result of industrial deforestation of Indigenous land is severe (Simpson, 2004, p. 378). Additionally, depletion of natural resources such as air, water, and soil; the destruction of ecosystems; habitat destruction and the extinction of wildlife; and pollution are all part of environmental destruction. Within the last 40 years, our pattern of consumption of earth's natural resources has more than tripled (United National Climate Report, 2016). If we carefully analyze the pattern of destruction and connect it to history, there's an obvious relationship to capitalism. In this process of feeding into capitalism, we become human colonial projects. We all have the responsibility to resist coloniality.

Let's take a minute to reflect on the Great Recession that started in the US and soon spread all over the world in 2007 and 2008 due to interdependencies of peripheries. Peripheries or the pheriphery countries are those countries that the western world categorises as less developed, underdeveloped or developing nations. In most cases these are former colonies that are being further colonized through globalization, which I will get into detail little later, structured to receive only a very small portion of the wealth distribution. Getting back to the question of the Great Recession, what do you suppose is the cause of the capital market crisis? Kotz (2009, p. 305) says that

> . . . the financial and economic crisis that began in the United States in 2008 indicates the start of a *systemic crisis of neoliberal capitalism*. The same institutional features of neoliberal capitalism that promoted a series of long economic expansions over several decades also created long-run trends that have led to a systemic crisis.

My perspective on this is that globalization, issues with wealth distribution, and huge wage disparities continue to grow, where the rich are getting richer and the poor are getting poorer, all reinforcing the colonial practice that was rooted in the settler colonialism. Moreover, those who were impacted by the market crisis weren't CEOs or the top management, who are generally White privilege men and women, but those frontline workers who are racialized or marginalized workers. Bringing in Kotz's argument above on the 2007/08 recession and the capital market crisis was due to colonized structures that are built on capitalism. Hence, my argument here is that capitalism perpetuates ongoing human colonial projects by creating structural divisions, wage gaps, and unequal wealth distribution. Dei (2013, p. 3) argues that "the articulation of racism comes to be contextualized through the ontological presence of capitalist modes of production." In other words, these human colonized projects are racialized bodies that are victims of racism rooted in capitalism build to suit White colonizers who are holding higher positions in corporations. The history of European colonization, led by European heterosexual males (Grosfoguel, 2002, p. 219), formed a hierarchical structure of inequities.

The capitalist world-system approach sheds light on the case I am making here. At the core of this approach is global capitalism and the global division of labor. This approach provides a robust foundational framework to reimagine the modern colonial world, though there are some limitations of this model (which I will not discuss in detail here). An important aspect of this approach is being able to debunk the argument that the "world has been decolonized" (Grosfoguel, 2002, p. 204) and differentiate the impact of capitalism in the global north versus global south. This approach will further strengthen my argument about the continuity of human colonial projects in the modern colonial world.

While I recognize the fact that capitalism is here to stay, if we are to mitigate the worst effects of capitalism, we need to talk about the decolonization process. Fanon (1963, p. 2) describes the revolutionary aspect of "decolonization, which sets out to change the order of the world." But I am not sure how feasible this is. My optimistic thinking, coupled with anti-colonial principles, is that there is a possibility for change if we rethink capitalism as it is here to stay. I acknowledge that this might be a stretch, I also feel we need to engage in talking about the possibility of changing the current colonial structure. I recognize that many anti-colonial practitioners would argue that the only path to decolonization is to dismantle capitalism. I am not certain if we can do that to a power structure that is rooted in settler colonialism in over 500 years of history. But there is power in utopian thinking and dreaming for a better world for our future generation through creating possibilities of "profit with a purpose." Touching on our Indigenous land teaching of building communities of business owners while debunking neoliberal ideologies. I will bring in two case studies to create possibilities. I recognize this is the influence of my business education background; I also need to learn to be gentle on myself while I am unlearning my many years of foundational learning and relearning what matters most to humanity in this day and age: social justice. This is not an easy task, but I am genuinely committed to a path of anti-colonial praxis towards decolonization, starting with my mind and soul cleansing.

Positioning

In positioning myself in the article, I am a human resources (HR) practitioner with over 15 years of experience in various industries. I have an undergraduate degree in corporate governance and an MBA, both from the United Kingdom. My MBA thesis was on the Enron and Worldcom failures. If I were to theorize what I wrote through my anti-colonial lens now, it would express my frustration with neoliberal capitalism. Due to a lack of knowledge of anti-colonial or decolonial praxis, I could not articulate my frustration in this way. Instead, I focused on the failure of the board and the CEO. This was my first experience resisting the idea of capitalism.

Coming back to my years of experience, I always knew there is something wrong with human resource practices. Every aspect of what I do every day contributes towards the argument of coloniality, where employees are human colonial projects. Every policy and practice that is adopted contributes towards profit in mind, hence producing and reproducing neoliberal capitalistic ideology at the expense of human well-being. I hear organizations talking about "people are our biggest asset" or "people are our strength." Yes, they are, as long as they contribute to increase profit margins. The minute they slack off due to various reasons— sickness, family obligation, or any other reason that hinders their ability to be at work—then they become the targeted human colonial subject. This is a micro-level impact of capitalism and the damage to human lives.

Let us look at the macro-level impact: How about the environmental impact due to capitalism? Deforestation of Indigenous land due to industrial activities, resulting in environmental destruction (Simpson, 2004) that preserves the continued colonization of Indigenous people and their land. I am concerned about depleting green spaces and protected land from corporate capitalism; we all have a responsibility to protect it from further human destruction, not just for today, but for our future generation. While I wouldn't call myself an environmentalist yet, as I am part of the problem with my consumption pattern, I am heading in the trajectory of environmental activism by changing my consumption pattern. So, this is my attempt towards resisting capitalism that is negatively impacting our environment and world in general.

Impact of Neoliberal Capitalism

The Corporate sector(s) around the world is a multitrillion-dollar venture that contributes towards world economic growth. When I hear the term economic growth, I have mixed feelings, as I am not certain as to who decided economic growth, on what basis and at what cost. The rise of capitalism, as part of settler colonization, as a global system and mobility, marks the formation of the uncertain of the modern world since the fifteenth century. This process of universalization of capitalism, however, entailed:

- forcible capture of people, land, and natural resources,

- transportation and deployment of labor (slavery), post seventeenth century (please note transatlantic slave trade began in the fifteenth century),

- distorted patterns of global migrations,

- economic exploitation of the global south, and

- finally, racist domination and political, social, and cultural oppressions organized by the colonial and imperial systems under European settler dominance.

While all of the above is problematic and contributes towards colonization, but I am going to more focus on one aspect, which is labor exploitation of the global south in the form of the international division of labor, and its consequences and the internal policies, processes, and procedures that are applied to result in and upholding colonized practices. According to Frobel, Heinrich, and Kreye (1994, p. 832) this "new international division of labor has already arrived and that it has turned Western investment toward the underdeveloped countries creating severe unemployment in industrial countries but *supposedly* benefiting the countries receiving this capital." According to the same authors, the reason why they are divesting the investment is because of:

- Cheap labor in developing countries. Hence the lower cost of production results in a higher profit margin.

- Longer working hours (days, week, and year) than the western world due to less stringent labor laws.

- The productivity of labor is equivalent or comparable to the western world *(this is an important point as this is part of capitalistic "isms" myth that whiteness is superior).*

- Workers can be hired and fired without restraint. Among other things, this means that labor can be consumed at a faster rate, and new workers can replace burned-out workers almost without restrictions.

- This existence of an available reserve army of labor permits the optimum selection of the most appropriate labor force according to age, sex, ability, discipline, etc. In other words, upholding all forms of "isms" and discrimination.

Professor David Barkin (1990, p. 13) provided a Marxist perspective on the discourse of the new world economy. He argues that "because of its international character, we call this process of expansion of capitalism, the internationalization of capital. This phenomenon has been in process for several centuries, but only just recently has it assumed global proportions." Post-fifteenth century, a global movement of capital and people has been free flowing, voluntarily or involuntarily (slavery). The above analysis on why the capital is being shifted to the developing world is very problematic as it is a visible indication of humans are being used as continuing colonial projects, affirming coloniality as a result of capitalism. The exploitation of workers by providing lower wages and less than desired working conditions, manipulation of facile labor law, and above all, being able to discriminate in the hiring process is all contributing towards coloniality.

Quijano and Wallerstein (1992) in their work explore the international division of labor, the global racial or ethical hierarchy, and the hegemonic Eurocentric epistemologies in the modern colonial world system (Grosfoguel, 2002, p. 205). However, the colonial administration has ended its influence on the colonial Eurocentrism on the current global system, resulting in coloniality, which is a colonial form of domination and exploitation. We saw this in the case of the 2013 Bangladesh factory collapse and lack of responsibility or action taken by Jo Fresh or Loblaw. This is problematic as it is an indication of real problems with capitalism, which is being used to colonize humans from developing countries. The result is affirming hegemonic Eurocentric epistemology that upholds world capitalism or the global south. On the flip side, if we bring our attention to the Western world or the global north, those who are impacted by shifting capital are those who are marginalized, racialized, or colonized people facing discrimination in the process and becoming human colonial projects. The fact of corporate work is Eurocentrism, or upholding White supremacy ideology. The face of the marginalized racialized colonial project is people of color in the north.

In talking about global capitalism and the international division of labor, it is important to bring in the capitalist world-system approach and coloniality of power. In exploring this approach, the distinction between coloniality and colonialism becomes an imperative aspect. As explained, coloniality is a continuation of the colonial situation of domination and exploitation. The colonial situation here refers to the cultural, economic, and political oppression of the racialized or colonized by the dominant. Colonialism is a colonial power enforced by the presence of colonial administration. According to Grosfoguel (2002), coloniality of power refers to a "crucial structuring process in the modern/colonial world-system that articulates peripheral locations in the international division of labor, subaltern group political strategies, and third World migrants' inscription in the racial/ethnic hierarchy of metropolitan global cities" (2002, p. 5). Grosfoguel (2002) description of the coloniality of power becomes an essential aspect of the capitalist world system and the exploitation of people from the global south. The myth that the world has been decolonized as the colonial situation ceased with the downfall of colonial administration is problematic as it negates the racialized or colonial hierarchy and makes coloniality unnoticed and invisible, especially in capitalism and corporate world.

During various stages of capitalism and in this process, including taking away the crucial resources (such as land and natural resources), the oppression of racialized or colonized peoples, and their direct or indirect exploitation by capitalists, remain the typical characteristics of the phenomenon of colonialism. We can continue to talk about these terms, but the reality is such exploitation of the global south exist in the world in various forms. In this respect, how can we even begin to talk about the multinational elites' league for "looting the third world, a sort-of global super-ministry of the colonies" (Degoy, 2006). In defending imperialist capitalist nations (global north) by protecting industrialization by opening up free market access to resources in the global south without giving the south access to markets in the north. This is somewhat an "apartheid on a world scale" (Degoy, 2006), affirming coloniality.

Capitalism and colonialism are inseparable, more specifically, the imperialism of the global south. Colonization of the Indigenous people of North America by the Spanish and Portuguese, followed by the French and the British, is the major scheme of modern imperialist colonization. This is a fierce form of colonization resulting in the genocide of the Indigenous population and the beginning of black slavery. If we carefully follow the path of colonization through history, we can see the linear relationship on how capitalism has constructed through the system of capitalist exploitation and the periphery. Grosfoguel (2002, p. 208) explains that the "colonial axis between Europeans or Euro-Americans and non-Europeans is inscribed not only in relation to exploitation (between capital and labor) and relations of domination (between metropolitan and peripheral states) but in the production of subjectivities and knowledge." Grosfoguel's argument is an important aspect of talking about the impact of capitalism in the global south as often the subaltern is excluded, and the knowledge production is based on dominant Western ideology. Let's bring our attention a bit to the work of Immanuel Wallerstein. He makes it clear that "a world-economy to survive must have a capitalist mode of production, and inversely that capitalism cannot be the mode of production except in a system that has the form of a world-economy (a division of labor more extensive than anyone political economy)" (Wallerstein, 1984, p. 60). I wrote about the division of labor above and the continuity of coloniality in the global south.

Capitalism has a larger futuristic impact that is often talked about very little. Let us look at the cause of environmental destruction and global warming. While a conservative like President Donald Trump can continue to believe and argue that global warming is illusory, the reality is far from what the conservative capitalists believe it. Think about the following facts:

- Each year, we extract an estimated 55 billion tons of fossil energy, minerals, metals, and biomass from the Earth for human consumption. This depletes natural resources for the benefit of capitalism, thus feeding into colonial practices.

- The world has already lost almost 80% of its forests in the form of industrialization, and we are continually losing them at a fast phase each day.

- At the current rate of deforestation, 5–10% of tropical forest species will become extinct every decade.

- Every hour, 1,692 acres of productive dryland become desert due to global warming.

- Approximately 27% of our coral reefs have been destroyed. If the rate continues, the remaining 60% will be gone in 30 years. There will be a point when our future generation would not even know what coral reefs are.

- A garbage island floating in our ocean, mostly comprised of plastics, is the size of India, Europe, and Mexico all combined. Think about the environmental destruction caused by plastic, which takes up to 1000 years to decompose.

- We are consuming 50% more natural resources than the Earth can provide. At our current population, we need 1.5 Earths, which we do not have.

If we analyze the cause of all these, one undeniable thing is capitalism and commodification of our natural resources. Let us go back in times of history. Tuck and Young (2012, p. 5) argues that in settler colonialism, the most important concern is natural resources. There is a very strong connection between settler colonialism, natural resources, and capitalism. When European settlers came to North America, they made Indigenous land their new home and source of capital (Tuck & Young, 2012), and also because of disruption of Indigenous relationship to the land, which is the beginning of the environmental destruction. Indigenous people knew how to protect the land. The land is not just the colonial notion of physical land and/or property, which is pretty much a capitalistic approach. For Indigenous peoples, land means more than that, representing their history, culture, connection to the environment, etc.

For neoliberal capitalists, globalization, with its relationship to ecology and environmental destruction, is just the latest phase of the process of capital accumulation (Baganh, 2001, p. 138), based on the endless commodification of natural resources across the globe. This globalization, which dictates human relationships to the environment, has led to a systemic socio-ecological crisis and the catastrophes we are currently experiencing. The crisis emerges through the exhaustion of these very "organizational structures" of modernity, with its emphasis on "material" accumulation (Arrighi 1994; Moore, 2011). The crisis is such that it delegitimates current systems of governance within the global capitalist socio-ecology. This means that the current failure to address environmental destruction and the problems reflect the exhaustion of the organizational structures that form interactions within the capitalist socio-ecological system. Hence, my argument that capitalism plays a vital role in environmental destruction is rooted in the history of colonialism and the negative impact on human lives becoming human colonial projects.

Rethinking Capitalism (Utopian Thinking)

My intention here is not to undermine the necessity of capitalism. Capitalism is dangerous in that it is rooted in a strong concrete Eurocentric foundation stemming from settler colonialism. As hard as it is to accept, it is here to stay with its over 500 years of history. But we also cannot forget the fact that the world did not begin after 1492; there was a world that existed even before that. So, I cannot stop and indulge in blue-sky speculation of "what would have been" if colonization was not part of our history.

My intention here is to see what can be done with what we have: to start shaking the Eurocentric capitalist foundation, a thinking process that requires an element of anti-colonial principles, debunking mainstream capitalism and building communities. I have discussed the international division of labor as a form of coloniality that would prevent the process of decolonizing the world while ensuring Eurocentrism. I am a Sri Lankan, a native Tamilian, who has faced forms of discrimination and oppression. Since my birth, all I knew was oppression. With my new knowledge, I see things differently. I see vulnerable women working in free trade zones being paid less than $1 per day with less than desirable living conditions and a rising cost of living. This is a form of coloniality. Dominant Sri Lankan politicians advocate trade to better the economy, but now I ask at the expense of what and whom? I see the dying cultural roots and the domination of Western culture. I see the disappearance of the middle class. This trend is happening both in the north and the south. As explained above, capitalism plays a big part in this widening gap between the rich and the poor or the upper class and the working class.

I cannot stop thinking about Paulo Freire's *Pedagogy of Hope* as a kind of utopian thinking. While I am not going to give a detailed *Pedagogy of Hope*, I will use some of its principles throughout this section. Let me get to the point. I have carefully chosen two case studies as a basis for my idea here, one from service-based industry and other from the product-based industry.

G Adventures

G Adventures was founded by Bruce Poon Tip, who is a Trinidadian-born Canadian entrepreneur. In 1990, G Adventures was launched with the belief that travelers around the world could experience "*authentic adventures in a responsible and sustainable manner.*" The company has grown from a one-person show to more than 2,200 employees worldwide in 28 offices around the world. They started with a handful of trips in Latin America to more than 700 adventures spanning around the globe. Each year G Adventures carries over 200,000 travellers from 160 countries with the focus of "real-world" exploration. So, what is different about G Adventures? It is their passion for making sure travelers get behind the scenes to experience the real world in an authentic and sustainable manner, rather than the typical mainstream travel. G Adventures is also known for its responsible approach to travel and has a non-profit partner, Planeterra, which was founded in 2003. Together, G Adventures and Planeterra have built more than 50 social enterprise projects into their itineraries to support local people and local economies in the destinations they travel to, with a focus on sustainability.

G Adventures prides itself on its commitment to "responsible travel." Here's what they believe is a responsible travel partner consists of:

> "Planet Earth is an amazing place, but it's far from perfect. Since the very beginning, G Adventures has operated under the belief that *travel is an exchange, not a commodity.* As a social enterprise, the planet is our product. Its social and environmental welfare is fundamentally important to us—not just as a business, but as human beings, too. When you travel with us, you're giving back as much—if not more—than what you take away, often in ways you'd never expect" (G Adventures, Responsible Travel).

Here are some examples of how they do responsible travel:

Planeterra. Founded in 2003, Planeterra is a not-for-profit organization and a subsidiary of G Adventures. According to Bruce's first book *Looptail*, the idea for Planeterra came from the frustration trying to work with bureaucratic NGOs and not-for-profits due to various kinds of red tape involved in helping local communities. He was committed to helping local communities that the company benefited from in their travel itineraries. Planeterra's mission is to connect local social enterprises to the tourism marketplace by providing catalyst funding, capacity training, and a market link for small businesses supporting women, children, youth, and Indigenous communities. With operating costs coming from G Adventures, 100% of public and corporate donations are invested in local social enterprises in various countries across the world. One such venture is that when you travel with G Adventures, travelers do not just stay in big hotel chains; instead, they stay in these local communities who host travel guests. This creative process not only ensures funding but is also focused on the sustainability of local communities that they are funding.

G Local. One of the commitments G Local makes is to "keep things local" on each travel. The company works with small, locally-owned businesses rather than big international chains, supporting local entrepreneurs and small businesses focused on strengthening local communities and raising the overall quality of life through sustainable businesses and continued local income. Approximately 112,000 people are employed globally by G Adventure's contracted service providers. Being a small entrepreneurial organization, this is a considerable number.

Responsible Travel with Indigenous People. Connecting curious travellers with Indigenous communities is an essential part of G Adventures travel. They are committed to respecting the rights, history, and culture of Indigenous peoples around the world while ensuring that tourism supports their well-being. In 2016,

G Adventures partnered with George Washington University to develop a set of practical, international guidelines. Any travel company can use these guidelines and ensure business relationships, tours, and experiences are developed and operated in an ethical and respectful manner. Very importantly, these interactions are required to uphold the communities' traditions and customs. G Adventures has also invested in local projects protecting children and animal welfare in addition to various other local projects. Just imagine if big travel companies could do something similar to this? Wouldn't there be a real change towards closing the income disparity gap globally?

People Tree

A big part of our consumption as human beings is our clothing. The apparel industry is worth an estimated US $1.3 trillion global retail sales each year. This is huge, given they are a big part of the problem concerning the international division of labor and promoting coloniality in developing nations. Moreover, environmental damage this manufacturing is causing environmental pollution is much larger than we know, and the larger impact is still invisible, as it is not spoken about widely by the capitalists.

I found People Tree's philosophy in promoting sustainable and free trade fashion very impressive. This is a UK-based company founded in 1991 that continues today to be the pioneer of fair-trade fashion internationally, promoting environmental justice and fair trade. People Tree is recognized by customers and the fashion industry as a pioneer in an ethical and environmentally sustainable fashion. Since its inception, People Tree has partnered with Fair Trade producers, garment workers, artisans, and farmers in the developing world to produce ethical and eco-fashion collections. Fairtrade is about creating a new way of doing business: creating access to markets and opportunities for people who live in the developing world and providing equal opportunities with fair and equitable wages.

So, why is a fairtrade company such as People Tree any different from other garment producers across the world? One could say that they are still part of the problem of promoting capitalistic coloniality through the international division of labor. Here are some facts as to why I see them as promoting utopian thinking in the fashion industry:

- The majority of its purchases are fair trade products from marginalized producer groups in the developing world. They guarantee most of their purchasing is committed to the World Fair Trade Organization and fair-trade standards. Being committed to fair trade puts people and the environment at the center of doing business and also recognizes, promotes, and protects the cultural identity and traditional skills of small producers as reflected in their craft designs and other related services.

- Their priority is to support producer partners' efforts towards economic independence and control over their local environment and community. They maintain a long-term relationship based on solidarity, trust, and mutual respect that contribute to the promotion and growth of fair trade. When needed, they help producers with access to pre-harvest or pre-production finance, ensuring sustainability.

- They use natural resources throughout the production to promote environmentally responsible initiatives for a sustainable future. People Tree only works with certified producers and their supply chains from the raw material to the finished fabric and garment. To be certified means that producer's textile products have been produced in factories adhering to strict environmental and social standards. Certification organizations are responsible for ensuring that these standards are followed and respected. If a brand or producer is certified, it ensures that they are environmentally-friendly and socially responsible. Importantly, in the production of organic cotton, no pesticides or harmful chemicals are used during the process.

People Tree Foundation is an independent charity working alongside People Tree, which brings benefits to an even greater number of farmers and artisans through scaling up training, technical support, and environmental initiatives and through raising awareness and campaigning for fair and sustainable fashion. While I am certain other organizations are committed to a sustainable business promoting the concept of "profit with a purpose," I found these two companies work as a base for real social change in the capitalistic colonial world. I found some of their work as a form of inclusion of anti-colonial principles and a path towards decolonizing the global south from its dependencies by building local capacities. Dei and Asgharzadeh's (2001) anti-colonial discursive framework allows for the "effective theorizing of issues emerging from colonial and colonized relations by way of using Indigenous knowledge as an important standpoint" (p. 300). I see, even in these cases, priority is given to Indigenous knowledge, giving colonized Indigenous groups a strong voice that they need. Founded in 1989, current membership with the World Fair Trade Organization (WFTO) stands at 324 organizations in over 70 countries, which is just a very small fraction from the capitalist free market. Just imagine if every business out there in the Western world joins the WFTO and becomes certified? Would that mean that the capitalist world has been decolonized?

Conclusion

Any social justice advocate would agree that there is a danger associated with capitalism that promotes and continue coloniality. It is one of the most obvious side effects of colonialism. The settlers' main interest was the trade and movement of goods and people (slaves). This trend spread to the corporate world in the form of modernity and coloniality in the name of the international division of labor. Capitalists' primary focus is a low cost, high profit. In addition to colonizing the workers in developing nations or the global south, those in the north are also impacted in two ways by capitalism. First, due to the outsourcing of labor to the global south, those who are affected by the loss of jobs are often marginalized/racialized communities. Second, even if you manage to keep the job, these marginalized/racialized bodies are being colonized by the organization through various Eurocentric internal policies, processes, and procedures. I see this every day in my HR career. In all these cases, people become human colonial projects.

One of the most important aspects of capitalism is the environmental damage and the capitalist relationship to the socio-ecological system. We all have the responsibility to protect our natural resources by being mindful of our capitalistic consumption pattern that feeds into environmental destruction and coloniality. Environmental destruction is also due to dying Indigenous knowledge that is a result of capitalist settler colonization and the focus on Eurocentric knowledge as valid and being spread widely, normalizing its history. If we do not rethink our responsibility towards protecting the environment, it is our future generations that will have to pay a larger cost. How do we rethink environmental destruction? Finally, the question above leads me to the two case studies that I discussed. I went into my utopian thinking mode to explore these case studies to rethink capitalism in the form of sustainable, environmentally responsible institutions, building a global community to sustain Indigenous knowledge and culture. I firmly believe through such scholarly work and exploration, we academics can make a difference in rethinking capitalism and a pathway to decolonization.

References

Arrighi, G. (1978). Towards a theory of capitalist crisis. New Left Review, 111, 3–24.

Arrighi, G. (1994). The long twentieth century: Money, power, and the origins of our times. verso. Retrieved online from https://books.google.ca/books?id=cFfKtpgn4fkC&lpg=PP1&ots=D-qfpXasRIH&dq=Arrighi%2C%20G.%20(1994)&lr&pg=PP1#v=onepage&q=Arrighi,%20G.%20(1994)&f=false

Barkin, D. (1990). Proletarizacion global. Universidad Autonoma Metropolitana, Mexico pp.13.

Degoy, L. (2006). Samir Amin: Colonialism is inseparable from capitalism. Translated by Patrick Bolland. Humanité. Retrieved online from https://www.humaniteinenglish.com/spip.php?article70

Dei, G. J. S. and Asgharzadeh, A. (2001). The power of social theory: The anti-colonial discursive framework. The Journal of Educational Thought (JET) / Revue de la Pensée Éducative, 35(3), 297–323.

Dei, G. J. S. (2013). Reframing critical anti-racist theory (CART) for contemporary times counterpoints. In G. J. S Dei and M. Lordan (eds.), Contemporary issues in the sociology of race and ethnicity: A critical reader (pp. 1–14). New York, NY. Peter Lang.

Grosfoguel, R. (2002). Colonial difference, geopolitics of knowledge, and global coloniality in the modern/colonial capitalist world-system. Review (Fernand Braudel Center), 25(3), 203–224. from www.jstor.org/stable/40241548

Kotz, D. M. (2009). The financial and economic crisis of 2008: A systemic crisis of neoliberal capitalism. Review of Radical Political Economics, 41(3), 305–317.

Moore, J. W. (2011). Ecology, capital and the nature of our times: Accumulation and the crisis in the capitalist world-ecology. Journal of World System Research 17(1), 107–146. doi.org/10.5195/jwsr.2011.432

Quijano, Anibal & Wallerstein, Immanuel (1992). Americanity as a Concept, or the Americas in the Modern World-System, International Journal of Social Sciences, No. 134, 583-91.

Simpson, L, R. (2004). Anticolonial strategies for the recovery and maintenance of Indigenous knowledge. American Indian Quarterly, 28(3/4), 373–384.

Tuck, E. & Yang, W. (2012). Decolonization is not a metaphor. Decolonization: Indigeneity, Education & Society, 1(1), 1–40.

Wallerstein, I. (1984). Patterns and prospective of the capitalist world-economy. Contemporary Marxism, 9, 59–70.

Wallerstein, I. (1984). The politics of the world-economy. Cambridge: Cambridge University Press.

Wallerstein, I. (1991). Unthinking social science. Cambridge: Polity Press.

Chapter Six

Bandung to Tkaronto: Anti-colonial and Decolonial Lessons for Community Work and Organizing

Coly Chau

Introduction

My first encounter with the word "Bandung" was in Robin D. G. Kelley's *Poetics of Anti-Colonialism* (Kelley, 2000), as it preceded a discussion of Aimé Césaire's *Discourse on Colonialism* (Césaire, 2000). Kelley (2000) listed global anti-colonial uprisings, revolts, and gatherings, including that of "Bandung." Without much thought, I flipped through the pages, continued reading, and forgot about it. In the Fall of 2018, I re-encountered the same Kelley and Césaire readings, but later the word "Bandung" reappeared in the form of an anthology called *Meanings of Bandung: Postcolonial Orders and Decolonial Visions* (Phạm & Shilliam, 2016).

Grounded in my spirituality and belief of *yuan fen* (緣分), which can be understood as a Chinese folk belief in destiny or "chance or fateful coincidence" (Fan & Chen, 2014, p. 569), something called me to pick up the book on Bandung. For me, *yuan fen* (緣分) governs the sacred interactions and relations in my present lifetime. I understand these interactions and relations range from short acquaintances to those of family members, ancestors, and places, and even to texts and words I encounter as a result of what I have yet to learn. In encountering Bandung, I also learned that the memory of Bandung remains absent. Within my communities, my classes and my circles, we could commonly and readily recall other Western Euro-American histories and events, such as the Cold War or nation-specific events, but there was no idea what the Bandung Conference was or what it had meant. I wondered and continue to wonder about what this present gap in our collective memories can signify. What would be different if the Bandung Conference had some significance in our lives and the work we do? I question what can be learned from the Bandung Conference.

Kelley (2000) powerfully wrote on Césaire's poetic work, describing it as a "declaration of war" on the old order—as old European empires were facing their impending downfall and Africa, Asia, and Latin America were entering an era of decolonization. Kelley (2000) in his book *A Poetics of Anticolonialism* describes how five years after Césaire's publishing of *Discourse on Colonialism*, the Bandung Conference came to be, with "representatives from the Non-Aligned Nations gather[ing] in Bandung, Indonesia to discuss the freedom and future of the third world" (p. 8). The Bandung Conference, also known as the Afro-Asian or Asian-African Conference, took place from April 18–24, 1955, where twenty-nine African and Asian nations, representing over half the world's population, met to discuss their fates. As Non-Aligned nations of mostly former colonies, they sought to distinguish themselves from the predominant American and Soviet divide of power at that time (Cho, 2007; Kelley, 2002). The Bandung Conference was seen as a threat to their former colonizers, vilified and doubted by the West. But the Bandung Conference took place and developed an existence beyond the duration of the event, beyond the physical locale, as well as, beyond what it set out to do. It lived and breathed in poetry, writing, and art, in bodies, in minds, on the streets, and around the world, during the conference and for decades that followed (Agathangelou, 2016; El Alaoui, 2016; Muppidi, 2016; Opondo, 2016; Phạm & Shilliam, 2016).

In this chapter, I attempt to reread and reinterpret the Bandung Conference for what it was and what it meant, but more so, what it can mean. Through this rereading and reinterpretation, I attempt to understand and make sense of what lessons the Bandung Conference offers for reimagining and building community spaces in Tkaronto, where I presently work and organize, and elsewhere.

I start by socially locating myself, as the entry points into my inquiry on Bandung and community spaces. Next, I give a brief overview of what the Bandung Conference was and what it meant. The chapter then articulates for the need to reread and reinterpret Bandung, to open up discussions about the potential for anti-colonial and decolonial lessons from Bandung. With my rereading and reinterpretation of Bandung, I explore how Bandung privileged anti-colonial praxes by delinking from modernity and coloniality. Next, I explore the significant use of poetic knowledge and its embodiments at Bandung. In rereading and reinterpreting Bandung, I explore the conference's projects of decolonial solidarities and futurities. Finally, I end with a reflection, particularly thinking about the romanticization, the many contradictions, refusal, and material realities of Bandung, and what remains to be asked and learned.

Locating myself and this work

My family and ancestors come from the Guangdong province (廣東), specifically Hong Kong (香港), a former British colony from 1842 to 1997; and Macau, a former Portuguese colony from 1557 to 1999; Vietnam and Cambodia, former French colonies; and Singapore, a former British colony. I was born in Hong Kong and migrated to Turtle Island at a young age. I identify as a queer, racialized, migrant woman learner, community member, worker, and organizer. I recognize my complicity as a migrant in the settler-colonial state of Canada, as well as my responsibilities of being an uninvited guest to the Dish with One Spoon Territory.

I am in the process of actively learning and unlearning, reclaiming my humanity, culture, and spirituality. For most of my life, I had been unable to express my worldviews, as it did not fit neatly into a category of "religion," and it had been deemed "superstition." When I learned that the words "religion" (宗教) and "superstition" (迷信) were only introduced into China by the West, through Japan, in the late nineteenth century (Yang, 2008), it helped to liberate me. It allowed me to revalidate the ways of knowing, being, and doing that have been passed down to me by my family and ancestors.

It is with this knowledge of my responsibilities and knowledge of my ancestors' and my lived experiences that have pushed me to engage with others within my communities. For the past decade, I have engaged in different ways with my different communities to address social issues, including anti-Black racism; settler-colonial violence and complicities; Islamophobia; anti-refugee and anti-migrant sentiments; homophobia and transphobia; gendered and sexual violence; decriminalization and support of sex workers; as well as, pushing for food and environmental justice. Communities have always been vital spaces of learning for me, outside of my family and schooling. They have allowed me to work, learn and grow in relation to others around both politics and identity. I write on my community work and organizing not to exceptionalize it or myself, but to utilize it as a place of reflection.

Recently, I have become increasingly conflicted and have found myself feeling quite disconnected from some of the previous community work and organizing I had engaged in. Perhaps, it has been my awareness of my spiritual injury, since reading Shahjahan's (2009; 2005; 2004) work on spirituality in the academy. Not only within the academy but also within community spaces, I felt a fragmentation and dismembering of my whole self. I have had to leave a part of myself at the door perpetually, as I entered into different communities; at times, it was my spirituality and my identities, and at times it was my politics. On occasions, entering such spaces I deemed to be my communities came at a great cost—I would not be able to fully express myself nor connect with others in ways meaningful to me or in ways that nourished me. The resulting disconnect spiritually, intellectually, emotionally, and physically, would continuously tug at me. This eventually became particularly restricting because at the core, I know and understand the importance and centrality of my communities, my community work and organizing in my life, but yet, there was a failure to encompass all of me.

At times, within some of these communities, we worked and organized through the same Western structures, theories, logics, goals, and outcomes. The community work required as much of our bodies and labor as capitalism did, and in the end, made us disposable. At times, we repeated the same lack of transparency, distrust, hierarchies, masculinities/heteropatriarchy, competition, reification of settler-colonial states and nationalism, and same professional and political motivations, as those from which we tried to disassociate from. We continued to degrade and dehumanize ourselves and those within our communities. It is with this in mind that I inquire about the opportunities to learn from the Bandung Conference on a community level. In the following sections, I utilize the Bandung Conference to think through some of these challenges.

Rereading and Reinterpreting the Bandung Conference Through Anti-colonial Praxes

Kelley's (2000) introduction to *A Poetics of Anticolonialism* provokes the need to reread and reinterpret global anti-colonial and decolonial uprisings, revolts, gatherings, and movements that followed Césaire's publication of the *Discourse on Colonialism* in 1950, including Bandung Conference. Kelley (2000) describes Césaire's work as a declaration of war and a manifesto for the third world. This work was deeply impacted by Negritude, which was about the reclamation of Blackness and ultimately the universal emancipation of peoples worldwide (Kelley, 2000). Reclamation of Blackness and the roots of Negritude was and is about transforming "Blackness as something to yearn for and to be achieved through an intellectual and political reimagining, re-visioning, and revelation to change the existing social order" (Dei, 2017, p. 122). The revolt incited in *Discourse on Colonialism* (1950) was ultimately about reimagining our beings, our relations, and the world.

In Phạm and Shilliam's (2016) introduction to their anthology *Meanings of Bandung*, they also write of this need to reread, reinterpret, and make sense of the Bandung Conference, beyond and preceding the Cold War context, to think even further back in history to understand Bandung's connections to earlier global anti-colonial movements throughout space and time, like Haitian Revolution and Independence, struggles for independence in Latin America, and the Māori King Movement's against settlers in Aotearoa (New Zealand). In Phạm and Shilliam's anthology, Agathangelou's (2016) chapter starts by thinking of the interconnectedness of contemporary critical internationalist revolutionary movements, from the Arab revolutions and Indigenous insurgencies to anti-racist, feminist, queer struggles and Black Lives Matter.

It is necessary to ask, then, what happens when we reread and reinterpret seemingly distinct or separated events, movements, and projects, in order to understand how they are interrelated, connected, or informed by one another? Or what are the opportunities to shape the present and future understandings and knowledges? My rereading and reinterpreting of Bandung Conference is about "de-islanding," as Kumarakulasingam (2016) beautifully and poetically puts it: to undo the colonial processes that saw islands and natives that inhabit them as non-relational, rather than knowing they are connected by oceans. It is also about what we know or do not know and what we affirm or forget, as Lowe (2006, 2015) describes: the delimiting of knowledge that has resulted in the categorization, separation, and hierarchization of archives and disciplines, and that ultimately prevents us from fully understanding the violent and interconnected impacts of imperial and colonial projects. Lastly, this rereading and reinterpretation are also prompted by thinking through Andrea Smith's (2006) writing on women of color organizing and on oppressions that reify hierarchies and white supremacy. Smith (2006) reminds us that thinking in these categories and hierarchies keeps us complicit in the oppression and colonization of other communities and countries, rather than focusing on the ultimate dismantling of white supremacy and heteropatriarchy. Rereading and reinterpretation of Bandung is about understanding the interconnectedness and the potentials to transform the present by being able to tackle the ever-changing systems that continue to degrade and separate us.

The Bandung Conference stands out as privileging, engaging, and centering anti-colonial discourses and practices. Even in the early beginnings of Bandung, the conference sought to recognize and address colonial impositions and dominations as disruptions to the society being colonized. A letter written by Indian president Jawaharlal Nehru leading up to the Bandung Conference and the opening speech at conference by Indonesian president Sukarno attest to their stance on colonialism. Both Nehru and Sukarno recounted the painful and violent experiences of colonialism. Their addresses on colonialisms were necessary as starting points for the conference, in particular to oppose revisionist histories of colonialism that either described colonialism as necessary and justified, or that colonialism solely existed in the past (Opondo, 2016). As Césaire (2000) writes in *Discourse of Colonialism,* the colonial encounters were not about human contact but about relations of domination and submission, about draining and destroying spiritualities, cultures, arts, societies, lands, worldview, systems, and possibilities. Colonialism was a process of "thingification," where colonized peoples would only be instruments of production (Césaire, 2000). In his speech, Sukarno also added how colonial processes continue to be present and have taken on new forms (Asia-African Conference, 1955). These acknowledgements of colonial pasts and presents enable speaking of the legacies and lingering presence of colonialism, thus providing bases for anti-colonial ruptures and imagining decolonial futures.

Beginning the conference with this historicism allowed for the process of regeneration of those who have been denigrated and dehumanized through the "thingification" that Césaire (2000) describes. In this manner, anti-colonial practice emphasizes the importance of addressing histories and naming the past that the post-colonial fails to do. The post-colonial can be understood as devoid of historical specificity, which prevents us from asking and addressing the question of how we can ensure that the spaces we create after the break with colonization can allow for "other epistemological possibilities" (Suleri, 1992, p. 759). By marking the colonial as the disruption, and not the end or imminent ways of proceeding, we allow for unearthing and reclaiming other ways of knowing, being, and doing. Where the post-colonial reinscribes Western thought and theory, the anti-colonial centers Indigenous and local epistemologies and evokes articulations from specific geographies, histories, cultures, traditions, and spiritualities (Dei & Asgharzadeh, 2000). Through anti-colonialism, we are reminded that colonial pasts and disruptions do not foreclose the future; instead, there remain alternatives rooted in Indigenous and local epistemologies.

Sukarno's opening speech continued by speaking of moving beyond victimization and fear, and the invocation of the many different religions, spiritualities, desires, cultures and beliefs that spanned the geographic spaces of the conference and of the nations represented at the conference to begin imagining the futures (Asian-African Conference, 1955). Sukarno's speech also recentered spiritual beliefs and religion by declaring their importance in understanding the world and in working towards achieving freedom. The invoking of Indigenous and local epistemologies, ontologies, and axiologies on a platform and scale such as Bandung validates the reclamation and reassertion of non-Western knowledges. Agathangelou (2016) writes of how Mao Zedong drew from Chinese folklore and Wu Cheng'en's novel *Journey to the West,* written in the sixteenth century, to describe his feelings

71

towards the Bandung Conference. Mao utilized the example of the Monkey King revolting and throwing away the Heavenly Rule Book, a story rooted in folkways of Chinese culture and folk religions or spirituality, and non-Western understandings of the world, to incite revolt at Bandung (Agathangelou, 2016).

The evoking of Indigenous and local ways of knowing throughout the Bandung Conference aligns in some ways with Mignolo's (2007) urging to delink from the rhetorics of modernity and the logic of coloniality. The use of Indigenous and localized knowledges and spirituality first allows for delinking from an imposed modernity that focalized Christianity and the European enlightenment, humanism, secularization and rationalism that accompanied it (Mignolo, 2007; Wynter, 2003). Further, the use of these forms of knowledge delinks from the logic of coloniality: its emphasis on totality, hierarchies, and subjugation of knowledges (Mignolo, 2007; Quijano, 2007). Delinking then can be understood not only as undoing what has been imposed, but also demystifying the superiority of Western knowledges and ways of being in relation to one another. In delinking from modernity and coloniality, it allows for the emergence of geopolitics and body politics of knowledges—epistemologies based on intimate relationships among people, language, and land (Maldonado-Torres, 2004), as well as epistemologies that are derived from history, locations, lived realities, and experiences of places, bodies, and cultural memories (Dei, 2017; Mignolo, 2007). Delinking, then, is a process of restructuring, reimagining, and rebuilding of life and communities post-"thingification" (Césaire, 2000). It can be understood as a process of liberation from the confines and degradations of modernity and coloniality, and thus, a process of rehumanization.

Anti-colonial is about transforming subjectivities. As Dei and Lordan (2016) describe it, it is about creating selves from history, culture, and Indigeneity. The Bandung Conference, therefore, served as a space for invoking the history, culture, and Indigenous or local knowledges in order to remake one's identity and collectively remake the subjectivities of former colonized third world nations after the dehumanization and degradation of colonization. The Bandung Conference enabled the creation of a space where the process and understanding of an individual's identity and the collective's identity were set by their own terms and not by that of the West. As Dei (2017) writes, "claiming subjectivities and identities as entry points to knowledge creation is political" (p. 121). It is this crucial act of reclamation of one's identity and one's agency that enables for creating and validating ways of being, knowing, and doing, beyond the previous imposition and domination. It is a return to one's self, a refusal to allow colonial disruption to dictate present ways of being, and a commitment to exist on one's own terms.

Further, in rereading and reinterpreting the Bandung Conference, it also calls for thinking about the subjectivity of the Bandung Conference itself. The Bandung Conference was about existing on its own terms, rejecting Cold War and Euro-American notions of subjectivity, and affirming that peoples and nations can and do exist outside of colonial subordination (Muppidi, 2016). Pasha (2016) proposes that rereading, reinterpreting, and rewriting Bandung allows for Bandung to exist in its own archive.

Within my own communities—the many iterations of community that I mentioned earlier—we have experienced different and multiple processes of colonization, dehumanization, degradation, migration, wars, and revolutions that sought to destroy history, culture, and spirituality. In an attempt to stop reproducing the rhetorics of modernity and logic of coloniality, what and how can we learn by privileging the anti-colonial? What is enabled by delinking from coloniality and modernity? In naming and addressing these pasts, can we collectively act to heal and move beyond victimization? Can we reclaim our identities and invoke Indigenous and local epistemologies, ontologies, and axiologies to ground ourselves, as well as, our community work and organizing? Can we set our terms of how we define ourselves for and by ourselves, and not on the terms imposed on us? I often think of Audre Lorde's (1984) *Sister Outsider: Essays and Speeches*, where Lorde writes on how Black women, men and people must define themselves, or they will be defined and used by others. Can we set these terms for ourselves, but also in relation to others and the other liberatory work that need to be done? What opportunities are opened when we allow for this remaking of ourselves and our communities? How do we rehumanize ourselves and our work? Where do we go from here? As Dei (2017) insists in *Reframing Blackness and Black Solidarities through Anti-colonial and Decolonial Prisms*, "claiming, naming, and representations of identities are vital, but what we do with our subject positions and identities is more crucial" (p. 121).

Bandung's Poetic Knowledge and Its Embodiment

The Bandung Conference was noted as having exuded poetic knowledge—from what the representatives of the nations expressed during the conference, to how it was being celebrated on the streets in other parts of the world. In this section, I explore the significance of anti-colonial poetic knowledge and the embodiments of it. In my personal reading and viewing of clips of the Bandung Conference, I also experienced some similar emotional, bodily, and mental reactions to those I had read about. Even for those who could not be in attendance, such as African American novelist and poet Richard Wright, there was longing to be there and to experience Bandung. Wright described the feelings that emanated from Bandung: they "smacked of tidal waves, of natural forces," and he spoke of his "desire" to be there (Wright, 1954, as cited in Muppidi, 2016, p. 27). According to El Alaoui's (2016) research on the poetry of the Bandung Conference, including that of Egyptian poets Fuad Haddad, Abdel Rahman Al-Sharqawi, Hashem Al-Refa'i, and Salah Jahin; Turkish poet Nazim Hikmet; and Sudanese poet Taj al-Sir Al-Hassan, all these poets described vividly the spirit of Bandung. The Bandung Conference was able to evoke particularly poetic knowledge and feelings beyond those in attendance; the poetic knowledge and feelings were also experienced elsewhere. Part of the significance of the Bandung Conference lies in this past and continued visceral and "felt" component of the conference. Through the poetic knowledge and its embodiment, many scholars have noted how it has informed other ways of sensing and expressing views and stances on colonialism (Agathangelou, 2016; El Alaoui, 2016; Kumarakulasingam, 2016; Pasha, 2016; Muppidi, 2016; Opondo, 2016; Phạm & Shilliam, 2016).

As with Césaire's *Discourse on Colonialism*, poetic knowledge allows for certain feelings to be felt and to be passed along. Poetic knowledge demands in the body a felt reaction, and an action, that differs significantly from rationality and logic. Césaire writes that "poetic knowledge is born in the great silence of scientific knowledge" and that it will enable the world to move beyond its current crises (as cited in Kelley, 2000, p. 17). As such, poetic knowledge is part of the delinking from false assumptions of modernity and allows for reclamation and unearthing of our beings, spirits, and selves that is needed to move forward. At times, these poetic knowledges can only be felt, but not quite described fully by words. As Césaire (as cited in Kelley, 2000) describes it, poetry is beyond intelligence; instead, it is an experience. Black feminist writings like Lorde's (1984) book *Sister Outsider* have extensively "highlighted poetic knowledge and its feelings, particularly spiritual and erotic ways of knowing, as powerful ways of knowing, despite their subjugation in the West." Where rationality has been ascribed to the great West and to white men, in reality, rationality and modernity are "road[s] that begin nowhere and end nowhere" (Lorde, 1984, p. 100), and reproduction of such Western ways "will never dismantle the master's house" (Lorde, 1984, p. 110). Therefore, it becomes necessary to ask, what are the potentials for these feelings? And were these feelings from poetic knowledge and its embodiments, felt liberation and revolution?

Writing on Césaire's work, Kelley (2000) states, "it is poetry and therefore revolt" (p. 28). In both Césaire's writing and the work of the Bandung Conference, poetic knowledge is part of the revolution. When poetic knowledge invokes Indigenous and local ways of knowing, being and doing, it incites revolution in and beyond the body, spirit, mind, collective, and the land. Poetic knowledge can help distinguish and bind together these seemingly separate and dismembered parts of ourselves and the world. It seeks to address and heal where the colonial imposition and domination has taken place. As Batacharya and Wong (2018) write, there are internal legacies of colonization that have been stored in our bodies. Poetic knowledge in Césaire's work and Bandung result in these affective and corporeal reactions, as it can be understood as the undoing of stored tensions and legacies of dehumanization and degradation. It speaks to and from the body. But further, poetic knowledge is also about Indigenous and local ways of knowing and expressing ourselves—in and beyond words, so extend beyond bodies, onto land and the immaterial.

Poetic knowledge is fluid and has the ability to go beyond limitations and boundaries (Stewart, 2008), which can explain why it can be expressed in one location, but felt and further expressed in other spaces, places, sites, and at different times. Thus, poetic knowledge, in how it is felt and expressed, is an embodied way of knowing and understanding, and as Dei (2017) posits, embodied ways of knowing are about one's body politics, emerging from the process of delinking from the rhetorics of modernity and logics of coloniality. Tuck and Yang (2012) articulate how "freedom is a possibility that is not just mentally generated; it is particular and felt" (p. 20). Poetic knowledge and the embodiment of it are crucial in anti-colonialism, allowing for freedom from subjugation, domination, and dehumanization to be genuinely felt in the body. As Algerian poet Malek Bennabi expresses, freedom is not only of the land but of the human spirit (El Alaoui, 2016).

If poetic knowledge and its embodiments can have profound impacts at Bandung, what are their potential for our communities? Perhaps, anti-colonial poetic knowledge and the embodiment of it can counter the continued spiritual injuries sustained from harmful community work and organizing. If we can feel and express beyond restrictions and Western ways, by invoking and allowing one another to evoke Indigenous and local ways of knowing, being, and doing, what are the potentials for our work and organizing? The late Roxana Ng questioned the adequacy of ideologies and politics that only centered on intellectuality without attention to emotion, body, and spirit (Ng, 2004, as cited in Batacharya & Wong, 2018, p. 7). What are the potentials for anti-colonial poetic knowledge and the embodiment of it in our community work, our organizing, and our politics? How can poetic knowledge situate and put into relationships our bodies, spirits, minds, collectives, and the land? How can Indigenous and local knowledges inform our poetic knowledge and multitudes of expressing it? What are the potentials when we can bring our whole selves, particularly through embodied ways of knowing, into our community work and organizing?

Projections of Decolonial Solidarities and Futurities

As Pasha (2016) writes, Western observers questioned, "How could former colonials forge a common language seeking an alternative world order?" (p. 203) There was much doubt and skepticism from the former colonizers about what Bandung Conference could mean or what it could achieve for the former colonies. As Muppidi (2016) writes, Western criticisms often infantilized non-Europeans and imagined a permanent dependency on European modernity. In this section, I focus on the forging of decolonial solidarities and futurities of Bandung. The Bandung Conference was about forming the third world language and terms to achieving a future that deviated from past and present colonial conditions. It was about moving away from and beyond relations of "thingification," that would allow one to determine their fate, but also recognize the interlinking of fates.

As previously explored, Bandung marked an opportunity to rethink human relationality, beyond colonial relations. In the remaking of subjectivities of formerly colonized people, it also enabled the remaking of intersubjectivity and collective subjectivity. Bandung was meant as a space of solidarities. Solidarities, as defined by Gaztambide-Fernández (2012), can be understood as the relationship amongst people or groups, where there is a sense of obligation to one another in their commitments and is realized through actions and duties. It was understood that there was a need to seek common goals and grounds, despite different histories, and political, social, and spiritual ideologies (Kumarakulasingam, 2016). In gathering together, the nations aimed to develop that common language to envision and create their futures within the framing of larger collective futures.

Gaztambide-Fernández (2012), in writing on pedagogies of solidarities, describes how intersubjective interaction, the encounters of peoples and groups, allow for transformation into subjects. At the Bandung Conference, there was an understanding that for the newly independent nations in attendance, the remaking of one nation or people's subjectivities was in relation to the other nations or peoples, among which there existed a deep interconnectedness. As Agathangelou

(2016) writes, by exhibiting solidarities through poetic knowledge, the Bandung Conference was a "site of new idioms and experimentation . . . using verbs, tropes, and strophes to challenge and transform the consciousness of peoples" (p. 102). It was through poetic knowledge that this consciousness of interconnectedness and intersubjectivity was expressed and realized. Further, this speaks to the creative pedagogical solidarities that Gaztambide-Fernández (2012) describes—an imagining, producing, and promising of new ways to be together. The Bandung Conference was about developing new ways of being together that addressed the past, but also, as I discussed previously, envisioned futures not dictated by the violent "islanding" that made colonized nations and people non-relational (see Kumarakulasingam, 2016).

At Bandung, there was an explicit understanding that solidarity was not about uniform thoughts or action but an acknowledgement of differences and power relations (Kumarakulasingam, 2016). Although the peoples represented at Bandung all had different experiences, and thus different desires and goals, there was a recognition that the platform could still be meaningful. That solidarity could be built not simply because of homogenous experiences, desires, and abilities to actualize desires, but built on relationships that both recognized and validated differences and power relations. This process involved the recognition that there was and continues to be a need to restructure and dismantle overarching systems and hierarchies that have created the unequal power relations and present conditions. Thus, these solidarities were created for decolonial futurities. As scholar and labor rights activist Winnie Ng (2012) writes, solidarities created through struggles and resistance are acts of hopefulness, and projects of decolonization.

In such, decolonial futurities cannot exist without relations, and gatherings like the Bandung Conference existed in recognition of this. As the work of Dei and Asgharzadeh (2000) and the work of Dei, Hall, and Rosenberg (2000) prompt me to think, collective and collaborative knowledges and futures will often be subjected to oppositional perspectives, but anti-colonialism is a focus on processes. It is a focus on the process of undoing past domination, imposition, dehumanization, and degradation, and working towards multiple ways of knowing, being, and doing, and multiple futures. As a process, it is also important to note that solidarities are not about static relations or positions. As Gaztambide-Fernández (2012) states, solidarity is a transitive act that requires reflecting on positions, and the differences and power relations involved in solidarity will change throughout time.

By moving forward relationally and developing a common language, the Bandung Conference was ultimately about a process of creating alternative futures. Alternative futures not through use of Western thought or theories, or Western understandings of relationships, but rather, futures that reclaimed and were grounded in Indigenous and local epistemologies. As Césaire (2000) writes, it is not about returning to old civilizations nor repeating them, but going beyond them: "It is not a dead society that we want to revive. We leave that to those who go in for exoticism. Nor is it the present colonial society that we wish to prolong, the most putrid carrion that ever rotted under the sun. It is a new society that we must create . . . . (p. 52).

Insistence on decolonial solidarities and futurities were crucial for the Bandung Conference, but how can this help to inform present life and spaces? Our communities, our work, and organizing cannot continue to be siloed. Our futures cannot be imagined as distinct from each other, either. Our relations cannot continue to dismiss differences and existing power relations. How do we imagine our futures in relation to other communities? How do we produce futures through the reclamation of our subjectivities and Indigenous and local knowledges, in relation to the subjectivities and reclamation of Indigenous and local knowledges of other communities? How do we work towards these multiple alternatives and multiple worlds and futures, in relation to others? In our community work and organizing, what is the language or modes of expression that can help us articulate these new human relations? Further, as Ng (2012) proposes, we need to creatively build solidarities that reflect our embodied knowledges and experiences, it is necessary to sustain us in our movements toward the futures we imagine.

Reflections on Romanticization, Contradictions, Refusal, and Material Realities of Bandung

Bandung was and continues to be a complex event with a complex legacy. Thus, it is important to detail the layers and nuances. Rereading and reinterpreting Bandung is not about romanticization, or the claim that the Bandung Conference was perfect or the ideal. Rather, Bandung was filled with contradictions. The Bandung Conference was not about producing utopia, but about producing possibilities of different futures. At the same time, we can question the dismissal of romanticism. In one of my Fall 2018 classes, the instructor (Dr. George Dei) prompted me to think that there is nothing wrong with romanticism, that we can allow romanticism to be our fuel for getting us towards these alternative futures. Rather, we should question where critiques of romanticization come from, and on whose terms these critiques of romanticism are on. In Phạm and Shilliam's (2016) edited collection *Meanings of Bandung*, many of the authors explored the "excess of meaning" that exuded from Bandung, particularly its symbolic, poetic, and visceral meaning, and its almost utopian promises. I question, can these meanings be quantified? Is it possible to move away from Western notions and capitalistic framings, where meanings can be seen as quantifiable, and as as a result, in "excess"? Aside from this thought, it remains important to learn from the achievements and significances, but also from the failures and the broken promises of Bandung. I continue in this last section to write and think through some of the contradictions of the Bandung Conference, and what remains to be learned. As Phạm and Shilliam (2016) write, we need to move beyond just romantic or pessimistic gestures. Moving beyond both can allow for more intentional reflection and can allow for alternative rereadings or reinterpretations.

Although Bandung centered the anti-colonial, it also reproduced many of the same structures and relations (El Alaoui, 2016; Opondo, 2016; Pasha, 2016;). Notably, it reified and pronounced the dominance of the nation-state and relations between nation-states rather than the importance of "peoples." Without dismantling of the nation-state, there will continue to be domination and imbalanced power relations. Nation-states continue to violently dictate, through both symbolic and material ways, who belongs and who does not. It is also essential to think of who was at Bandung, and who was not. Although Bandung deemed itself an Afro-Asian

Conference, there were many nations and peoples not in attendance or represented. The conference was dominated by representatives that embodied hetero-masculinities, while women and people of other genders or sexualities were not represented, nor young people. As Smith (2006) reminds us, heteropatriarchy also reinforces the nation-state. Many artists, poets, thinkers, communities, learners, and people globally who wanted to be in attendance were kept out of Bandung. This speaks to who was and continues to be able to decide on the futures of people. We must refuse to seek recognition from nation-states that neglect us or demean us, and we must continue to refuse empires that try to speak of and for us (Simpson, 2014; Simpson, 2007).

As Dei and Lordan (2016) write, we must be critical of anti-colonial projects that continue centering nation-building and continue to oppress certain peoples. As with our community work and organizing, we must ensure we are critical of our complicities in the nation-state. Particularly, be critical of when we are attempting to reclaim our subjectivities on occupied and stolen lands; when members of our communities are seeking professional and political motivations complicit in nation-building and capitalist state; as well as, what we mean by communities—who do we continue to keep out of our communities?

Further, as Opondo (2016) writes on the sixtieth anniversary of Bandung, what happens when some of the former "wretched of the earth" become those reproducing the wretchedness? It was only six decades prior that China had supported Black liberation, formed the Afro-Asian People's Solidarity Organization, criticized American racism, and been vocal about global struggles against colonialism and imperialism (Kelley, 2002). Since then the Chinese state's exploitation of Africa, the Americas, Asia, and even internal exploitation have continually been exposed. Kelley (2002) writes that Chinese foreign policy was actually more about strategic alliances than a commitment to the third world revolution. Further, as noted by Phạm and Shilliam (2016), what does it mean for Bandung to have taken place at the same time that Indonesia was usurping Western Papua (New Guinea)? Can solidarities exist when identities from anti-colonial struggles are not evenly formed (Simmons & Dei, 2012)?

Can solidarities exist if domination and impositions continue to dictate relations? Within our community work, we must move away from performativity or self-centered interest. We must challenge what is meant when we are in "solidarities." We must be critical of our desires, and how we can be complicit in oppression and colonization. As Gaztambide-Fernández (2012) writes on transitive solidarities, we must be reflective of our non-static changing positions. We must remember that

> solidarity in relationship to decolonization is about challenging the very idea of what it means to the human, and by extension, the logic of inclusion and exclusion that enforce social boundaries, including notions of social, political and civic solidarity. It is about imagining human relations that are premised on the relationship between difference and interdependency, rather than similarity and a rational calculation of self-interest. (Gaztambide-Fernández, 2012, p. 49)

Ultimately, we must return to the land and the material world (Batacharya & Wong, 2018; Dei, 2002; Dei & Lordan, 2016; Tuck & Yang, 2012). Anti-colonialism is as much about spirit, histories, cultures, and knowledges as it is about the land. The land is deeply connected to our understandings of ourselves, our relations, our knowledges, our existence and survival. How do we unearth Indigenous and local ways of understanding and reconnecting with the land? How do we develop new relationships to the land that are also not bound by relations of "thingification"? The land, the earth, the water, the air, the plants, the animals and other non-human beings are interconnected in our liberatory work. Our community work and organizing must ultimately address our relationship with the land.

I end this chapter by thinking about the need to continue rereading and reinterpreting of global anti-colonial and decolonial uprisings, revolts, gatherings, and movements, such as that of the Bandung Conference. We must reclaim Indigenous and local ways and find new interconnected ways to make meaning of the world, that exceed Western epistemologies, ontologies, and axiologies, and what has been prescribed to us. We must move beyond disciplines; beyond interdisciplinary work, we need to be transdisciplinary in our decolonial work (Ng, 2018; Pasha, 2016). In our community work and organizing, we must continue to unearth and find new ways to come into and return to our work.

References

Agathangelou, A. M. (2016). Casting off the "heavenly rule book": Bandung's poetic revolutionary solidarities. In Q. N. Pham & R. Shilliam (eds.), *Meanings of Bandung: postcolonial orders and decolonial myths*. London, UK: Rowman & Littlefield International Ltd.

Asian-African Conference. (1955). *Asia-Africa speaks from Bandung*. Djakarta, Indonesia: Ministry of Foreign Affairs.

Batacharya, S. & Wong, Y.-L. R. (2018). Decolonizing teaching and learning through embodied learning: Toward an integrated approach. In S. Batacharya & Y.-L. R. Wong (eds.), *Sharing breath: Embodied learning and decolonization*. Edmonton, AB: AU Press.

Césaire, A. (2000). *Discourse on colonialism*. New York, NY: Monthly Review Press.

Cho, H-Y. (2007). Revitalizing the Bandung spirit. In K.-H. Chen & C. B. Huat (eds.), *The inter-Asia cultural studies reader*. New York, NY: Routledge.

Dei, G. J. S. (2002). NALL Working Paper #9: Spiritual knowing and transformative learning. Retrieved from https://nall.oise.utoronto.ca/res/59GeorgeDei.pdf

Dei, G. J. S. (2017). *Reframing blackness: Anti-blackness and black solidarities through anti-colonial and decolonial prisms*. New York, NY: Springer.

Dei, G. J. S. & Asgharzadeh, A. (2000). The power of social theory: Towards an anti-colonial discursive framework. *Journal of Educational Thought, 35*(3), 297–323. https://www.jstor.org/stable/23767242

Dei, G. J. S., Hall, B. L., & Rosenberg, D. G. (2016). Introduction: Envisioning new meanings, memories and actions for anti-colonial theory and decolonial praxis. In G. J. S. Dei Hall, & D. G. Rosenberg (eds.). *Anti-colonial theory and decolonial praxis*. New York, NY: Peter Lang, vii–xxi.

Dei, G. J. S. & Lordan, M. (2016). Envisioning new meanings, memories, and actions for anti-colonial theory and decolonial praxis. In G. J. S. Dei & M. Lordan (eds.), *Anti-colonial theory and decolonial praxis*. New York, NY: Peter Lang.

El Alaoui, K. (2016). A meaning of Bandung: An Afro-Asian tune without lyrics. In Q. N. Pham & R. Shilliam (eds.), *Meanings of Bandung: Postcolonial orders and decolonial myths*. London, UK: Rowman & Littlefield International Ltd.

Fan, L. & Chen, N. (2014). "Conversion" and the resurgence of indigenous religions in China. In L. R. Rambo & C. E. Farhadian (eds), *The Oxford handbook of religious conversion* (pp. 556–577). New York, NY: Oxford University Press.

Gaztambide-Fernández, R. A. (2012). Decolonization and the pedagogy of solidarity. *Decolonization: Indigeneity, Education & Society, 1*(1), 41–67.

Kelley, R. D. G. (2000). *A poetics of anticolonialism.* New York, NY: Monthly Review Press.

Kelley, R. D. G. (2002). *Freedom dreams: The black radical imagination.* Boston, MA: Beacon Press.

Kumarakulasingam, N. (2016). De-Islanding. In Q. N. Pham & R. Shilliam (eds.), *Meanings of Bandung: Postcolonial orders and decolonial myths.* London, UK: Rowman & Littlefield International Ltd.

Lorde, A. (1984). *Sister outsider: Essays and speeches.* Trumansburg, NY: Crossing Press.

Lowe, L. (2006). The intimacies of four continents. In A. L. Stoler (ed.), *Haunted by Empire: Geographies of intimacy in North American history.* Durham, NC: Duke University Press.

Lowe, L. (2015). *The intimacies of four continents.* Durham, NC: Duke University Press.

Maldonado-Torres, N. (2004). The topology of being and the geopolitics of knowledge: Modernity, empire, coloniality. *City, 8*(1), 29–56. DOI: 10.1080/1360481042000199787

Mignolo, W. (2007). Delinking: The rhetoric of modernity, the logic of coloniality and the grammar of de-coloniality. *Cultural Studies, 21*(2–3), 449–514. https://doi.org/10.1080/09502380601162647

Muppidi, H. (2016). The elements of Bandung. In Q. N. Pham & R. Shilliam (eds.). *Meanings of Bandung: Postcolonial orders and decolonial myths.* London, UK: Rowman & Littlefield International Ltd.

Ng, W. (2012). Pedagogy of solidarity: Educating for an interracial working-class movement. *Journal of Workplace Learning, 24*(7/8), 528–537. DOI: 10.1108/13665621211261007

Ng, R. (2004). *Embodied pedagogy: New forms of learning.* Workshop at the Department of Sociology, Umea University, Umea, Sweden, 5 May, and presentation at Gavle University College, Gavle, Sweden, 10 May.

Ng, R. (2018). Indigenous resurgence: Embodying all our relations pedagogy. In S. Batacharya & Y.-L. R. Wong (eds.). *Sharing breath: Embodied learning and decolonization.* Edmonton, AB: AU Press.

Opondo, S. O. (2016). Entanglements and fragments "by the sea." In Q. N. Pham & R. Shilliam (eds.). *Meanings of Bandung: Postcolonial orders and decolonial myths.* London, UK: Rowman & Littlefield International Ltd.

Pasha, K. P. (2016). The Bandung within. In Q. N. Pham & R. Shilliam (eds.), *Meanings of Bandung: Postcolonial orders and decolonial myths.* London, UK: Rowman & Littlefield International Ltd.

Phạm, Q. N. & Shilliam, R. (2016). Reviving Bandung. In Q. N. Pham & R. Shilliam (eds.), *Meanings of Bandung: Postcolonial orders and decolonial myths.* London, UK: Rowman & Littlefield International Ltd.

Quijano, A. (2007). Coloniality and modernity/rationality. *Cultural Studies, 21*(3), 168–178. DOI: 10.1080/09502380601164353

Shahjahan, R. A. (2004). Reclaiming and reconnecting to our spirituality in the academy. *International Journal of Children's Spirituality, 9*(1), 81–91. DOI: 10.1080/1364436042000200843

Shahjahan, R. A. (2005). Spirituality in the academy: Reclaiming from the margins and evoking a transformative way of knowing the world. *International Journal of Qualitative Studies in Education, 18*(6), 685–711. https://doi.org/10.1080/09518390500298188

Shahjahan, R. A. (2009). The role of spirituality in the anti-oppressive higher-education classroom. *Teaching in Higher Education, 14*(2), 121–131. https://doi.org/10.1080/13562510902757138

Simmons, M. & Dei, G. J. S. (2012). Reframing anti-colonial theory for the diaspora context. *Postcolonial Directions in Education*, *1*(1), 67–99. https://www.um.edu.mt/library/oar/handle/123456789/19585

Simpson, A. (2007). On ethnographic refusal: Indigeneity, "voice" and colonial citizenship. *Junctures*, *9*, 67–80.

Simpson, A. (2014). *Mohawk interruptus: Political life across the borders of settler states*. Durham, NC: Duke University Press.

Smith, A. (2006). Heteropatriarchy and the three pillars of white supremacy: Rethinking women of color organizing. In INCITE! women of color against violence (eds.), *Color of violence: the Incite! anthology*. Cambridge, MA: South End Press.

Stewart, S. (2018). Poetry: Learning through embodied language. In S. Batacharya & Y.-L. R. Wong (eds.), *Sharing breath: Embodied learning and decolonization*. Edmonton, AB: AU Press.

Suleri, S. (1992). Woman skin deep: Feminism and the postcolonial condition. *Critical Inquiry*, *18*(4), 756–769. https://doi.org/10.1086/448655

Tuck, E. & Yang, K. W. (2012). Decolonization is not a metaphor. *Decolonization, Indigeneity, Education & Society*, *1*(1), 1–40.

Wright, R. (1954). *Black power: Three books from exile: Black power; the color curtain; and white man, listen!* New York, NY: Harper.

Wynter, S. (2003). Unsettling the coloniality of being/power/truth/freedom: Towards the human, after man, its overrepresentation—an argument. *CR: The New Centennial Review*, *3*(3), 257–337. DOI: 10.1353/ncr.2004.0015

Yang, M. M.-H. (2008). Introduction. In M. M.-H. Yang (ed.), *Chinese religiosities: Afflictions of modernity and state formation*. Berkeley, CA: University of California Press.

Chapter Seven

A Look at English Language Futurity in the Post-colonial State

Cherie A. Daniel

Introduction

In writing this chapter, I believe that it is beneficial to the reader for me to locate myself to provide context. I was born in Canada to immigrant parents. My mother is South American born from what was known then as British Guiana (Guyana) and grew up speaking "British English." My mom makes it clear that the language that was spoken in Guyana (pre-independence) was what she knows. In Guyana, there is what is considered a broken or pidgin English. It is effortless to understand and spoken by many with an accent or tone that is very distinct from so-called British English. The pidgin English is mostly spoken by what the upper class believes are the lower, uneducated class in the country. Growing up among my family, I was able to crack the code of language and slang at an early age. I recall early on hearing my aunts and uncles speak in what we coined "Guyana language" and were in awe of and would mimic its words that we did not know the definitions for. My mom would scold me, saying, "You do not have to prove you are Black and speak like that." At that time, I could not understand what my mom was saying because I thought I was speaking Guyanese, the language of my maternal ancestors and heritage. However, from a mother's point of view, the tone and accent of my speech linked to something bigger. I can now see that in her mind if I continued to speak in a manner that was not close to the dominant, I would be setting myself up to be treated as less than who I was destined to become. My father, on the other hand, spoke Creole from Grenada. The words he used were closely aligned to the French language, and I also could decipher some of what he would be saying when he spoke with his family members in my presence. He would only speak English to me and refused to teach me Creole. He never spoke it at home, but in contrast to my mother, he would not make a big deal if I mimicked a word or asked him what it meant. I must confess that I felt cheated out of the heritage, and I chalked that up to the colonizer mentality that my mother unintentionally possessed. Allsop (2010) also speaks on this point:

> For hundreds of years, people have looked at Creole speakers as having less value than Standard Language speakers. "Creoles and creolized varieties of English are associated with low ethnic, social, political, and economic status."... People have believed that the people who spoke such languages were inferior to those that spoke Standard English. (p. 2)

Following Allsop's comment and my own experience, in this chapter, I intend to explore language in contemporary times, taking a closer look at what the past and present have to offer and examine the future of the English language. With the move to global education and migration of people at a vast rate to other countries, it is possible that English could be replaced as the dominant language in a far shorter time than ever imagined.

What Does the Past Offer?

Heller & McElhinny (2018, p. 73) note, "from a historical perspective, that the overwhelming number of European languages may reflect a bias towards languages documented in the context of large-scale European mobility". These languages also reflect the impact of Western European imperialism and the creation of a (specific, nuanced, particular, specialized) inequitable condition for language exchange. Further, the authors suggest that the practices used to manage and enslave people to ensure that there was no opportunity to revolt included mixing people with different language backgrounds (making language exchange - or in other words - communication, ambiguous). In large plantations, for example, Europeans would make up small numbers of speaking English, Spanish, or French so that the enslaved people would have limited access to native speakers of those languages of power; languages they spoke to one another would have to been drawn on many linguistic and cultural inputs (felt knowledge, blood knowledge, cultural memory, rebellion, etc).

Historically, the English language represented power, influence, and wealth, becoming the dominant language adopted by the world as the global standard for communication and trade. David Grewal notes:

> Nowhere are the dynamics of network power clearer than in the domains of language and money. Within a single linguistic or monetary community, we take these systems of exchange for granted. Language and money are inescapable .... When one language or one currency gains great network power, the disruption it generates focuses attention on an otherwise obscure process. (Grewal, 2008, p. 70)

From a purely economic standpoint, it is true that the top currencies in the world are also linked to the English language. This is clear evidence that power and money are linked to language. Colonizers have used this method of language to dominate and create divisions among communities based on wealth, well beyond the time when color barriers were outlawed. An additional means of ensuring that the dominant role of the English language is preserved takes place in the homes of the affluent class. For instance, there has been historical evidence in the mid-twentith century that White children being cared for by Black nannies were learning Creole as their first language, a language which is perceived as degenerate than European languages. Such children symbolized a fear of the form of White degeneracy due to living in the tropics and in proximity to colonize and racialized people (Heller & McElhinny, 2018). I tend to agree because there was no issue for Black people (women specifically) to become nannies for the privileged White children, but when the influence become more than childminding it was met with difficulies. There have been stories that I recall where White children that grew up in the islands with the Black nannies would speak of them as momma or terms related to the close bond they shared. One could foresee that the influence would be so significant that the White children would, in a way, become surrogate children to the Black nannies, which in turn would lead to a cross-cultural link in both culture and language.

Alternatively, language was historically in the hand of the oppressor. This is why, early on, colonizers would make sure to separate those who communicated through a or common language from each other. In other words, it can be illustrated that the colonial method was a means to separate and further divide through language and not unify.

> [The fact that] the British Empire encompassed one-quarter of the world's population... explains why English is an official or dominant language in 60 countries ... the current global position of English is the result of more than a few centuries of outright conquest. In the past few decades ... it has grown rapidly in importance as the language of international commerce, governance, and technology. (Grewal, 2008, p.73)

It is clear that the effects of oppression historically continued to force people who were not always versed in the English language to immigrate to the dominant English speaking countries to learn English and gain access to better opportunities. However, more often than not, these folks would find themselves left feeling devalued and displaced based on the barriers surrounding their knowledge of the language in their 'new country'. As a result of these experiences resulted in intergenerational trauma, Elders are becoming more and more removed from their communities. I remember the days when the Elders in families historically had pride in their rich oral history and the connection this knowledge established for the identity of their community. Communities would gather and celebrate their unique, rich culture and leave a legacy of a strong connection to language and land. Families would ensure the connection of younger generations with the older generations and customs, but the colonial past continues to destroy when one is displaced to another country. Since language is tied to one's social status, one is forced to use the colonizer's language of English to progress, whether in your country or a foreign country. Therefore, it is fair to argue that once colonizers realized that language is critical in affirming one's identity and economic emancipation, they carefully executed plans and infiltrated those countries that became British colonies and created language barriers, through which they were able to gain power over the people. These barrier continues to exist today in one form or other, resulting in lingering divisions between the lower, middle, and upper classes, or in the division between proletariat and bourgeoisie.

Indigenous Canadians and Language Rights

While language rights are entrenched in law s.16 of the *Charter of Rights and Freedoms*, the only official languages in Canada are still English and French. Section 16. (1) reads, "*English and French are the official languages of Canada and have equality of status and equal rights and privileges as to their use in all institutions of the Parliament and Government of Canada.*" Prima facie, the law suggests that Canada embraces instead of erasing language rights. However, it simultaneously sends the message to Indigenous people that their languages are not validated. It is important to note that although the Dominion of Canada gained Independence on July 1, 1867, it was not until April 17, 1982, that those language rights were officially entrenched. It was not by coincidence that it was English (the dominant) that was recognized; and, because of the necessity of persuading representatives from the Province of Quebec to be signatories to the Charter, French was also recognized as an official language. However, what does this suggest to Indigenous Canadians who have been further alienated by having their languages denied official recognition? This further suggests erosion of whole communities and stemming from the year of systemic racism. It is a clear mimicry of the colonization mentality. There are no levels of quality, but rather, in this case, a further divide between three parts of Society, the English-speaking Canadians, the French-speaking Canadians, and the Indigenous people. Even with the truth and reconciliation report, in my opinion, there is a growing number of Indigenous communities, who are questioning this right and its inclusion towards them. Droogendyk and Wright (2017) speak to the issue of Indigenous peoples and North America and resistance. They argue, "Indigenous peoples in North America have resisted colonization for centuries, fighting for survival, recognition, and sovereignty—despite the attempts of colonial governments to eliminate their cultures and way of life" (Droogendyk & Wright, 2017, p. 303). What has the government's response been toward the further ignoring of the language rights of Indigenous people? It has been recognized that the effects of residential schools are still being felt today. The loss of land and the continued fights for recognition are still contentious issues and a source of conflict from both sides. Language rights have also become more important because the new generations are looking for reparations for the consequences of further losses. These reparations are crucial to preserve the culture of people that is based on rich oral history and risks becoming extinct. Droogendyk & Wright (2017) speak on this point as well:

> In this examination of resistance by Indigenous peoples, we explore the role of one critical element of Indigenous culture—language. Language is not only a vehicle for communication but the medium by which cultural knowledge is transmitted. But more than this, a language holds in its vocabulary, structure, and delivery the traditions, views, and ways of thinking that are a group's cultural uniqueness. (p. 304)

Even with everything discussed above, many still believe strongly that Indigenous culture is now becoming more and more recognized. However, it is false that, because of truth and reconciliation, which ended in 2015, conversations are no longer required. However, it was not until 2019 that the United Nations declared the International Year of Indigenous Languages. This was apparently an attempt to acknowledge Indigenous languages while at the same time attempting to protecting those who speak it. On January 12, 2019, a post on the United Nations website notes:

> Language plays a crucial role in our daily lives. They are not our first medium for communication, education and social integration but are also at the heart of each person's unique identity, cultural history and memory. The ongoing loss of Indigenous languages is particularly devasting, as the complex knowledges and cultures they foster are increasingly being recognised as strategic resources for good governance, peacebuilding, reconciliation, and sustainable development. More important, such losses have negative impacts, Indigenous peoples' most basic rights. (United Nations, 2019, para. 1)

The movement toward recognition of Indigenous language and reclaiming ownership of the land has become an insurgence towards retracing history and breaking the dominant narrative. Could reclaiming language be a step in the right direction of reclaiming history? Does it not make sense that the original people should be restored to their original state? Would the restoration of language rights give power back to a nation that was essentially erased from history and forced to lose their identity because of the colonized state of existence? Or would official recognition of language merely appease Indigenous groups rather than rectify years of oppression? And if so, if the dominant continues with its failed attempts to "right this wrong" without consultation of Elders or other members of all Indigenous communities, what could be the future result? Droogendyk and Wright (2017) comment on the perceptions of injustice:

> The process of decolonizing the mind might also facilitate resistance in other ways; for instance, a colonial mindset that justifies Indigenous oppression is inconsistent with Indigenous cultural knowledge and experience. To the degree that a re-emergence of an Indigenous worldview can offer a clear alternative, decolonization of the mind can serve as a basis for questioning the legitimacy of the colonial structure, making the collective struggle seem increasingly legitimate and worthy of participation. (p. 307)

Creole Languages Versus English Language

Allsop (2010) contends that there is a great divide between the public's opinion of Creole languages and linguists' opinions of Creole languages. If the majority of the public were to hear the Creole language, they might find it "broken" or a sign of being uneducated. They may even believe the following: "Pidgin ranks right up there with Ebonics" (Allsop, 2010, p. 3). The manner in which pidgin and Ebonics are similar is because both are made up of various English words. Through a shortening or tone change it becomes its own identiy. The langue mostly spoken by Black people. The idea is that it is a negative value to speak this language, however in today's society Ebonics has been called "African-American English". In fact in 1995, "the Oakland Unified School District has declared Black English a second language, making it the first district in the nation to give the controversial dialect official status in programs targeting bilingual students." (Woo & Curtius, 1996) This mentality is not far from the colonizer since that is what their thoughts were for colonization in the first place. This attitude of superiority towards language goes hand in hand with the prevalent idea of the White savior coming to the rescue. When something questions the existence of the dominant voice, the colonizers respond with an attempt to "fix" the problem, which lies with the colonized. In his discussion of "The Negro and Language," Fanon (1967) observes, "To speak means to be able to use a certain syntax, to grasp the morphology of this or that language. Still, it means above all to assume a culture, to support the weight of a civilization" (p. 1). This, to me, is an excellent summary of what the English language was, but I would argue this is no longer the case. The imposition of English was the key for colonizers to fight resistance among the colonized, forcing them to adopt the value system of the dominant culture, to erase their own languages, and to be further robbed of their cultures and ways of knowing.

In the United States, reports Allsop (2010), "There are now more Creole speaking students in the USA than ever, and educators need to be prepared to teach in this unique educational situation" (p. 4). This proves to me that the current post-colonial collective is taking back charge of their voice and reclaiming the existence of their ancestral voices and language. Green and Smart (1997) provide some reasons for the move toward an alternative to the English language, explaining that the development of a Black vernacular has been an essential form of resistance. Since 1973, the term "Ebonics," coined from "ebony" and "phonics," has become a controversial but common label for Black vernacular(s) in the United States (Green & Smart, 1997, p. 521).

Additionally, outside of the United States and Canada, it is becoming clear that the languages in the Caribbean have evolved into many different forms of the English language. By merely looking around university campuses and the international cohort, one can see an increase in students from India, Jamaica, and China, who hope for their families back home to join them. Parents are following trends in their community in wanting to send their children to foreign lands for better opportunities. The level of the English language used by international students has developed through language classes within their home country, via online methods, or by private tutoring. By showing competence in English, immigrant students hope to ensure assimilation in Society.

Native Jamaicans, too, participate in this trend of taking language classes. It is clear that when many think of Jamaica, they automatically think of its famous patois. Many do not want their children associated with a language that is considered broken or the voice of the uneducated. Historically, Jamaican and other Caribbean dialects are each known for a distinct accent (usually attached to the pronunciation of certain words). There is a stigma or shaming that is associated with speaking these dialects. As a result, there is a strong movement toward ensuring that the "Queen's English" becomes the standard. Due to the lingering effects of colonization, the belief is that to excel in life and open up opportunities, you need to be closer to the dominant language. While this may have been true for the Baby Boomers, I feel that for the Generation Xers onward, there has been a movement towards reclaiming their heritage. Evidence of this could be seen in 2001, when the Ministry of Education and Culture of Jamaica began to use the term "transitional bilingualism" in the elementary years of schooling.

This initiative was meant to assist young children to engage in school by using the language and dialect that may be familiar to them from their home life. As it generally understood, engaging learners in familiar dialects from a young age ensures that they will have more motivation toward academics generally. Although Standard English is still the preferred method of instruction and expression with the students, this is beginning to change, for there is a mobilization toward expressing themselves in their mother tongue that is felt to be effective, a return to the methods of years before the imposition of Standard English. There are continued stories that have been passed down to generations where teachers in the Caribbean would not allow children to speak their Creole languages. Instead, children were led in the direction of Standard English. This led to a disdain for their own culture, ensuring distance between that culture and the dominant language, and created a situation where more opportunities were lost.

The rise and popularization of the Jamaican Creole or Patois can be traced to Bob Marley, who unified language through music across all cultural borders. Almost everybody knows the words of "One Love" or "Three Little Birds" and also realise that Bob Marley was singing in his own version of English. The increasing activities of tourism have also allowed for more people to be exposed to the Creole language. This is clear when people from all over arrive at the airport in Jamaica and are being transported to their all-inclusive resort. As they board the bus, the tour guide instantly goes into a script that includes teaching words to speak like a Jamaican. You hear things like, "Say it with me: Yahhh Mon," which means "Yes," or "Everything is IRIE," which means "all good" and, of course, my favorite: "Whaaa Gwan?" which means "What's going on?" As I experienced this on a recent trip to Jamaica during the language lesson, I saw people from the Netherlands, United Kingdom, Canada, and the United States united for that moment on the bus. Now, while I do not assume to be in anyone's mind, I was able to observe that people were happy and smiling and that they were repeating the words with great difficulty. I stopped and thought to myself, what an irony it is learning this Creole language! What must it be like for non-native English speakers to grasp the language without a guide, outside the space where their pronunciations are accepted?

Now their acceptance of this mini linguistic lesson does not erase the views of the same people on the bus when they return from their magical vacation in the islands. They want to assimilate and learn more and more and can be seen around the resort mimicking the words and trying very hard to ensure the right pronunciation. To me, the popularity of the Jamaican Creole is both a positive and negative development: while I am very happy for the boost to economy that the all-inclusive trips have brought to Jamaica, I would argue that it comes at a cost as well. The detrimental aspect of this promotion of Jamaican Creole is to other islands, where tourists automatically think Jamaican is spoken. Or the assumption that I personally have been subjected to: someone greets me with "Whaa Gwan" and before I can answer, follows up with "Which part of Jamaica are you from?" It takes a moment for them to process my response of "I am not Jamaican," which leaves them looking clearly confused, but they go on to say, "Where are you from then?" I, therefore, take this to mean that I could not possibly be from anywhere else in the Caribbean and most certainly not born in Canada.

Does this mean that the older generation will be accepting of their children and grandchildren speaking in this manner? In 2005, a study titled "The Language Attitude Survey of Jamaica: Data Analysis" was undertaken by the Jamaican Language Unit of the University of West Indies Mona (University of the West Indies (2007). The survey gave some insight into people's perception of language in Jamaica. From the sample of individuals that were consulted, there was a positive view of *Patwa*. In fact, "the majority felt that Patwa was a language and that parliament should make it an official language alongside English."

Furthermore, moving towards the idea of bilingualism by making English and Patwa official languages of Jamaica was supported by the majority of the people. Therefore, to me, the study suggests moving in the direction of many that are looking to re-establish the historical language of the majority of people in a nation. This suggests English still has a place, but people do not accept that English as the only language that should be used. This is also examined in Wassink's (1991) paper "Historic low prestige and seeds of change: Attitudes toward Jamaican Creole." Wassink (1991) cites a finding from Pauline Christie, who notes, "[r]ecent discussions among both Jamaican scholars and laypeople suggest that Jamaicans' attitudes toward Jamaican Creole are changing. This change, some suggest, has accompanied the increased popularity of Dancehall culture and nationalistic 'consciousness-raising' efforts" (p. 1). This further proves the point that language has no choice but to follow Jamaican music's worldwide acceptance and be itself accepted, either consciously or unconsciously, by everyone. In a paper presented on March 25, 2007, Grewal (2007) also illustrates the connection between the Caribbean and the English language.) a woman from St. Lucia who explains that "We don't speak a real language, we just speak broken French" (p. 1). He observes that even after she has mae this comment to him, the woman "didn't seem sad or angry in explaining her situation." To me, that was sad, as it symbolized the long-term effects of colonization on the language of her people. These effects have been the case for all Caribbean nations as well as other colonized nations. There is no doubt that this is something she was taught in the English language by someone who was either not from the Caribbean or was trained in a foreign country. The purpose of this teaching was to continue this narrative of non-acceptance of one's self, language, and culture. Frank (2007) further notes that " [t]hose responsible for propagating such unfair and inaccurate assessments are generally speakers of the standard languages, and particularly members of the education establishment, who would rather see the patois wiped out and replaced by the standard English language" (p. 1).

What Does the Present Offer?

Language historically has been linked with power and class; there is no doubt about that. Oxford English Dictionary picks a word of the year and notes a few words as worthy to add to the Dictionary. In 2015 the Oxford Dictionary's Word of the Year was for the first time a pictograph, officially called the "Face with Tears of Joy" emoji (Oxford Languages, 2015). When this was first published, I was not surprised, because although emojis have been around since the 1990s in one form or another, they became more popular as technology of communication in the telephone industry boomed. If one looks at the history of language, it was clear that written language was not limited to the form of letters or the alphabet that we know. The manner of communication was often in symbols. There was no need to have phonetic representations.

I would argue that hieroglyphics and the use of symbols to communicate persist in the present time in the form of emojis. With the links between historical forms of communication clearly defined, I believe that language is becoming simplified. While others may think that short forms of words and emojis are new and generational, I tend to disagree and feel that the communication of the past is gaining a rebirth. What is happening is that those who constantly update and create these digital emotions are forming their own language. What is also interesting is that emojis also do not have any form of verbalization within the communication. This method of communication is continuing to grow and also create a dominant form of communication.

What About Futurity? (What Does the Future Bring?)

With the population in non-English speaking countries growing at a rate higher than the United States, what will the future hold for the English? Using China as a case study, Lustig (2018) states that "more people are speaking English as a second language than Americans speaking their first" (para. 2). What does this mean? I believe that the English language is losing its worldwide hold. With the dawn of technology that can instantly have the ability to interpret languages both written and oral, there may not be a need for English in a manner in which we communicate. As more domestic students take opportunities to travel and learn about cultures abroad, they are savvier in undertaking to learn the language of the land before going to the land. They are not relying solely on the English language. With this in mind, perhaps there is room for a global language, one that is not linked to any country in particular but that allows a commonality between those that speak with regardless of culture or social status.

In 1997, the British Council commented on the future of English:

> English is widely regarded as having become the global language—but will it retain its pre-eminence in the 21st Century? The world in which it is used is in the early stages of major social, economic, and demographic transition. Although English is unlikely to be displaced as the world's most important language, the future is more complex and less certain than some assume. (Graddol, 1997, p. 2)

Here we are twenty-one years later and still looking at this issue. The findings note:

> The economic dominance of OECD countries—which has helped circulate English in the new market economies of the world—is being eroded as Asian economies grow and become the source, rather than the recipient, of cultural and economic flows. Population statistics suggest that the populations of the rich countries are aging and that in the coming decade's young adults with disposable income will be found in Asia and Latin America rather than in the US and Europe. Educational trends in many countries suggest that languages other than English are already providing significant competition in school curricula. (Graddol, 1997, p. 2)

When I first came across this information, it hit home for as my now my 8-year-old daughter came home from school with a survey discussing the possibility of introducing other languages over and above French and English to the students. I sat back and thought about the implications of the fact that her English-speaking school curriculum did not have room for Grammar. However, there was a push to learn and incorporate other languages into her overall learning . It was not surprising that Mandarin and Spanish were the popular of languages offered. This, to me, signaled a change towards the idea of global education and classroom. In a recent blog article is has been already suggested that "Spanglish, a mixture of English and Spanish, is the native tongue of millions of speakers in the United States, suggesting that this variety is emerging as a language in its own right" (Horibin, 2015, para. 5). In my opinion, with the continued migration of immigrants and the accompanying shifts of language and customs, there will be a future of people who may not speak English as their first language because it is no longer the dominant voice. I think that the change is coming sooner than we think, and what the future holds are variations of English that will be so changed and different that they could be called "broken language."

Conclusion

This chapter explored the past, present, and future of English language in the post-colonial states. The chapter revealed that with the advent of global education and mobility among younger people, English as we know it may become extinct sooner than ever imagined. What is clear is that we are well entrenched in the texting revolution, as evidenced by the already shortened words that are used in English. As noted in the above discussion, emojis are taking over. We are no longer left with "etc.," but we now have to contend with 'k" for "okay" and "cya" for "see you." The erosion of the English language has already begun. As young people start to gain more knowledge about shared culture and history that was lost, so will English be lost. We also see the gender neutrality becomes more and more accepted and adopted. The language barriers are slowly becoming language identifiers that develop alongside new forms of communication and resistance.

Note

English Creole Languages are derived from English and share a majority of their vocabulary with English. However, grammar and pronunciation can be very different and can make Standard English and Creole English mutually unintelligible. English Creoles are widely spoken throughout the world, including Central America (Belize), the Caribbean (Jamaica, Barbados, Trinidad and Tobago, and more), Africa (Sierra Leone and Liberia), and Australia. English Creoles are also spoken in the United States, for example, Village English, spoken by Native communities in Alaska (Wong), the Gullah language spoken in South Carolina and Georgia, and Hawaii Creole English. (Allsop, 2010, p. 3)

References

Allsop, S. (2010). Assisting Creole-English and non-standard dialect speaking students in learning standard English. (https://minds.wisconsin.edu/bitstream/handle/1793/39100/Allsop.pdf?sequence=1

Droogendyk, L. & Wright, S. C. (2017). A social psychological examination of the empowering role of language in Indigenous resistance. *Group Processes and Intergroup Relations, 20*(3), 303–316. https://doi.org/10.1177/1368430216683532

Fanon, F. (1967). *Black skin, white masks.* New York: Grove Press.

Frank, D. B. (2007). We don't speak a real language: Creoles as misunderstood and endangered languages. Paper presented March 25, 2007, at a Symposium on Endangered Languages in College Park MD, sponsored by the National Museum of Language.

Graddol, D. (1997). The future of English: A guide to forecasting the popularity of the English language in the 21st Century. Retrieved from https://swsu.ru/sbornik-statey/pdf/learning-elt-future.pdf

Green, C. & Smart, I. I. (1997). Ebonics as cultural resistance. *Journal of Peace Review, 9*(4), 521–526. https:// doi: 10.1080/10402659708426103

Grewal, D. S. (2008). *Network theory of power: The social dynamics of globalization.* New Haven and London: Yale University Press.

Heller, M. & McElhinny, B. (2018). *Language, capitalism, colonialism: Toward a critical history.* Toronto: University of Toronto Press.

Horibin, S. (2015, Nov. 10). What will the English language be like in 100 years? Retrieved from https://theconversation.com/what-will-the-english-language-be-like-in-100-years-50284

Lustig, R. (2018). Can English remain the 'world's favourite' language? Retrieved from https://www.bbc.com/news/amp/world-44200901.

Oxford Language (2015). Word of the Year 2015. Retrieved from (https://en.oxforddictionaries.com/word-of-the-year/word-of-the-year-2015)

United Nations (2019). 2019 International year of Indigenous languages. Retrieved from https://www.un.org/development/desa/indigenouspeoples/news/2019/01/iyil/

University of the West Indies (2006). The language competence survey of Jamaica: Data analysis. The Jamaican Language Unit Department Of Language, Linguistics & Philosophy Faculty Of Humanities & Education University Of The West Indies, Mona. Retrieved from https://www.mona.uwi.edu/dllp/jlu/projects/The%20Language%20Competence%20Survey%20of%20Jamaica%20-%20Data%20Analysis.pdf

Wassink, A. B. (1999). Historic low prestige and seeds of change: Attitudes toward Jamaican Creole. *Language in Society, 28*(1), 57–92, www.jstor.org/stable/4168895

Woo, E. & Curtius, M (1996, December 20) Oakland school district recognizes Black English *La-Times* retrived from https://www.latimes.com/archives/la-xpm-1996-12-20-mn-11042-story.html)

Chapter Eight

Resisting the Colonial Matrix from Within as a Scholar:
Everyday Resurgence for the Anti-colonial Scholar

Arthi Erika Jeyamohan

> *The Black Scholar must pursue our liberation in the academy (and within all institutional spaces) by developing a warrior spirit; a spirit in combat.* (Dei, 2014)

Introduction

As I entered the Anti-colonial Thought and Pedagogy course, I had no idea about the importance of anti-colonial work or what differentiated it from post-colonial work. Until taking this course I was not even aware of the extent to which settler colonialism and racial capitalism affected people. A lot of questions concerning my own identity and position as a scholar kept resurfacing for me through the class discussions. I was learning how to unlearn, after all. I start with an important question: How has this personal and intellectual journey unfolded for myself in terms of responsibilities and roles in the academy? First, I became aware of my complicity in settler colonialism and racial capitalism, leaving me with this responsibility to unlearn all that I have internalized through oppressive and dominant narratives. This unlearning that took place at an intellectual level is in direct opposition to what is largely taught and normalized in colonial educational spaces. The hypocritical nature of participating in the colonial matrix of education proved to be extremely difficult for me to navigate while pursuing anti-colonial thought and work. How could I authentically produce anti-colonial work while being a complicit part of a colonial system?

Furthermore, how could I do this, while retaining my goal to bring that very system down? Was it even possible for students in my position to do this while prioritizing their authenticity? As one of many solutions, I start focusing on forming strategic alliances to accomplish such a daunting task. As a disabled, queer-womxn of color, I often find myself struggling to meet the expectations of this capitalist society (capitalist education system) we live in. How would I then successfully produce "valid and authentic" work through that uphill battle as an "othered" identity? My roles in the academy began to shift, from one that sought individual validation to a position that sought to participate in something more substantial, be a part of a movement—initially pursuing my degree for a career and financial security, quickly transformed into a desire for systemic change, and solidarity against oppression. I began discussing many of these questions and feelings with my fellow peers. The conversations that began in the classroom often continued well into the late hours beyond and outside of it. This showed me the potential that other spaces beyond the classroom had for education, spaces that also transcend physical limitations, into the spiritual realm. Another leading question for me and my colleagues that night was, how do we make sense of such an oppressive and complex system while being complicit? Education systems reproduce the colonial relationship by embedding many disadvantages and distractions for subaltern scholars, such as impossible performance expectations, the cost of tuition, books and living, health care, etc. This can arguably be considered a form of "politics of distraction" (see Corntassel, 2012) that shape-shifting colonial entities employ to ensure they remain in power. This, in the end, comes back to the same argument and questions those who wish to dismantle this system keep asking themselves. Is it even possible to resist from within? And how does one do this without losing sight of the goal?

Using my own experiences and peer/class discussions, I will attempt to show how to dismantle a system as complex and overwhelming as the colonial matrix; anti-colonial scholars must adopt daily resistance practices as a form of resurgence. I will expand on this idea of daily, sustainable resistance by exploring the following: (1) responsibilities and roles in the academy; (2) the power of trialectic spaces and unlearning; and (3) the importance of community and strategic alliances. This next section discusses the responsibilities and roles in the academy.

Responsibilities and Roles of Anticolonial Scholars in the Academy

After the all-day conference for the Anti-colonial class organized by the course instructor, some of the students and I decided to go out to one of the local bars in downtown Toronto to decompress and continue some of our interesting conversations. As we entered the space, everything there—from history and decor to menu and even service—was very much exclusively catered to White people. As we sat down to order, we immediately began discussing the overbearing and oppressive nature we subconsciously felt sitting in that space. The discussions and examples that came out of the night represent the arguments I would like to make in this chapter. The night as a whole resonated very deeply with myself. It was a symbolic experience that gave me a real taste of what it meant to reflect on the past, present, and future of anti-colonial work with allies, even in colonial spaces.

As we sat there in discussion, I used a word that one of my classmates felt was problematic. Another classmate encouraged her to speak about it and educate the rest of the group (including myself) as to why it was problematic and how a better word could have been used. This learning moment showed me that identifying as an anti-colonial scholar meant going beyond the (limited) colonial understanding of the word "scholar." My responsibility as an anti-colonial scholar meant that the educational process is not limited to a paid, standardized classroom lecture. Rather, it took place in spaces and forms that didn't fall within the colonial and capitalist binaries of the educational system—binaries that often restrict and limit what type of knowledge is acceptable and valid, and what is not. The ways in which those conversations took place were educational and reflective for the students in that space. Leading me to realize the importance of pursuing that type of knowledge and critique in my everyday life beyond the school walls. That process of being a scholar can be taken beyond that binary understanding into a more plural one. As Elabor-Idemudia (2011) puts it, "Knowledge is a power that begins with the self and in interaction with others" (p. 142). As we discussed so often in the classroom, decolonization begins with the mind. Therefore, as an anti-colonial intellectual, I must focus on continually situating myself while being accountable for my complicities. I must reclaim the understanding of what it is to be a scholar but not through the gaze of the dominant. Dei (2014) argues that "The anti-colonial is primarily about decolonization and that decolonization cannot happen solely through Western European scholarship/science" (Dei, 2014). To speak from the anti-colonial perspective requires us to be critical of the hegemonic ideologies we encounter constantly. Learning to unlearn and learn differently is also a huge part of this process of decolonizing the mind. As a scholar, my own experiences have shown me that learning isn't a fixed, one-time experience but a continuous process that can take place not just in the physical realm, but in the spiritual one as well. Since the education system has long been prey to the neoliberal market regimes, with their increased regulation of what types of knowledge are produced and validated, students are immediately disadvantaged within non-market focused or non-dominant knowledge fields (Wagner & Yee, 2011). This speaks to how spaces such as universities become increasingly subaltering for certain student bodies and their work (Basu, 2013). In these spaces where education is market-focused, even a department such as Social Justice Education is dependent on funding, affiliation, and regulations, with its fundamental frameworks rooted in colonialism. This takes us to the next section, which discusses exploration of trilectical learning spaces and unlearning.

Power of Trialectic Spaces and Unlearning

The process of unlearning and relearning is one that can be promoted in many ways, and is also an important step for the anti-colonial scholar. In accordance with trialectic spaces of learning, I would like to observe how the mind, body, and soul are involved in the educational process. Trialectic space or suahunu is described as "a space for intellectual and political dialogue as well as concrete practice for social change to happen" (Dei, 2012, p. 824). The interconnectivity of knowledge in almost all aspects of human life means that education or being a scholar can be taken out of the physical limitations of the colonial one and pursued through an anti-colonial lens. Unlearning is encouraged in this space as a method of coming to know in different ways. Educational experiences in trialectic spaces can transcend just the physical and take on the spiritual. This type of learning or trialectic space connects the physical body with the mind and the soul, since trialectic space gives an understanding of many aspects of experience: "The trialectical space concerns the temporal as well as the ensuring relations, human conditions, histories, epistemological ways of knowing as imbued through space, time and memory" (Dei, 2012, p. 824). This really speaks to the significance of creating spiritual spaces of learning, that enhance the knowledge acquisition in a way that isn't demarcated by grades, or specified font styles and margin measurements. The intuitive and spiritual learning that occurs in Indigenous communities for many years have been invalidated through colonial education systems. The type of knowledge that comes from being in a space for long historical periods of time is very much a spiritual knowledge that is stored in the bodies and minds of Indigenous peoples and is often overlooked in hegemonic spaces of learning. This type of thinking also lends this open-mindedness in accepting multiple ways of knowing and coming to know. According to Dei, "When we open the space for multiple ways of knowing and understanding, we begin to undo colonial knowledge regimes" (Dei, 2012, p. 825). This type of learning fostered in trialectic spaces reaffirms the subversion of Eurocentric knowledge production by using Indigenous knowledges as a positive starting point while allowing for a consciousness of the historical and social contexts of the self in respects to identity and spatiality.

Fanon maintained that theory and the intellectual talk were not a good substitute for action, practice, and reality (Dei, 2014). This calls scholars' attention to the importance of action/practice-based anti-colonialism, beyond an exclusive focus on knowledge. Being a student has largely been related to narratives of socio-economic vertical mobility, whereas being an anti-colonial student, can be seen, understood, and lived as an experience starting from you. This form of scholarship becomes more about a spiritual and intellectual journey of everyday, lived reality, such that knowledge becomes a tool of survival and emancipation rather than a commodity. Education within trialectic space engages mind, body, and soul in a way that is instinctual and sometimes spiritual while also being grounded in the physical world of our bodies and nature. Radically re-envisioning what it means to be an anti-colonial scholar in general, a student can help position oneself more authentically. It is the anti-colonial intellectuals' duty and responsibility to re-define education and what it means to be a scholar/intellect. It is important to mention here that re-envisioning and re-defining education can mean different things for different anti-colonial scholars as well. Still, unlearning must always involve re-conceptualizing education outside of the dominant gaze.

As our night went on and we ordered our food, most of the students continued their conversations in a passionate manner, eliciting looks and whispers from surrounding patrons. The genuine discomfort that arose in this space only further legitimized our conversations, emboldening our spirits to keep doing the work. Our topics, "authenticity of white people and allyship" and "struggles of living in a capitalist/neo-colonial world," weren't what the regular patrons of that establishment would consider "bar talk." So, our very presence and conversation topics, in that predominantly white bar, was a form of resistance that disrupted the norms of that hegemonic space. My second subtopic, "disturbing hegemonic spaces and practices," is a way that anti-colonial scholars can continue to resist the colonial matrix on a day-to-day basis. This is one of those roles and responsibilities that arose from my own experiences as a student who has understood and seen things that have gone beyond the point of no return. As Grosfoguel (2002) says, the dominant imaginary is still colonial. Therefore, the act of simply seeing, thinking, and believing beyond this imaginary is resistance.

The education system is as hegemonic as the rest of the colonial systems we live in. It has long been dominated and centred on euro-western ideals and philosophies. This is problematic, especially to the anti-colonial scholar, as these spaces not only continue to be spaces of subaltering but also spaces of oppression. This brings us back to my initial questions: How does one do anti-oppression work, while being oppressed? Anti-colonial scholars whose main motivation is to dismantle this system often end up sidelined by the very consequences they are trying to fight. This can seem overwhelming, as an individual, but the idea is not to take the system as a whole (nor alone) but rather to resist in authentic ways that are sustainable daily and that are resonant with our entry-points and positionality. A classmate brought up the idea of how people of colors' very existence in certain spaces is an act of resistance. So, much like resisting the hegemonic space of Maddy's, our position as anti-colonial scholars in the (colonial) education system is, in fact, a daily act of resistance. So, re-envisioning and reflecting on that idea can provide more power to those who are otherwise disadvantaged in these spaces.

It is important to note that hegemonic spaces are not limited to physical spaces but can be practices and ideologies as well. This speaks to the advantages of trialectic learning spaces that consider body, mind, spirit, and soul.

> Specifically, the trialectic space is constituted as a space for learners to openly utilize the body, mind and spirit/soul interface in critical dialogues about their education and social change... a space that nurtures intellectual and political conversations while valuing the importance and implications of working with a knowledge base about the society, culture and nature nexus. (Dei,2012, p. 826)

Using an anti-colonial perspective, it is easy to understand how hegemonic spaces can be reproduced even in the way individuals create and legitimize work, create conversations, provide social services, etc. (Dei, 2014, 2012, 2011; 1996; Grosfoguel, 2002). This means there are several ways (and opportunities) to resist those spaces as an anti-colonial scholar. What is important is to define what this means for us individually. A great example of this is wearing culturally traditional clothing in otherwise "white" spaces. Another example is choosing to create work that is non-traditional or in our own languages to disrupt the hegemonic narratives of what type of work is constantly being produced as "knowledge." It is powerful to think of how unlearning with these intentions in mind can be a great starting point in the anti-colonial scholar's journey. This takes us into our last exploration: the importance of community and strategic alliances.

Importance of Community and Strategic Alliances

Creating a community-learning experience versus the individualized one for which western education is known is also a way in which anti-colonial scholars can resist hegemonic colonialism on a day-to-day basis. An illuminating personal experience of this everyday resistance was through the conversations students from the course chose to engage in outside and inside of the classroom. Learning in different spaces and allowing that learning to be multi-dimensional returns to the previous topic I discussed: expanding the idea of being a scholar beyond the colonial definition can also lead to the creation of solidarities and communities. Creating a community with the other scholars, as well as their friends and families, meant that there was a support system that ran deep. This type of community-based learning that takes place in various capacities is a powerful counter to colonial narratives in education systems. This brings the conversation to the last subtopic in regard to anti-colonial scholars re-envisioning their resistance: the importance and vital need to(re)build communities and solidarities.

At the end of a long night of anti-colonial conversations, a look of hope glowed on everyone's faces. We exchanged how happy and relieving it was to be able to have that experience and connection with each other. We spoke of how we have been searching for ways to connect, build relationships, and unite together to resist and dismantle colonial forces. I could not help but say out loud to everyone, "United we stand, divided we fall." As I said those words, and as I write them here, I feel a spiritual connection to all those fighting the system. The empowerment and unity we felt in those moments brought us together, made us stronger, allowed us to give each other permission to feel, and, more importantly, permission and space to heal. On this note, Corntassel (2012) states, "if colonization is a disconnecting force, then resurgence is about reconnecting…" (p.97). With this exploration of (re)connection, it becomes key that scholars engage actively in creating interconnected relationships between people and their work. As Smith (2016) discusses in her article, people of color who organize must focus on making strategic alliances and connections, but not solely based on shared victimization, but also based on where they are complicit in the victimization of others. This speaks to how community and solidarities open up an opportunity and duty to critique each other as well as empower each other. This demands that anti-colonial scholars not be complacent in our resistance and decolonization of our minds; after all, decolonization is a fluid and ongoing process (Dei, 2019). Through the strength we find in (re)building communities and solidarities, there can be deeper and widespread healing.

By focusing on strategic alliances, a subject of solidarity comes into play and leads to more questions: What does it mean to stand in solidarity with other oppressed communities, and why is it so important? Again, focus on communities and solidarities as anti-colonial scholars allows us to create social networks and organize against the oppressive forces. It leaves the room and creates space for knowledge outside an academy that isn't accessible to all. Bringing this information back to the community and finding common ground mean that solidarity can be formed where people from different entry-points to the plight of colonialism can come together to resist against it. It also provides scholars with a robust epistemological community to work and move forward with. This allows us to disturb the hegemonic spaces and practices in greater numbers, which in turn is a way of taking the process and understanding of being a scholar outside of the classroom walls. This brings the re-envisioning of daily resistance full circle to answer the questions I had initially begun the semester with. What does it mean to be an anti-colonial scholar while being complicit in the colonial matrix? How does one resist and continue to dismantle a system that is so far ingrained that its roots touch everything? The answer to that is by creating an equally complex daily resistance that works on multiple levels with and alongside other members of marginalized communities (Corntassel, 2012).

Conclusions and Thoughts on Futurity

I began my own identity-based inquiries stemming from being an anti-colonial scholar with what seemed like an impossible and overwhelming task, but the result is a renewed perspective on my own identity as an anti-colonial scholar. My idea of who I am had changed significantly from just a few months ago when I first embarked on my anti-colonial journey. The questions that kept returning me to square one revolved around how I, as an individual, would take on the system of colonial oppression. Through unlearning and relearning differently, I was able to understand that it wasn't my responsibility alone to take on this whole system but rather to be a part of a bigger movement. My responsibility as an anti-colonial scholar is to decolonize my mind and re-define what it first meant for me to identify as an Anti-colonial scholar. This task resonates with Fanon's call for decolonization of the mind: "Frantz Fanon (1963,1967) charged Black and colonized bodies to remove our 'White Masks' and pursue a project of liberating ourselves from ourselves. This is about reclaiming our authentic selves and still remaining true to that self" (Dei, 2014, p.174). Within a colonial framework, this may seem impossible at first, but only if taken on as a singular task. Applying this idea of the plurality to question of how one can resist proves to be an optimistic perspective and approach.

As mentioned in the first subtopic, it is important to reimagine what this resistance means outside of the colonial gaze. This type of work requires that anti-colonial scholars take into consideration the importance of positionality in knowledge production. Secondly, this resistance can develop into something a bit more action-based but also something spiritual, to resist hegemonic spaces and practices in our own ways, whether that means being our authentic selves in predominantly white spaces, or whether that means re-defining hegemonic practices, the actions (as little as they may seem) have power when renewed daily. It is important to remember the idea of the "ripple effect" brought up many times in class. Anti-colonial work isn't necessarily always about the BIG SPLASH effect, but rather about the ripples that are created with enduring and positive effects. Lastly, creating those solidarities, connections, and unity through communities is an extremely important part of the fight. A politics of refusal needs to be taken up by those involved in the decolonial project, to imagine the possibilities of delinking from modernity and coloniality. These communities are where the support, healing, and spiritual (re)connectivity begin and are sustained. Physical, intellectual, and spiritual spaces serve a large purpose to motivate individuals while healing and teaching communities. Working within these communities allows us as anti-colonial intellectuals to contribute directly where it matters in hopes to counter colonial forces at every turn.

To go back to the quote by Dei (2014) at the beginning of this paper, to be an academic warrior is more than being simply an "intellectual." As Professor Dei (2019) has also mentioned in class, "A warrior fights, contests, resists and subverts... a warrior sacrifices the self for a larger cause." This position of an anti-colonial scholar is the position of a warrior—it is not simply a title that is given but earned. This fight is not limited to the classroom but extends to everyday life, bringing forward the importance of the everyday renewal of our resistance practices and refusal. As we speak out and continue forward in this fight, we transform. That transformation, no matter how little it may seem in the moment, is powerful for the way we imagine our futurities. As maintained in the last class, when it comes to anti-colonial work the project of futurities is very much a daily discussion. These daily discussions and ponderings on the past, present, and future provide anti-colonial bodies with an awakening to move away from the Eurocentric dominant. It is important to hold on to the imaginary, fantastical, and unique aspects we bring to these spaces when speaking about futurities and revolutions: the importance and value of knowing differently.

References

Basu, R. (2013). Multiplying spaces of subalterity in education: From ideological realms to strategizing outcomes. *The Canadian Geographer / Le Géographe Canadien, 57*(3), 260–270.https://doi.org/10.1111/cag.12029

Corntassel, J. (2012). Re-Envisioning resurgence: Indigenous pathways to decolonization and sustainable self-determination. *Decolonization: Indigeneity, Education & Society, 1*(1), 86–101.

Dei, G. J. S. (1996). Theoretical approaches to the study of race. In G. J. S. Dei (ed.), *Antiracism education in theory and practice*. Halifax: Fernwood.

Dei, G. J. S. (2011). *Indigenous philosophies and critical education: A reader*. Bern, Switzerland: Peter Lang.

Dei, G. J. S. (2012). "Suahunu," the trialectic space. *Journal of Black Studies, 43*(8), 823–846. https://doi.org/10.1177/0021934712463065

Dei, G. J. S. (2014). The African scholar in the Western academy. *Journal of Black Studies, 45*(3), 167–179. https://doi.org/10.1177/0021934714525198

Dei, G. J. S. (2019). Comment made in class: Anti-colonial thought and pedagogical challenges, September 2019.

Elabor-Idemudia, P. (2011). Identity, representation and knowledge production. In G. J.S., Dei (eds). *Counterpoints, Indigenous philosophies and critical education* (pp. 142–156). New York, NY: Peter Lang.

Fanon, F. (1963). *The wretched of the earth*. Amsterdam, Netherlands: Amsterdam University Press.

Fanon, F. (1967). *Black skin, white masks*. New York, New York: Grove Press.

Grosfoguel, R. (2002). Colonial difference, geopolitics of knowledge, and global coloniality in the modern/colonial capitalist world-system. *Review (Fernand Braudel Center), 25*(3), 203–224. Retrieved from http://www.jstor.org/stable/40241548

Smith, A. (2016). Heteropatriarchy and the three pillars of white supremacy. In INCITE! women of color against violence (eds.), *Color of violence* (pp. 66–73). Durham, NC: Duke University Press. https://doi.org/10.1215/9780822373445-007

Wagner, A., & Yee, J. Y. (2011). Anti-oppression in higher education: Implication neoliberalism. *Canadian Social Work Review, 28*(1), 89–105. https://www.jstor.org/stable/41658835

Chapter Nine

Never Assimilated in Turtle Island

Ciro William Torres-Granizo

Introduction

In my process of adventure and learning to know myself and the world around me, I have been exposed to at least three Western-European cultures: English, German, and French. In my naiveté, I thought that by learning the languages and immersing myself in their manners and sophistication, I could be accepted. The reality is that even though I could try my best to meet their expectations, I will always be missing something. They will use any excuse not to treat me as an equal. As part of my plan to improve myself academically, I decided to pursue a Masters of Education degree, with a major in Social Justice Education. To be honest, choosing my subjects was not a question of selecting those that most appealed to me, but rather choosing those where I could be accepted. I was fortunate to be accepted in the Fall of 2018 in a course titled SES3914, Anti-Colonial Thought & Pedagogical Challenges.

From the first class I found the course very absorbing because, in my process of learning the different theories, listening to classmates disclose their very powerful personal experiences, and taking part in the analyses we made with the course instructor (Professor George Dei), I came to understand more clearly the substance of each philosophy we studied, and, more importantly, to see racialized people show sympathy towards each other in a manner that made me really believe that I have to do something, through my humble knowledge, to change in some way the quality of life experienced by the colonized. Before I took this course, I knew that the way some colonizers treated me was not right, but I thought I was oversensitive. After finishing this course, I know exactly what is the entitlement or sense of superiority involved in White supremacy, and that gives me the courage to disclose very hurtful personal experiences in this essay.

I hypothesize that once you are deemed to be a colonized body, you never stop being one. It doesn't matter how hard you try to assimilate yourself into Euro-American culture (Fanon, 1952). At the end of the day, you always come back home to see yourself as underpaid, underestimated, under-respected, under-integrated, undervalued, under-wanted, underpaid, and under-loved. In this paper, I want to explore some of the painful experiences that I went through during the quest to assimilate and belong. I will start by discussing how I came to learn English as my third language and how I ended up in international business school in Quito, Ecuador. I will share with the reader some of the discriminations I encountered throughout my journey to self-discovery. I will share with the reader my experiences at an Italian restaurant in Toronto, a community college, and an Ontario government agency—experiences of constant rejection for lack of one thing or the other.

I understand how my brown identity was constructed. I experience feelings of dependency and inadequacy. My self-perception as a brown person who left my native cultural origin behind and adopted Canadian culture produced an inferiority complex in my mind. I try to appropriate and imitate the colonizer culture. This behavior is evident in educated brown people who can acquire status symbols of the colonial world's "white masks." I am unable as a brown person to fit into the norms dictated by White society. There is an unconscious and unnatural training of brown people from an early age to associate brownness with wrongness (Fanon, 1952). I am amazed at the way Fanon's psychoanalysis applies to my own reality. I have tried to mimic Whites so much that I came to believe their twisted narratives about browns.

Most of my life, I have given my best efforts to assimilate into the Western culture, but for the most part, I have received aggression and been told repeatedly that I don't belong. I want to belong to White culture, but when I do belong, I belong to the other. As a consequence, my hypothesis becomes my thesis.

Butler (2008) holds that gender as identity is not something that one is born with and that dictates how to act. Quite the contrary, everyday activities mark the good or bad in one's identity, and in a similar way, everyday activities elaborate gender (Butler, 2008). In the pursuit of cleansing ourselves from colonial contamination, everyday activities count, such as avoiding the materialism and individualism encouraged by capitalism, neoliberalism, globalization, and whatever name colonialism will take in the future. Just as Butler (2008) claims the necessity of revisiting Western philosophy that gives predominance to the masculine, so the history of Western colonialization must be reread from the perspective of the heretofore excluded, that is, from the perspective of the colonized themselves (Butler, 2008).

After almost twenty-two years of wasting my life, I understand the authentic meaning, interpretations, and relevance of place. Place has a paramount role in my self-definition as an Indigenous person. Place has supreme importance in the consolidation of my identity, and my resurgence and resistance to colonial imposition so that I can recover my Indigeneity. Modernity, colonialism, and capitalism mutate themselves through time, namely into neoliberalism and globalization and some other, future form. As a constant, however, they erode the metaphysical links between place and everything in it, including people. Through unconscious techniques, they damage direct interpersonal relationships, bringing as consequences dysfunctional families, diminishing employment standards, environmental damage, and an uneven playing field for disadvantaged groups. For Aboriginal people, the reality is very depressing: lack of identity, heteropatriarchy, pollution, high murder rates of women and a larger proportion of Indigenous people incarcerated. The next section discusses learning English as a third language.

Learning English as a Third Language

I began to learn English at the age of eight in Ecuador. Before that, I began learning German when I was four years old. My mom made an effort to enroll me in a German-immersion school with her belief that to endure German discipline would be a positive influence on my personality and improve my life possibilities. As I matured, I traveled to different countries, learned to know their cultures, and become a global citizen. I was fortunate to live and study in Switzerland and travel in Europe for three years. I am happy about my mother's idea. I do not regret the time I invested in learning multiple languages and being at ease with German culture. However, I do regret not having the opportunity to devote time to learn the most important native language in my own country, Quechua.

When I was a child, my mom planned weeks-long summer trips to the countryside to see the difference between life in the capital and small farm towns. We lived a simple life with farm families, sharing their activities and providing them with foods they could not produce themselves, such as salt, sugar and cooking oil, plus clothing, and other goods we no longer needed. I am not Indigenous Quechua, but from those experiences I learned to speak the basic Quechua language, especially through interaction with native children. Even at an early age, I could perceive a special connection between Aboriginal language, land, identity and their very meaningful implications and interrelations.

Christina Jaimungal explores the construction and colonial legacy of whiteness in the context of English, a dominant colonial language, as second language instruction (Jaimungal, 2016). She exposes the link between teaching English as a second language and its intrinsic connection to Whiteness (Jaimungal, 2016). I partially agree with Jaimungal (2016), but the dominant colonial language need not only be English: it can also be another Western European language, such as French, Spanish, Portuguese or German. In my personal experience, since I was a child, I have been exposed to Western languages and culture. Still, at the same time, I received a strong influence from my mom to be very sure who I am, to value and respect the native blood I carry, and to love Indigenous cultures, their resistance and tenacity. That was the reason she exposed me to life on the farms: so that I would learn to value Indigenous knowledge. She did not want me to be consumed by cultures and lifestyles of the people living in the capital, and of the wealthy, privileged people around me at my school.

In an International Business School

In 1995 I was studying in the international business school in Quito, Ecuador, an overseas, elitist school serving the children of expatriate Germans living in Ecuador and also accepting Ecuadorean students. At the same time, I tutored private students in English, German and mathematics. Our weekly schedule included three days of classes from 7 AM to 4 PM and two days of internship with German companies associated with the school. Every two weeks, we had a student-teacher meeting to discuss issues in our programs. I missed one of these meetings, and my accounting tutor reported my absence to the Dean. Consequently, I was reprimanded and warned not to miss future meetings. Subsequently, in those meetings, my tutor sat close to me and began to demonstrate an amorous interest in me.

At the Christmas party that year, she insisted on dancing with me, although I was reluctant to do so. She later asked me to accompany her to her apartment to retrieve marked exam papers and deliver them to my classmates. While we were in her apartment, she invited me to have lunch, and I accepted. Then she asked me to have some wine, which I refused, after which she began to play music on her piano. When I attempted to return to classes, I discovered that she had locked the entrance door; she told me she really liked me and that if I didn't have sex with her, she would not allow me to leave. I accepted, thinking that this would be a one-off experience, but she continued approaching me both in school and at the company where I was working to the point that we established a relationship. One weekend we went dancing in a discothèque where we met a secretary from the school who later reported to the Dean that she had seen us together. After confronting us, the Dean was not so concerned with the moral issue (because I was older than 18 at the time) but imposed an administrative penalty on my tutor and demanded I go for some hours of psychological treatment at my expense. It was remarkable that the psychological treatment was basically brainwashing about accepting the superiority of Europeans and encouraging me to focus on people of my own race in future relationships.

Over a two-year period, we studied economics, accounting, information technology and other subjects as part of the business administration program. Additionally, we applied theoretical learning to work in associated German companies. At the end of the program, we completed a comprehensive accumulative examination to determine if we could graduate and receive a diploma. All of us were studying intensively to meet the exigencies of the examination. When we received our results, some of us were not entirely satisfied because we hoped for a higher mark. Then the secretary addressed us and explained that we were really good students, considering that our German classmates, who received higher marks than we did, had been coached before the examination and had even been given the exam questions. No disciplinary action was taken because the parents of the students in question were closely connected to the management and administration of the business school. We preferred to focus on our futures rather than wasting energy in a hopeless complaint.

Those experiences bring to my mind what Bonds and Inwood (2015) describe in their paper "Beyond White Privilege: Geographies of White Supremacy and Settler Colonialism." By giving special attention to the German students, and even allowing them to look better on the final examinations, the managers were emphasizing the benefits they assumed White students should receive. My experiences indeed demonstrate *White privilege* accorded to German students. Additionally, they go beyond the concept of White privilege to reveal the *White supremacy* on the part of the German managers, which informed the practices and policies of the school (Bonds & Inwood, 2015).

Encounters in GTA: Love, Work, and School

In the summer of 1997, I was walking in downtown Toronto and decided to go into a bar. A White woman was looking at me, so I went over to her, and we began to talk small talk. Eventually, we became cozier. Then we decided to move to somewhere more private and went to a hotel. In the hotel, we began foreplay and ultimately made love. Later, I began to caress her to demonstrate intimacy and tenderness. She stopped because she didn't want to create expectations of something more than the carnal, because she couldn't think about a relationship with someone who was not White. I was shocked by her response to my tenderness, and now I connect this event with Fanon's "thingification" theory. The person thought of me as a "thing," just as colonizers reduced the colonized to non-humans (Fanon, 1963).

In 1998, I began working in an Italian restaurant in Toronto, a year after arriving in Canada. I got this job by responding to a "Help Wanted" advertisement in the restaurant window. A lot of people responded to the advertisement, but my language skills brought me to the top ten applicants. At the interview, one of the owners was positively impressed by my remark that I was very flexible with schedules and ready to work long hours and learn what they wanted to teach me. I was happy to be hired, and immediately they sold a uniform to me. During my first week, I was scheduled for twenty hours, and as I demonstrated my dedication, commitment, and attention to customers, I was given full-time hours and sometimes overtime.

I was happy about the number of hours I worked and the consequent stability and peace-of-mind that followed, but then the managers began to overload me with tasks and miscalculate my hours of work when calculating the payroll. The situation turned more difficult when they didn't want to provide safety equipment like gloves and asked me to perform dangerous tasks. If I was feeling overwhelmed by the greed of the owners, who tried to squeeze out a few more pennies, the situation was even worse for people who were illegal immigrants. Some of them had no English skills, the majority were not well educated, and they were desperate to save money to send back home.

In this harsh work environment, I learned to defend my rights and to be on my guard, but it upset me when I saw the abuse of the most vulnerable employees. Some of them, after working very hard for two weeks, were dismissed and not paid for the time worked. The owners claimed invalid deductions from the pay of illegal immigrants, such as the cost of cleaning uniforms and income tax and Canada Pension Plans, even though the workers had no Social Insurance Numbers. The restaurant foreman was very aggressive, and when an employee didn't understand what he wanted done, he would physically abuse them. The situation became unbearable when I expressed to management that, even though I was not the target of the most extreme treatment, I was deeply offended by being exposed to it. They replied that we were to work hard and provide them with a good profit, and that's all they cared about. They had no concern about our sensitivities and considered us as part of the furniture, saying, "You came here voluntarily—just face the music and dance. If you don't like it, go back home."

These experiences bring to my mind what Dei (2017) highlighted in his paper "So Why Do that Dance?" where he talks about neoliberalism at work in Canada's economy. Racialized people are inserted into the economy as exploitable labor and generators of profit who perform crucial jobs but do not enjoy the benefits and protections of Canadian society (Dei, 2017). The way that vulnerable employees of the Italian restaurant were abused makes me think of invisible chains imposed on them by the insatiable greed of the owners. I could see very clearly how the evils of colonialism mutated into the realities of neoliberalism.

In September 2009, I read in the local newspaper that paralegals were a profession in demand in the law industry. I went to enquire at a community college where a Latin American- Canadian admissions officer explained that I could apply for their Paralegal Degree program. When I asked for information at the Registrar's office, a clerk advised me that there were no positions available and that I should pursue a less difficult program such as haircutting, cooking, or carpentry. I enquired a second time from the admissions officer, and he checked the college's system and verified that there were still places available in the paralegal degree program. I returned to the Registrar's office with my documents and asked to be included in the list of applicants. When I checked my status on the college website, I found my status as "Missing Supporting Documents." When I complained to the Registrar's office, they granted me admission to the program after realizing their errors and discrimination. The episode is related directly to White supremacy, which, without the staff admitting it, acted to exclude me from admission to the college on racial grounds. This colonial aspect of White supremacy involves "taking or appropriation….of land, wages, life, liberty, community, and social status" (Pulido, 2015).

Applying to an Agency of the Ontario Government

In April 2012, while studying at college, I attended a networking event to provide practice in the art of interacting with people to expand business connections and find a sponsor for my mandatory internship. Potential employers from the public and private institutions were invited to the event. I made sure I was adequately dressed for the occasion and brought my updated curriculum vitae and documents. I approached a representative of a government agency, let her know that I was a student in the fourth semester seeking to do the mandatory internship required for my graduation, and began to summarize my skills. Then this employee of the government agency truncated my interaction with her by saying she could not understand what I was talking about, adding that I spoke terribly accented English, and asked me if I was Canadian. I replied in the affirmative. She then asked where I came from, and I replied that I was from Ecuador. Then she dismissed me and commented that there was no possibility for me to be hired in her agency. I complained to the Dean of my school, who was also my administrative law professor. Just a few weeks before, we had been studying the conditions necessary to sue the government. I reminded him that I had the conditions to sue in this case since I experienced discrimination based on my race.

The Dean passed my concerns to a government employee. Months later, I applied to that agency and was surprised that I was offered employment. This memory invited me to think about the unconscious bias that the employee was demonstrating. Unconscious bias consists of attitudes or stereotypes affecting our understanding, actions, and decisions in an unconscious manner. Unconscious bias can come from natural instinct, culture, upbringing, life experience, background and identity. The insidious cycle triggered by unconscious bias leads to differential treatment of certain groups, which in turn leads to unequal outcomes and attitudes and assumptions about those groups. Types of bias include stereotype, gender, and racial prejudice (Turner, 2018).

In an Agency of the Ontario Government

During the summer of 2013, I worked as an intern in a government agency facilitating legal advice. That agency has a high demand for service since they are an option for people who cannot afford private legal counseling. I was very conscious of my position there, because in the past, when I was acquiring my Residence Status, I went to the same agency for advice. I had the attitude to repay the benefits I had received from them. I worked more hours than were required of me and made translations of documents to facilitate procedures. One afternoon I was disgusted when I saw a staff member shred some intake documents without any processing being done, showing a complete lack of professionalism and not providing empathy or the slightest gesture toward natural justice. I reflected that through irresponsible acts like that, she could be harming the applicants, participating in a kind of "necropolitics." Some of them were fleeing countries to which they could return only by risking their lives. The person who shredded the documents may have endangered lives just as do the mafias in Africa (Mbembé, 2003). The destruction of the documents was potentially just as lethal for the applicants and as the use of social and political power to control the lives of African people.

You Don't Have Canadian Studies. You Don't Have Canadian Work Experience

I was getting frustrated working in restaurants because, regardless of the level of the establishment, the common characteristic was the abuse of personnel, so I began to apply for career jobs. I applied to be a flight attendant, hotel front desk clerk, bank teller, and other positions, trying to present the best of my skills and personality. I also attended seminars about preparing a curriculum vitae and preparation for interviews, even receiving direction from a psychologist specializing in human resources. Going through numerous applications and interviews, the answer was inevitably the same: "You don't have Canadian studies. You don't have Canadian work experience." After hearing that, I felt humiliated and inadequate. I thought it was necessary to apologize to the interviewers for my lack of credentials, becoming convinced that Canadian education and experience were exceptional and far superior to my credentials from other countries.

I decided to improve my proficiency in French so that I could apply for bilingual positions. I studied French at a well-known academy of French language instruction for two years. I did my best learning the French language and culture, but I ended up frustrated simply because they didn't want to teach. They seemed to care only about the money I paid, not the quality of instruction or my needs for development. They encouraged me to take grammar, conversation and pronunciation, and even to attend cultural events. After I made my calculations, I realized that with the money I paid to them, I could have done French immersion in France, with the benefit of complete exposure to the language. I am still waiting to have the time to do that, but so far have not found it, and I am afraid of the famously arrogant and unwelcoming French people (Poirier, 2005).

Afterward, I applied for a Bachelor of Education in the Concurrent Teacher Program at the University of Toronto. After going through a complicated procedure, the university denied me admission because on my English proficiency exam, I scored 89/100, and they expected 90/100. Having the possibility of applying again the following year, and in the meantime improving my English, I decided to apply for the Bachelor in Applied Arts, Paralegal Studies degree program at a community college. After encountering complications, aggravation and discrimination, I practically forced myself into that program! During the first two semesters, I gave my best efforts to my plan to apply again to the University of Toronto, but after I achieved a grade average of 90%, one of my college professors told me it would be a shame if I did not complete the program.

I finished the eight semesters to graduate with Honors with a grade average of 90%. Subsequently, it took me six months to get my Paralegal license from the Law Society of Ontario (LSO). I have applied for numerous positions in the legal industry in both the private and public sectors, but so far without success. The consistent problem is that I don't have enough Canadian legal experience, and no one wants to give me the opportunity to gain that experience. So far, I keep my license from LSO and enjoy the lectures they provide. It was to further enhance my academic credentials that I enrolled in the Master of Social Justice Education program at the Ontario Institute for Studies in Education (OISE).

My experience in seeking career employment in Canada leads me to relate to Dei's (2017) paper "So Why Do that Dance?" when he talks about the devil's circle of being unable to get employment because of a lack of Canadian experience, thereby losing the opportunity to gain that experience. This is nonsense and just a way to hide the real reason we are refused employment. To understand this project of racialization, we must look at the historical processes and trajectories that have allowed dominant groups to call upon culture, gender, ethnicity, language, religion and race as a way of distinguishing groups for differential and unequal treatment. This process of racialization allows White supremacist systems of domination to justify their attempts to suppress racial minorities as unequal and different (Dei, 2006). Twenty years ago, the famous excuse, "You don't have Canadian studies. You don't have Canadian work experience," was very popular. Nowadays, these statements could lead to legal action because of this discrimination.

Citizenship

I came to Canada in 1997, escaping a period of economic, social, and political instability in Ecuador. In 1996 in Ecuador, we elected a popular left-wing president, Abdala Bucaram, a politician without a defined political doctrine nor economic plan for his government. He detached himself completely from protocol to the point that he sang and danced for the people while drunk. From the beginning, his government was plagued by corruption and his management of international relations was chaotic and unplanned. Bucaram's mismanagement of the country provoked strikes and the blocking of highways by Indigenous people, with the result of provoking social disintegration and looting in cities and inciting people to civil war. At that time, I was studying Civil Engineering at the Catholic Pontifical University of Ecuador. Since the situation was deteriorating day by day, my mother decided that I should leave the country because I was young and single and would be among the first drafted by the military to fight.

I could have chosen between Switzerland and Canada and chose Canada because I sensed it was closer to Ecuador, and it was comforting to know that my mom would be cared for by my sister, who was a member of the National Police. I came to Canada with an Ecuadorian-Canadian family, but from day one I had to obtain accommodation and began to organize my life here. After four weeks, I got my first employment in a German restaurant in Etobicoke.

To make my first friends in Canada, I went to a downtown Anglican church. I became a regular there and volunteered in their program to provide meals to underprivileged people and developed a strong sense of commitment to that program because I could understand how important it was for people who have nothing more than problems and were rejected even by their own families. For them that church represented a place where they were accepted, heard, nurtured and loved. For me, it represented my adopted family and a place to pray and meditate and escape from my worries. The incumbent priest came to appreciate my Christian values, and I could confide my problems and worries in him. One day I told him that I was not sure how long I could continue volunteering because I did not have residence status and would eventually have to leave the country. He was the first person to encourage me to apply for Permanent Residence status. Armed with the legal advice I obtained through community centers, I began to navigate the labyrinthine Canadian immigration process and achieved Permanent Residence status in 2003.

In 2006 I applied for Canadian citizenship and in 2007 Immigration Canada asked for further information and asked for more forms to be completed regarding taxes, employment, an exact accounting of days of residence in the country in the last three years, and successful completion of the English language and Canadian culture tests. Finally, on April 13, 2007, I became a Canadian citizen.

The concept of citizenship is considered to be how membership in the nation is defined and practiced. According to Bloemraad, Kortweg, and Yurdakul (2008), the concept of citizenship has four dimensions: legal status, rights, political and other forms of participation, and a sense of belonging. Black bodies may have the ability to claim Canadian citizenship, but they are not treated the same under the legal system. In this way, belonging is not only determined by one's claim to the collective, one must also be considered as part of the national imaginary. We can track the history of Black displacement and disfranchisement within the nation. National imaginaries make real who is believed to inhabit and belong to space, who makes up the nation, and who can legitimately be questioned regarding their presence. These experiences serve as constant reminders of non-belonging (Dei, 2017).

I have not completely experienced the four dimensions mentioned by Bloemraad et al. (2008), but I know I have legal status, and I have participated in political and other ways. However, I do not feel that I enjoy the right to be treated as equal since, regardless of the Charter of Rights and Freedoms, people still discriminate against me, especially in employment and opportunities to study. I do not truly feel that I belong in this country since I have not yet been allowed to apply all my capabilities.

Conclusion

In my childhood and adolescence, I enjoyed the best of two worlds: the Western and the local life. I learned from both of them and felt I belonged in both. My experiences in the international business school were awakenings to how bad it could be dealing with the colonizers imposing White privilege through White supremacy. After I arrived in Canada, I came to understand that I could not demonstrate my tenderness to a White woman who did not even consider me a body with a soul. While working at the Italian restaurant, I experienced how vulnerable people were treated as chattels by the dominant capitalists, imprisoned by the evils of neoliberalism. In an agency of the Government of Ontario, an employee used language as an excuse for racial and colonial exclusion built around power and hegemony as a way of denying even my identity. The employee of an agency of the Government of Ontario was exercising necropolitics by her negligent act of shredding applications for service submitted by vulnerable people. The fact of giving unequal treatment to racialized people to justify domination is very evident in denying employment with dignity. I have not experienced completely the four dimensions of citizenship detailed by Bloemraad et al. (2008) when, after twenty-two years living in Canada, I consider myself under-employed and have no sense of belonging to this country. In my own interpretation, place has seven meanings: survival on scanty resources; essence of our identity; center of our relationships; links between past, present, and future; core of resistance against capitalism and its mutations; foundation of Indigenous claims to sovereignty; and the only way we are going to save our planet and humanity.

References

Bloemraad, I., Korteweg, A., & Yurdakul, G. (2008). Citizenship and immigration: Multiculturalism, assimilation, and challenges to the nation-state. *Annual Review of Sociology, 34,* 153–179

Bonds, A. & Inwood, J. (2015). Beyond white privilege: Geographies of white supremacy and settler colonialism. *Progress in Human Geography 2016, 40*(6), 715–733. https://doi.org/10.1177/0309132515613166

Butler, J. (2008). Performative acts and gender constitution: An essay in phenomenology and feminist theory. In A. Bailey & C. Cuomo (eds.), *The feminist philosophy reader* (pp. 97–107). Boston: McGraw-Hill.

Dei, G. J. S. (2006). Introduction: Mapping the terrain—Towards a new politics of resistance. In G. J. S. Dei & A. Kempf (eds.), *Anti-colonialism and education: The politics of resistance*. Rotterdam: Sense Publishing.

Dei, G. J. S. (2017). So why do that dance? In *Reframing blackness and black solidarities through anti-colonial and decolonial prisms*. Berlin: Springer-Verlag.

Fanon, F. (1963). On national culture. In *The wretched of the earth* (pp. 145–180). New York: Grove Press.

Fanon, F. (1952). *Black skin, white masks*, C. L. Markmann (Trans.). Chippenham: Grove Press.

Jaimungal, C. (2016). A race to whiteness. *Revealing the colonial structure of English language education—What kind of education for all?* In G. J. S. Dei & M. Lordan (eds.), *Anti-colonial theory and decolonial praxis*. New York, NY: Peter Lang.

Mbembé, J. A. (2003). Necropolitics. *Public Culture, 15*(1), 11–40.

Poirier, A. (2005). You love us really. *The Guardian*. Retrieved February 3, 2020, from https://www.theguardian.com/world/2005/may/18/france.bookextracts

Pulido, L. (2015). Geographies of white supremacy and ethnicity 1: White supremacy vs. white privilege in environmental racism research. *Progress in Human Geography Online*. Retrieved November 30, 2018, from https://journals.sagepub.com.

Turner, T. (2018). Recruitment, retention & advancement: Countering unconscious bias. Law Society of Ontario workshop, November 24, 2018.

Chapter Ten

Arab Muslims: The Politics of Identity in the West

Heba Khalife

Introduction

Until 9/11, Arab Americans were invisible within the dominant United States discourse on race and ethnicity (Basma, 2016). Today, Arab Americans have become more visible than ever in media, which has and continues to stigmatize them as violent and barbaric people. This has resulted in further alienation and intolerance from both White folks and people of color, resulting in intolerance. Yet, Arab Americans remain officially invisible as they are still required to self-identify as White on the US census. Lobbying attempts by Arabs and Muslim American groups to add a Middle Eastern and North African classification on the United States Census have been repeatedly denied (Basma, 2016).

In this chapter, I will address some questions pertinent to the development of Arabs and Muslim identity in the West and how that affects this group. I will review how the notions of neoliberalism and multiculturalism affect Arabs' and Muslims' ability to have an authentic identity, and how these policies are perpetuating colonialism. I will look deeply into how some Arabs can benefit from a White supremacist system, how they are complicit in perpetrating colonial systems, and what their exact role in anti-oppression, resistance, and decolonization should be. As a first-generation Lebanese Canadian who has begun my journey into decolonization, I am approaching this subject with personal experience and with many questions. This is the starting point of my decolonization process, beginning with my mind and body, and I am starting to understand my complicity and contributions in perpetuating a colonial and oppressive system. This chapter intends to highlight my journey to decolonization, through questioning myself and others, through realizing my complicity and understanding the need to unlearn certain thoughts and behaviors, and through exploring ways of resisting.

History of Arab Immigration

To begin to understand why Arabs are classified as White in the USA, one needs to understand the history of Arab immigration. There were four major waves of Arab immigration to the US (Basma, 2016). Wave one occurred from 1880 to 1945 and was predominately Christians from Lebanon and Syria. Waves two and three were from 1925 to 1960 and 1960 to 1990, respectively, and those were the periods when Muslims began to immigrate to United States in search of better jobs and thriving economies; they were also able to enjoy more proximity to Whiteness, for some Arab Americans were invisible to an extent because of their light skin and White features. The final wave or wave four, is post-1990s and included many Muslim Arabs who were fleeing wars and identified as Arabs (versus White), which was in part due to plans to return to their homes and not assimilate into US culture.

In the first wave of immigration in the early 1900s, in order to gain naturalization in the US, a Syrian immigrant named George Dow convinced the government of United States to classify Syrians as White and as such qualify them for citizenship (Kayyali, 2013). He was successful, and this resulted in Arabs having to self-identify as White on the United States census, which remains a practice today despite multiple lobbying attempts to change this classification (Basma, 2016). Many of these immigrants also changed their names to pave the way to assimilate into American society fully. As more "brown" Arabs and Muslims began to immigrate to the United States, the process of racialization and vilification of Arabs began. Bonilla-Silva (1999) discusses how "racialization is a historical process that evolved in the United States. as a means to offer, or deny, privilege and opportunity based on physical appearance" (Basma, 2016, p. 24). As more Muslims and Arabs who did not identify as White immigrated to the US, the media ensured that they were seen as the other. The racialization, and therefore alienation and denial of opportunity, explicitly began.

Arab and Muslim Identity

With a prevalent narrative throughout the West that Muslims are violent and barbaric, a shift of identity amongst Arabs was inevitable. "Muslim" became an identity in itself, where Muslim Arabs and Christian Arabs became a dichotomy, and Muslim Arabs became separated from Whiteness. Christian Arabs became more likely to identify as White to separate themselves from the negative narratives. In contrast, Muslims Arabs, who previously would have liked to identify as White, may have found it more difficult.

Ajrouch and Jamal (2007) did a study in Dearborn and found that Christian Lebanese and Syrians were more likely to identify as White than Muslims, as Christianity is often associated with Whiteness in the West. This self-identification also depended on when they immigrated: those in earlier waves were more likely to identify as White as well. Through my interaction with Christian Lebanese people, I found that they are more likely to identify as White, as many believe they are Phoenician and not Arab. "Muslim" also becomes another layer of identity in itself, as even White Muslims who wear the *hijab*, for example, get classified as such as others.

Post 9/11, I was always hesitant to identify myself as Muslim. The question of "where are you from?" always made me nervous, and I would always respond with "Windsor," the small city where I grew up in Southern Ontario. In hindsight, my answer was to avoid being associated with Arab Muslims, and therefore having to identify with and defend the negative stereotypes that were then associated with being Arab and Muslim. I had internalized the racism that the media was perpetuating. I started believing that being Muslim and Arab was bad, or negative. By answering "Windsor," I was giving myself proximity to Whiteness, and therefore could be seen as a non-threat, and could be accepted as Canadian.

In looking at and understanding the politics of identity, I can see how Arabs, specifically Levantine Arabs who can often present themselves as White, become complicit in perpetuating colonialism and benefiting from White privilege. At one point within my career, my friends and I would experiment by changing our first name on job applications to something more White-sounding, and that was often successful in getting us job interviews. As a recruiting and HR professional, I knew first-hand that recruiters were more likely to call you if they could pronounce your name or if they got the impression that you were Canadian or proficient in English. This unfortunate action perpetuated my complicity, as I saw the political and economic benefits of identifying as White. If I could make more money, and all I have to do is name myself Heather, why wouldn't I?

Multiculturalism, Orientalism, and the Coloniality of Identity

In this section, I will review the Multiculturalism Act in Canada and define liberalism and neoliberalism. I will examine how they create binarism and individualism and do not allow for community or authenticity, which is a direct contradiction to the premise of these *isms*. I will also review the concept of Orientalism, which, according to Smith (2006) is a pillar of White supremacy because of "the West defining itself as a superior civilization by constructing itself in opposition to an 'exotic' but inferior 'Orient'" (Smith, 2006, p. 68). This, in parallel with multiculturalism, perpetuates identity crises.

According to Kymlicka (1995), liberalism and neoliberalism function under three main goals: individual rights and equality, self-fulfillment, and freedom. The notion of individualism in Canadian liberal society tells us that we can be successful and fulfilled if we work hard enough. It is a one-size-fits-all ideology that does not consider the systemic and institutionalized racism and violence against racialized folks. This individualism alienates those who come from cultures where the community is important and valued, such as Arab and Muslim culture. It does not allow people to be authentic and creates competition rather than solidarity. We are stronger together; however, we are placed into institutions where we are in constant competition and always compared to others, which in actuality limits one's success and impact. But how can we compete when Arab Muslims also have to fight against racism, discrimination, and other labels?

Neoliberalism claims public spaces to be "secular" and does not allow us to be aware of other folks' political views, religious, or cultural affiliations at school or work. School and work are the two significant places where people interact and socialize in their day-to-day lives. This alienation creates a binary of Canadians or "other" that further separates people from their communities, prohibits progress and growth, and limits multiple voices from one community being able to speak out. To fit in or be accepted into these institutions, one must present oneself as "Canadian."

The Multiculturalism Act, whose concept was initially introduced by liberal leader Pierre Trudeau as a policy, was officially enacted in Canada in 1988 by former Prime Minister Brian Mulroney. It was introduced to establish legislation to protect ethnic, racial, linguistic, and religious diversity within Canadian society. Multiculturalism, as St. Denis (2011) explains, "encourages social division…is regressive…and permits a form of participation on the…'cultural other' that is limited to decorative…" (p. 308). The reality, as many visibly racialized folks in Canada experience, is that there is an acceptable amount of diversity that is allowed, which is usually in a commodity or a form of consumption. Multicultural policies promote what Ramachandran (2009) refers to as cultural racism, a concept that does not focus on skin color or ethnicity per se, but instead sees non-White culture as the other, inferior to Canadian White culture. Ramachandran (2009) goes on to explain the underlying racism in liberal multiculturalism:

> Cultural racism does not negate biology and the inequitable treatment of people based on skin color. Instead, it builds on it and reframes the prejudice in terms of cultural differences. This serves two purposes: first, it establishes a civilized norm—in this case, embodied by Christian Eurocentric culture—and secondly, it provides a basis for discrimination which no longer identifies skin color as the cause for unequal treatment. By using cultural differences as the demarcation, racism is evacuated from the discussion allowing the Canadian nation-state to retain its particular brand of liberalism. (p. 35)

Cultural racism is another by-product of liberal multiculturalism that continues to enforce binarism—you are either Canadian (White), or you are not. You will either assimilate, or you will not succeed. You are with us or against us. The only community that multiculturalism truly allows you to be a part of is the White Canadian liberal community. The White liberal community promotes and values individualism over collectiveness. What are the implications that liberal multiculturalism has on Muslim Arabs? Multiculturalism enforces tokenizing, which can be seen as a result of orientalism, in that it allows non-White folks to celebrate only the commodified aspects of their culture.

Orientalism

Orientalism, which Edward Said (1978) describes as the way the West defines itself as superior to the East, is, according to Smith (2006), one pillar of White supremacy. This section will review how orientalism dehumanizes Arabs and Muslims, and I will discuss immigration and identity from this perspective as well. In Western contexts, the East is a construct of the Western imagination. The East is a hot desert, filled with exotic women and belly dancers, camels, and hookah. These types of perceptions construct the Middle East as inferior to the West, where people are dehumanized and reduced to imagery instead of humans you interact with. This dehumanization places Arabs as lower on the racial hierarchy, below

White folks but above Black folks, as Smith (2006) states that Black bodies are on the lowest part of the hierarchy. Racialized folks are looked at and accepted only for the aspects of our history and culture that can be commodified, consumed, or sensationalized in the media.

Orientalism affects the imagery of both Arabs and Muslims. While Arabs are seen as commodities, Muslims are perceived as barbarians. The West constructs Muslims as suicide bombers and in a constant state of war. Muslim men are perceived as misogynistic, violent, and evil, and the women are seen as silenced and in need of saving, as "uneducated, bound to tradition, and under continuous threat of violence from Third World Men" (Ramachandran, 2009, p. 35). Any violent act committed by a Muslim is seen as a result of a violent culture or religion, rather than as an act of mental illness. It is not called a result of systemic patriarchy, the actions of a lone wolf, or any other label that is afforded to White folks when similar crimes are committed.

When you look at both of these labels together—commodities and barbarians—Arabs and Muslims have two layers of identity inscribed by Westerners, both of which are meant to dehumanize: they are the other—the enemy, a threat to Western "culture" and ideologies. Claiming either of these identities in the West is a matter of politics of identity, where one must evaluate the repercussions, the labels, the stereotypes, and discrimination that will hinder being one's authentic self.

When White folks, and often other non-Arabs, non-Muslims, or people of color ask where I am from, a question I now proudly answer with Lebanon, the first thing I am told is that Lebanese women are beautiful. This is usually followed by professing their love of shawarma and baklava, and often a question of whether I am Muslim. When I answer yes, I usually get silence, an eyebrow raise, a quick "oh" and "but you are not like most Muslims," and that quickly ends the conversation. For folks in the West, being Lebanese is associated with food and women but not people.

Identity Crisis: Arab, Muslim, or Canadian?

Arab Canadians (or Canadians of Arab background) can often avoid being labeled as such by claiming Canadian as an identity. By not associating with their Arab ancestry, and instead choosing to claim Canadian as their identity, they bring themselves up the racial hierarchy. They can better benefit from a White supremacist system. Being Lebanese and first-generation Canadian who can pass as White due to my physical appearance, I can choose and control my place in this hierarchy of privilege. I can be Heather from Windsor, or I can be Heba from Lebanon, and this will dictate how I navigate through the systems, and the level of humanity Westerners give me. By choosing the former, I become complicit in the colonial system. I perpetuate the idea that you must be White, sound White, or act White to be accepted and successful in Western society. I become privileged and begin to benefit from White supremacist systems. As I started my decolonization process, I now proudly identify myself as Muslim and Arab, but many who choose to benefit from these systems do not.

As stated above, neoliberalism has taken away the opportunity to be authentic to oneself for immigrants and racialized folks, as institutions have been secularized and multiculturalism has limited this opportunity. This means one must act Canadian (White) to fit in and succeed today. This is done by creating what I will refer to as a survival identity, which is the perfect mix of one's ethnic and cultural background and White Canadian identity. The ethnic and cultural background that is acceptable is something that can be consumed or commodified, that does not make White folks uncomfortable. These "things," such as food or clothing, are what are expected to be brought to school or work on days like "multicultural day," which is seen as an attempt to celebrate diversity but once again limits and reduces one's ethnicity and culture to things that can be consumed and perpetuates tokenism.

Reasons for taking on a survival identity are plentiful and are perpetuated by things like overt racism, cultural racism, fear, and capitalism. Survival identity is a strategy that is used to both survive and thrive in Canadian society. Fear creates the need for a survival identity. With the political climate and media constantly referring to Arabs and Muslims as terrorists, there is a need to hide one's identity in fear of being discriminated against, persecuted, or worse—injured. Capitalism also is a factor. To make money, you need to survive the capitalist structure of our society by being accepted into certain universities and getting hired at high-paying companies. I will focus the rest of this section on how liberal multiculturalism is a reason for creating a survival identity.

Referring back to Edward Said's (1978) notion of orientalism, the survival identity strategy is needed to overcome the thingification and inferiority complex of Middle Easterners. It is a strategy used to subvert and perhaps resist this concept. A means for White Canada to view Middle Easterners as people instead of things, and to be accepted into Canadian society.

For Arabs and Muslims, it can be seen as a necessary step to be successful in both education and careers. Changing names to something "Canadian," for example from Mohammad to Mike, is one way to assimilate, as you are less of an "other" when someone can easily pronounce your name. Learning English vernacular and not speaking Arabic in public spaces is another example of taking on a survival identity. However, with regards to language, certain expressions can still be kept that have been adopted and accepted by White folks such as "yallah!," "wallahi, bro," and "habibi." Ash (2004), in reference to Kymlicka's vision of a multicultural society, states that "ethnic minorities are permitted to retain their culture but are, nevertheless, expected to integrate into the 'mainstream' liberal society" (p. 402).

Modernity and the Coloniality of Identity

Creating a survival identity can impact your connection with your true, authentic self and connection with your history and ancestry. It creates an exclusionary identity, where you become the other within your ethnic community, and you are also the other within white Canadian neoliberal contexts, putting your identity in limbo, or in-between.

Frantz Fanon states that we cannot copy the example of the West; however, many in Lebanon pride themselves of Western identity, as compared to other Arab countries. It is a country that has a mix of both Muslims and Christians, especially in Beirut, where you can freely wear whatever you want, and eat and drink whatever you like, which is close to Western ideals. Modernity in Lebanon has resulted in being able to wear short skirts and get drunk on the street, which is what defines freedom and civilization for many. Since this can often happen in Lebanon, Lebanese are seen as higher on the racial hierarchy than other more religious and darker-skinned Arab and Muslim people. Colorism is quite rampant in Arab communities and is why Lebanese folks prefer to identify as White.

People in Lebanon also pride themselves on being able to speak English and French, which was brought to Lebanon by French colonialism, over Arabic. The more educated or wealthy you are, the more you are likely to use all three languages, often within one sentence. This is viewed as having class and prestige, and superior to those who only speak Arabic. Language is part of the colonial project in Lebanon, where speaking the native tongue only often means you are poor, uneducated, or low class. It may be more comfortable for Lebanese folks to assimilate into Western society as a result of being raised in a colonized country that values Whiteness and non-native languages.

How can the Lebanese partake in anti-colonial praxis when the colonial practices that are embedded within them are a source of their pride and self-worth? How can a country referred to as the plastic surgery Mecca of the Middle East begin its process of decolonization when the authentic self and true identity is viewed as inferior? Am I perpetuating orientalism as someone who grew up in the West, with my views of Lebanon and the Lebanese constructed by family interactions and media only?

The politics of identity really highlights the coloniality of identity. It has become a site of struggle for many Muslim Arabs in the West and has resulted in many Arab Muslims and other racialized folks creating a survival identity. Having an Arab, Lebanese, Muslim woman identity results in a loss of career opportunities and therefore has economic implications. It results in having the identity of the "other," in being stigmatized within the educational and corporate systems, and in being alienated from my peers. Colonization has taken away the ability to freely identify with ourselves, our ancestors, and our history.

Politics of Refusal and Decolonization

The politics of refusal are multi-faceted. We need to claim back our ancestry, our history, culture, and religion. We need to reclaim our names, our traditional clothing, and our language. But at what cost? Those in the United States need to continue to lobby to have Middle East and North African (MENA) added to the census, to be recognized as a group of people who contribute to society, instead of being grouped in with White people. There should be a refusal to identify as Shiite on the census, and an active rejection of the privilege that comes with it. By identifying as White on the census, it is forcing those in the MENA category to identify as White, as something they are not. This further perpetuates identity crisis, can severely impact and reduce the representation of this population, which can also, in turn, affect policies and other statistics that affect this group.

Fanon (1963) claims that violence is the means and the end of anti-colonialism, but what effect does this have on a group of people who are already viewed as violent and barbaric? Violent acts result in further stigmatization of Arab Muslim people, more travel and immigration bans, and more bombs dropped on innocent civilians. As necropolitics dictates, those in power can decide who lives and who dies (Mbembe, 2003). In the West, and especially in the USA, Muslim and Arab bodies are both dispensable and are often referred to as collateral damage. This alone may prevent many from reclaiming their authenticity.

As Dei (2018) argues, the process of decolonization for Arab Muslims in the West has many different aspects. First, the decolonization of the mind must begin. For this to happen, as Fanon (1963) says, decolonization must start with us understanding our oppression, and the inferiority complex that has been created through colonialism and orientalism. Part of understanding our oppression will be to realize our complicity in colonialism, recognize the oppressor within us, and stop being seduced by Whiteness. Since we are often people who can benefit from White supremacist systems, part of the decolonization of the mind is to really understand that we are benefiting from this system, to understand the consequences of it, and to deny these privileges consciously.

Once the process of the decolonization of one's mind begins, there needs to be solidarity amongst the Arab and Muslim people, which is currently prohibited due to colorism and elitism. Stereotypes about other Arab people are often perpetuated within communities, such as people from certain Arab countries being known for domestic violence. One way to combat this discrimination, specifically for Muslims, is to truly embrace the spirit of Islam that prohibits discrimination based on ethnicity. Connecting with spirituality and religion can bring solidarity among Muslim people. Furthermore, a reconnection with ancestral land is an important aspect of decolonization that further helps to build community. Disalienation needs to occur as a part of reclaiming oneself and reclaiming humanity. Césaire (2000) believes that returning to the native homeland, speaking the language, eating the fruit off the trees and connecting to the land, learning the history, and speaking and re-learning the language are all a part of the process of decolonizing oneself and creating community and solidarity. Recognizing that being able to return to the ancestral homeland is a privilege many do not have, this solidarity will bring about a stronger community, which in turn can result in more people speaking up and out against colonial practices with less fear of retaliation.

This solidarity needs to occur not only with other Arabs and Muslims; the decolonization process should include a shared responsibility to have solidarity with other oppressed groups. Part of my decolonization process includes making friends with Arab Muslims, reclaiming my name, my home country, Lebanon, and actively making friends with Arabic speakers to practice the language. I have reconnected by learning and cooking recipes passed down from my grandmother. I ask my father, uncles, and other relatives about their childhood and how they grew up. I am currently relearning who I am, and where I come from, and will soon visit my parents' villages to connect with our land, the mountains, the valleys, and the sea. Furthermore, I believe speaking about the experience of first and second-generation immigrants is very important for the decolonization experience. The in-betweenness, and the survival identity that gets created, is a site of struggle for many Arab Muslims, specifically for women. Safe spaces need to be created to connect with others who are having the same experience, to allow the feeling of disconnect to be a tool to reconnect with each other.

Conclusion

Arabs are not White and will never be accepted as White in Western society. Some can continue to pass as White if they completely give up their identity, which includes their names, language, and connections to land, family, and community. In the United States, Arabs are forcibly made to self-identify as White, which is part of the coloniality of identity, and in Canada, Arabs are accepted under the farce of multiculturalism, while in practice, they continue to experience oppression. Internalized racism and colorism, which begins in Lebanon for me, must be recognized as such. Decolonization must begin by recognizing that colonialism has trained us to hate our authentic selves and emulate the French (or other White folks) by fueling classism through the coloniality of language and divisions of religious sect. As my search into understanding my identity continues, I am left with many questions. I am not accepted as Canadian, and I am not accepted as Lebanese. So, what and who am I? I am a non-practicing Muslim who struggles with some aspects of religion, whose ethnicity is somewhat ambiguous, whose name and eyebrows are definitely "foreign" or "exotic," and who has been able to navigate through the education and corporate system through creating a survival identity and through benefiting from certain aspects of White supremacy. Through my decolonization process of claiming my identity, I need to focus on understanding and accepting that there is no one definition of Arab or one clear example of how one needs to be.

References

Ajrouch, K. & Jamal, A. (2007). Assimilating to a White identity: The case of Arab

Americans. *The International Migration Review, 41*(4), 860–879. https://doi.org/10.1111/j.1747-7379.2007.00103.x

Ash, M. (2004). But where are you REALLY from? Reflections of immigration, multiculturalism, and Canadian identity. In C. Nelson & C. A. Nelson (eds.), *Racism, eh? A critical inter-disciplinary anthology of race and racism in Canada* (pp. 398–409). Concord: Ontario Captus Press.

Basma, D. (2016). *Invisible citizens to visible subjects: Multicultural counseling competence with the Arab American population* (Ph.D. thesis). Retrieved from https://trace.tennessee.edu/utk_graddiss/3892/

Bonilla-Silva, E. (1999). The essential social fact of race. *American Sociological Review, 64*(6), 899. https://doi: 10.2307/2657410

Césaire, A. (2000). Discourse on colonialism. In E. C. Eze (ed.), *African philosophy: An anthology* (pp. 222–227). London: Blackwell Publishers.

Dei, G. J. S. (2018). Comment made in class: Anti-colonial thought and pedagogical implication. Fall 2018. OISE, University of Toronto.

Fanon, F. (1963). *The wretched of the earth*. Trans. C. Farrington. New York: Grove Press.

Kayyali, R. (2013). US census classifications and Arab Americans: Contestations and definitions of identity markers. *Journal of Ethnic and Migration Studies, 39*(8), 1299–1318. doi.org/10.108 0/1369183X.2013.778150

Kymlicka, W. (1995). *Multicultural citizenship: A liberal theory of minority rights*. New York: Oxford University Press.

Mbembe, J. A. (2003). Necropolitics. *Public Culture, 15*(1), 11–40

Ramachandran, T. (2009). No woman left covered: Unveiling and the politics of liberation in multi/interculturalism. *Canadian Woman Studies, 27*(2/3), 33–38.

Smith, A. (2006). Heteropatriarchy and the three pillars of white supremacy. In INCITE! women of color against violence (eds.), *Color of violence* (pp. 66–73). Cambridge, MA: South End Press.

St. Denis, V. (2011). Silencing Aboriginal curricular content and perspectives through multiculturalism: "There are other children here." *The Review of Education, Pedagogy & Cultural Studies, 33*(4), 306–317. https://ir.lib.uwo.ca/aprci/268

Said, E. (1978). *Orientalism*. London: Routledge & Kegan Paul.

Chapter Eleven

Local Ghanaians' Resistance Against GM Crops

Suleyman M. Demi

Introduction

In 2014, Ghana's largest private radio station, Joy FM, broadcasted numerous stories with the same underlying theme: "Angry Farmers Hit the Streets Over GMO"; "Speaker Suspends GMO Deliberations"; and "GMOs, EPAs Signs of Neocolonialism; Farmers Cry." Such headlines captured the demonstrations of Coalition of Civil Society Groups against the introduction of a "plant breeder's bill" in 2014 that would initiate the growing of GM crops in Ghana. Anti-GMO advocates argue that the introduction of GM crops will impoverish peasant farmers and create health problems for Ghanaians (Rock, 2018, 2019). Ghanaians also are concerned about the involvement of corporate donors in the promotion of GM crops in Ghana, believing it is a form of neocolonialism (Rock, 2019). Equally worrying is the clandestine nature by which seed companies introduce GM crops through the auspices of Ghanaian scientists, all the while operating in the shadows. As some Ghanaian officials admit, "If Monsanto was the one pushing it, I'm sure that farmers would be a bit hesitant. Because it's being pushed by their indigenous research institutions...that's easier to accept" (Ignatova, 2015, p. 105).

Conversely, the pro-GMO camp counters that GM crops would lead to production of pest-resistant crops that reduce crop failure and hence lessen farmers' financial losses (Braimah et al., 2017; Moellenbeck et al., 2001); herbicide-resistant crops that reduce labor costs related to extensive physical and mechanic weed control (Brookes & Barfoot, 2014); and disease-resistant crops that reduce crop damage and increase productivity and ultimately farmers' incomes (Dahleen et al., 2001). In July 2014, I took a course titled "Environmental Health, Transformative Higher Education and Policy Change: Education for Social and Ecosystem Healing" at OISE, University of Toronto. As part of the course, we watched a film titled *The Genetic Takeover or Mutant Food* (Parent & Vandelac, 2000) that discusses the pros and cons of GM crops as outlined by eminent scientists, including biochemist and nutritionist Dr. *Árpád* Pusztai, who demonstrated the potential harmful effects of GM crops to humans based on research undertaken with rats. When

Pusztai stood against the suppression of his findings and made them public, he was ridiculed and sacked from his job. As American epidemiologist Devra Davis (2002) argues,

> In the ideal world, science works only if it remains objective, independent and outside politics. While the decision about what to study or even whether to study anything at all may legitimately come from the personal values of the individual scientist, the methods applied to the research effort are supposed to be isolated from those values. (p. 125)

After reviewing Davis's (2002) book as part of my course assignment, I asked myself two simple questions: First, are we living in an ideal world? Second, can we guarantee the objectivity of all findings, especially when corporate interest is involved? As these questions lingered in my mind, I decided to heed political philosopher Frantz Fanon's (1963) earnest prayer: "O my body, make of me always a man who questions" (p. 206). According to Banks (1993), despite its claim of objectivity, "modern science is not value free but contains important human interests and normative assumptions that should be identified, discussed and examined" (p. 5). Davis's (2002) quote above suggests the decision to study something depends on the values of the researcher, thus creating a subjective positionality. This explains, for example, why devoted Muslim scientists seldom carry out research on the productivity of pigs, or why devoted Hindu scientists refrain from research involving milk and beef production. Still, reading the various articles on GMOs, I felt compelled to contribute to the debate on GM foods in Ghana for reasons that will be made clear in this chapter, beginning with a brief discussion of how GM crops became such a major issue in food production.

The discovery of deoxyribonucleic acid (DNA) by Watson and Crick (1953) in the early 1950s heralded the transformation of biotechnology. Since its introduction and use, DNA technology has been applied in many fields—including agriculture, forestry, environmental mediation, medicine, and forensic science (Murphy, 2007)—yet it is its application in the creation of GM foods that has perhaps created the greatest controversy. Whitman (2000) describes GM foods as "crop plants created for human or animal consumption using the latest biology techniques. These plants have been modified in the laboratory to enhance desired traits such as increased resistance to herbicides or improved nutritional contents" (p. 1). The World Health Organization (WHO, 2002) in turn succinctly defines GMOs as organisms in which the genetic material has been altered in a way that does not occur naturally.

GM foods were met with fierce resistance, particularly in the Europe, and the debate whether to allow GM foods there is still raging. From a relatively modest production scale of 1.66 million hectares in 1996 (James, 2012), GM crops are currently adopted by 17 million farmers in 24 countries cultivating a total of 189.8 million hectares worldwide (International Service for the Acquisition of Agri-biotech Applications [ISAAA], 2017). Countries such as the United States, Brazil, Argentina, and Canada are the largest producers of GM foods globally, while South Africa and Sudan are the chief producers of GM crops in Africa (ISAAA, 2017; James, 2012). Currently, Africa has accepted mainly three GM crops (soybean, maize, and cotton) while other crops are on trials. Globally, the leading crops grown using GMO technology include maize, soybean, tomato, sweet pepper, papaya, canola, alfalfa, squash, sugar beet, and petunia, though the United States alone has over 40 varieties of GM crops (ISAAA, 2017). Maize and soybean constitute 83% of GM crop cultivation worldwide (ISAAA, 2017).

Some have argued that GMOs are not a new concept because traditional plant breeding (TPB) has produced genetically modified crops for years (Raman, 2017). In this perspective, GMOs represent an advancement in science designed to improve the laborious, time-consuming aspects of TPB (Raab & Grobe, 2003; Raman, 2017). Despite the seeming similarities, sharp differences exist between TPB and GMOs, including: (a) TPB does not traverse genes between plant and animal, but GMOs do; (b) there is little to no patenting of life in TPB, but such patenting constitutes core concepts in GMOs; and (c) TPB techniques occur in natural settings through field experimentation, while GMOs are essentially lab work before trials are conducted in the field.

In Africa, GMO advocates have argued that the introduction of GMOs will help address food shortages facing the continent. However, some African scholars challenge this assertion and argue it is borne of the coloniality of science (Mutva, 1999; Raschke & Cheema, 2007). According to these scholars, the pro-GMO argument fails to address the root causes of food insecurity in Africa, which is linked to the colonization of African and the introduction of foreign crops at the expense of African indigenous food crops (AIFCs) that are acclimatized to the local environment (Raschke & Chema, 2007). Hence, these scholars argue that since the European colonization of Africa, local knowledge of varieties of indigenous crops, food cultures, and local pharmacology have continuously been eroded (Mutva, 1999; Raschke & Chema, 2007). Indeed, many AIFCs have been devalued as so-called wild, uncultivated, primitive, orphan, or famine food (Dei, 1989; Vorster et al., 2007).

Although food-security monitoring measures help governments to plan, food security policies have several limitations. For instance, such policies pave the way for large corporations to control the food sector through the increased use of agrochemicals, resulting in soil acidity and nutrient depletion, which in turn accelerates the rate of crop deterioration (Demi, 2019a, 2019b). Also, the quest to reduce poverty and improve food security has resulted in a global rush for land in developing countries (Bello & Baviera, 2009; Robertson, 2010), thus displacing smallholder farmers and eroding indigenous food systems in rural communities (Amankwah, 2009; Center for International Forestry Research [CIFOR], 2011). Achieving food security through the introduction of GMOs aims to ensure food is always available and accessible to the people; however, in the process of meeting this goal, the following key social justice questions are ignored: What are the socio-economic conditions of the local food producers? Are food producers receiving commensurate wages for their labor? Do the methods of acquiring land to produce food benefit local people or worsen their plight? Are foods produced through an environmentally sound and sustainable manner?

Also ignored are the culture and tradition of local farmers who ostensibly are the beneficiaries of GMOs. The value of food in traditional settings extends beyond mere nutrition into complex issues such as beliefs and spirituality (Marzband et al., 2017; Pufall et al., 2011) and culture and identity (Dei, 1986; Demi,

2014). Though issues regarding beliefs and spirituality run parallel with the scientific principles of cause and effects, we must acknowledge that the world is inhabited by different groups of people and not by the scientific community alone. People's various beliefs must be respected, particularly because some GMOs are not explicitly labelled and therefore do not enable consumers to make informed decisions about their food choices.

Despite the agitation of Ghanaian smallholder farmers against the introduction of GMOs, GM cowpea and rice are being cultivated in Ghana (Rock, 2019). Studies have shown that a majority of Ghanaians oppose the commercialization of GMOs, considering the history of colonialism in Ghana (Buah, 2011; Rock, 2019). Buah (2011) assessed the perception of GM foods among a cross-section of Ghanaians and found that although more than 60% of respondents had heard of GM crops, their knowledge level was rated low or average. Furthermore, Buah's findings revealed that more than 80% of government workers across various ministries and ordinary citizens were unwilling to accept GM foods due to the unknown health effects and for ethical reasons. Such findings about consumers' poor knowledge of GM foods calls for further investigation into the effects of GMOs on smallholder farming households in Ghana. Hence, the objective of this study is to seek the perspective of smallholder farmers on the introduction and commercialization of GMOs in Ghana. The next section discusses the concept of the precautionary principle.

Applying the Concept of the Precautionary Principle to GMOs

While there are numerous definitions of the precautionary principle (PP), a consensus characterizes PP as follows: "when an activity raises threats of harm to human health or the environment, precautionary measures should be taken even if some causes and effects relationships are not fully established" (Freestone & Hey, 1996, as quoted in Kriebel et al., 2001, p. 871). The concept of PP started in Germany and became widely accepted in European environmental policies in the late 1970s. Since its acceptance, the PP has been integrated into many international treaties and legislations, including those pertaining to North Sea pollution, ozone depletion chemicals, fisheries, climate change, and sustainable development as a foundation for environmental decision-making (Freestone & Hey, 1996; Kriebel et al., 2001).

Arguably, the *Rio Declaration* (United Nations General Assembly [UNGA], 1992) is the most widely publicized international acceptance of the PP (Myhr & Traavik, 2002). According to the Declaration's Principle 15, "In order to protect the environment the precautionary approach shall be widely applied by states according to their capabilities. Where there are threats of serious or irreversible damage, lack of scientific certainty shall not be used as a reason for postponing cost-effective measures to prevent environmental degradation" (UNGA, 1992, p. 3). The Declaration guides most environmental policies, particularly in Europe, and countries like Denmark and Germany are leading the crusade against environmental harm. The threshold phrase for the PP includes "threats of serious or irreversible damage" and words like "harm" (Myhr & Traavik, 2002, p. 76). Kriebel et al. (2001) and the Toxics Use Reduction Institute outlined six components of the PP: (a) taking preventive action in the face of uncertainty; (b) reverse onus, placing the burden of proof on the proponents of an activity; (c) exploring a wide range of alternatives to possibly harmful actions; (d) increasing public participation in decision-making; (e) community right to information; and (f) a just transition to safe jobs and socially sustainable livelihoods.

Critics of the PP argue that acting without scientific evidence is tantamount to deviating from science (Holm & Harris, 1999). Others have also argued that numerous definitions of the PP reduce the principle to subjective value judgments, thus making it difficult to agree on what constitutes an inappropriate application (Royal Society of Chemistry [RSC], 2014). They further assert that the PP does not always result in societal or environment benefits (RSC, 2014). The critics fear that strict application of PP could impede technological innovations, and humans are likely to lose potential benefits of such innovations. However, life is too valuable to be subjected to risks and uncertainties. Again, the proponents of the PP address most of the criticisms. First, the PP is not anti-science but rather ensures that scientific innovations improve human life and ensure environmental sustainability. It also highlights the need for broader consultation with the beneficiaries of an action. The beneficiaries of innovations also deserve the right to know and participate in the decision-making process leading to the release and use of the innovations. In this respect, the PP rather promotes technologies or products that are acceptable to most people and ensures wider usage. It also saves companies from investing in products that will incur debts for their lack of use. Additionally, if we must make a wrong judgment, it should save us from danger rather lead us into harm. In 2003, the General Council for the United Church of Canada (GCUCC) met and agreed on a four-principle resolution on GMOs, the first of which states:

> If our best scientific evaluation turns out to be in error, it is better to err on the side of safety and lose potential benefits than to err by downplaying or dismissing real risks and suffering serious consequences as a result. In other words, it is preferable to forgo benefits of new Genetically Modified (GM) food variety by wrongly predicting health or ecological risks than to experience harms by wrongly failing to predict them. (GCUCC, 2003, p. 1)

The quote above highlights the significance of putting "life" first on the scale of safety measures because harm to life is irreversible. There are several instances where effects of substances were downplayed only to be accepted later as being harmful. For example, Rachel Carson (1962) in her groundbreaking book *Silent Spring* linked environmental pollution to cancers. Carson was ridiculed and criticized for being too radical in her thinking. Decades after her death, it has now been acknowledged that her revelation was true. Davis (2002) shows how the carcinogenic properties of chemicals such as lead, trichloroethylene (TCE), and butadiene were highly contested for decades before finally being banned. These contestations divided the scientific community into two: those who demanded definite proof of cause and effect and those who argued for the adoption of precautionary principles.

Despite the criticism of the PP, it is used as a guiding principle for the transboundary movement of GMOs, taking preventive measures in cases considered as a threat of significant reduction or loss of biological diversity (Myhr & Traavik, 2002). In its response to the inquiry on GMOs and application of the PP in Europe, the RSC (2014) notes:

There is no "right," "wrong" or "appropriate" way to apply precaution in Risk Management and it should not be surprising that individuals, organisations, member states and international bodies may reach different conclusions on Risk Management, even when based on identical risk assessments, since their underlying value judgements are unlikely to be the same. We should therefore not be surprised that national opinions on the use of GMOs should differ, since the outcome is determined by how the different value systems interpret the underlying scientific information. (p. 4)

The above quote necessitates the use of the PP in dealing with potentially harmful substances. Therefore, the fact that GM crops may have some merits does not prevent us from taking preventive measures. If we give corporations the right to engineer our food to meet their interests, we should be prepared to deal with the consequences when their interests change. In chapter 3 of this book, Zainab Zafar describes the coloniality of science and how science has been the foundation of racism. We know of the history of using science to commit crimes against racialized bodies—for instance, infecting the Black population in the U.S. with syphilis in the Tuskegee Study (Brandt, 1978; Howell, 2017) and the sterilization of Aboriginal women as a form of colonialization (Baskin, 2019; Stote, 2012). These points may sound trivial or pessimistic but are very important questions to ponder as we surrender our lives to corporations.

Methodology

The study was part of broader research undertaken for a doctoral thesis conducted in Ghana from March to June 2017. During the data collection period, the author decided to seek the views of research participants in Wenchi Municipality of Bono Region (BR) and Ga West Municipality of Greater Accra Region on the introduction of GM crops in Ghana. Data were collected through in-depth interviews involving 20 smallholder farmers, one agricultural extension officer (EO), and one representative of the Peasant Farmers Association of Ghana (PFAG). The qualitative data were analyzed through coding and thematization using NVivo software. Secondary sources of information were obtained through analysis of policy documents from Ghana's Ministry of Food and Agriculture (MoFA) and Ministry of Health (MoH), along with other reputable sources.

Results and Discussion

Results of the study revealed a majority of farmers were not aware of GM crops. Those who were aware had scanty information about the GM crops and sometimes conflated GM crops with hybrid crops, confirming other findings (Buah, 2011). Even with hybrid crops, farmers have serious reservations due to high demand for agrochemicals and high perishability. Farmers argue that the introduction of hybrid crops has accelerated the extinction of indigenous seeds, and they tie them to the seed companies. Participant Otumi made this point succinctly:

White people have spoiled us because they brought their seeds and proclaimed their seeds were the better ones. Truly, they added something little to make it appear so. So, we left our seeds and concentrated on Whiteman's seeds and now we have lost our old seeds. You see what is happening? We can no longer get the old seeds that we use to plant. ... Before the maize (verities) that we grow were not Agric (hybrids), they were local varieties, so they were not too sweet, so the insects do not feed on them very much. The Agric maize is too sweet, so you can't preserve the maize for very long time; that is why the Whiteman manufactured chemicals. So, unless you go to them before they give you chemicals to preserve the maize. That is where everything went wrong. So, before when you harvest maize, you can keep it up to five or six months, but now just two months, then the insects will start feeding on the maize and turn it into powder. So, in the olden days we set fire in traditional way but not the way we use coal pot and cylinder.

Otumi in the above quote recounts some of the limitations of the hybrid seeds, which were introduced to farmers with much euphoria to save farmers from poverty, but to no avail—the same way proponents of GMOs tout their merits (high yielding, drought tolerant, high nutritive value, etc.), all the while ignoring their limitations. Another farmer (Sebe) approached the topic from an economic point of view and argued that farmers cannot afford the hybrid seeds due to their exorbitant price, not to mention that of the GM crops themselves. Sebe notes:

That thing, to be honest, in some ways it has affected us, but in some ways too, it has helped us. It has worried us because that seeds when they come, I say it that they are using the seed to get money so when it comes it is very expensive, and they sell it to us [farmers]. You cannot replant your seeds. If you become stubborn and plant, they will not grow well so you have to buy new seeds [every season] and when you go to buy too the seeds are expensive. Even more expensive than the maize that you will sell after harvesting.

The above quote highlights the plight of peasant farmers in Ghana who cultivate crops to feed themselves and sell the surplus. Even with hybrid seeds, farmers sometimes find it difficult to break even, and they do not have economy of scale to generate a profit. So, the critical question is: Whose interest(s) will the introduction of GM crops in Ghana serve—farmers or corporations? Another concern that farmers such as Sebe expressed so vividly is their inability to save their own seeds when the GMOs are introduced. Farmers are worried they will relinquish their independence to seed companies, which they view as a form of neocolonialism.

Sebe's point was corroborated by the representative of PFAG, who voices the concerns of farmers:

The issue of GMOs itself is [a] very complex and controversial one. ... Traditionally the farmers prefer their own saved seeds and some of these seeds ... are able to withstand all those things we are talking about [drought, pest, diseases etc.]. [It] is just that some of these seeds are becoming extinct because gradually we are losing them. So that is what the farmers are used to, what they are getting. Now, if you will remember, now most of the time we use these hybrid seeds, okay?. Even the hybrid seeds farmers cannot afford them, they said they are expensive, okay. So, if you are trying to build a technology that is obviously going to be more expensive than the hybrid, which has been confirmed by them anyway, what are you trying to do with the smallholder farmers, okay? Are you not deliberating trying to gradually make an institution or the organization take over the seed industry? Okay, so we don't want that, we don't want them to lose what they have, okay.

According to the representative of PFAG, farmers face serious challenges in terms of post-harvest losses and lack of a ready market. He further argued that most indigenous seeds that are becoming extinct due to the introduction of hybrid seeds could address most of the challenges that the GMOs are purported to address, at a lower cost and in an environmentally friendly manner. He therefore called on the government to shelve the planned introduction of GM crops and instead focus on preserving indigenous seeds through the creation of indigenous seed banks in various regions for farmers to access them. Consequently, the introduction of GM crops is a new form of colonialism that ties the livelihoods of smallholder farmers to seed companies.

For his part, the Extension Officer (EO) who took part in the study was concerned about the health implications of GM crops and argued that yield should not be the only yardstick to measure the productivity of seeds: "We in the ministry, we are looking at the yield, but you cannot use just one aspect to conclude that it is good, like we know that for GMOs the yield that we want we can get it, but the health hazards that will also come." The EO's argument suggests that yield is just one aspect of many considerations when looking at the overall value of crops; there also are some intrinsic social and cultural values and consumer satisfaction in terms of taste and preference that are ignored. The EO acknowledged that GMOs are being tried in Ghana but suspected some GMOs have already been imported into the country, even though farmers prefer their local crops:

> Yes, it is true they are doing some trials and testing of that [GMOs]. We even heard that for cowpea they even started in the North. ... Of late the maize that we are importing from South Africa we don't even know, the pan 53, the yellow maize and that stuff that yields fast. ... Farmers are looking at it that eeye! Even when you chew it, [it] is not like our local maize because that one, you need to give it more fertilizer for it to yield more. So, farmers are anticipating that if it's GMO, they should tell us that this is GMO or something like that, ahaa.

The above quote suggests that farmers could find it difficult cultivating GM crops in Ghana due to poor taste, as most farmers produce food mainly for home consumption. Secondly, the clandestine manner in which GM crops are introduced is worrisome. Not even the officers working with the MoFA could provide definite information about the stage of GM crops in Ghana. Furthermore, overconcentration on the yield of GM crops at the expense of all other factors needs serious analysis.

Brookes and Barfoot (2014) estimated that $16.6 billion was realized as net profit of GM crops globally in 2012 and cumulatively $116.6 billion of net profit since their inception in 1996. They further estimated that the benefits of GM crops were shared almost 50% each for farmers in the developed and developing countries. However, the interesting revelation of their study is that 64%, 74%, and 84% of gains from soybeans, maize, and cotton, respectively, were from reduction in production costs (cost saving), with the remaining percentages derived from gain in yield. This requires us to be cautious in churning out figures to prove that GM crops are beneficial. It is important to note that production costs are not just money thrown away for no apparent reason, but rather monies paid to laborers, input suppliers etcetera.

Hence, income gained from reduced production cost is income lost to laborers and input suppliers. A holistic analysis in support of GM crops requires further investigation to assess the purported gains from GM crops against social costs before we can conclude that GM crops have brought about economic benefit. We must assess the impact of job loss to the laborers and their families in terms of their health, nutrition, and schooling. Essentially, apparent profit from GM crops halts income distribution and concentrates income into the hands of rich farmers and seed companies and widens the poverty gap. Shiva (2008) criticizes this type of assumption when she notes that "destroyers of work and employment always present destruction as liberation" (p. 139). According to Shiva, addressing the poverty situation in the world requires us to bring human energy back into production, respect and dignify physical work, and bring people back to agriculture to reclaim nourishment. Despite touting the economic benefits of GM crops and the need for them to be adopted by many countries, Brookes and Barfoot (2014) admit that GM crops have some setbacks:

> Some incidence of weed resistance to glyphosate has occurred and resistance has become a major concern in some regions. … As a result, growers of GM HT crops are increasingly being advised to be more proactive and include other herbicides (with different and complementary modes of action) in combination with glyphosate in their weed management systems, even where instances of weed resistance to glyphosate have not been found. … At the macro level, these changes have already begun to influence the mix, total amount, cost, and overall profit of herbicides applied to GM HT crops. Relative to the conventional alternative, however, the economic impact of the GM HT crop use has continued to offer important advantages. (p. 66)

Brookes and Barfoot thus confirm earlier studies postulating that agricultural pests would develop resistance to herbicides and create more problems than the latter were designed to resolve. Their findings further show the possibility of increasing production costs through the purchase of other herbicides to complement the glyphosate as well as compounding health problems caused by excessive use of chemicals from different constituents, as agrochemicals in fertilizers and herbicides have been linked to cancers and obesity (Bertell, 1999; Carvalho, 2017; Steingraber, 2010; VoPham et al., 2017). It is important to consider the implications to Ghanaians' health, especially when studies have found that chronic diseases are on the increase in Ghana (de-Graft Aikins et al., 2014; Demi, 2017; Kushitor & Boatemaa, 2018; Tannor et al., 2019).

Some scholars are eager to make cost and benefit analyses of GM crops and conclude that GMOs are profitable, safe, and could solve the food security challenges of the world; this eagerness persuades other researchers to believe that independent scientific research on effects of GM crops for human and animals consumption is limited (Brown et al., 2003; Domingo, 2007; Vain, 2007). In their review of GM crops between 1996 and 2012, Mannion and Morse (2013), though they are inclined to favor GM crops, conceded that the socio-economic benefits of GM crops are not verifiable:

> Socio-economic benefits of GM crops are less clear cut than agronomic and environmental benefits, especially in relation to debt issues; it is unclear at present what effects it may have had on society and whether it is worse for farmers producing GM crops than those producing conventional varieties. In contrast, trends are generally positive in relation to human health, notably fewer deaths and accidents with chemical pesticides. (p. 31)

Mannion and Morse's approach to the economic benefits of GM crops is more holistic because they considered social costs that Brookes and Barfoot (2014) overlooked. Still, one wonders how they concluded that GM crops promote health despite the preponderance of evidence to the contrary.

Henceforth, the commercialization of GM crops in Ghana should consider the peculiar nature of the country. First, more than 90% of farmers in Ghana are smallholder farmers, and a majority of them cultivate less than two hectares of land (MoFA, 2010). These farmers lack the economy of scale that will ensure they benefit from the adoption of GM crops. Because the increase in production costs related to the purchase of GM seeds, herbicides, and insecticides, farmers need to produce large quantities of crops in order to make a profit. Second, Ghanaian farmers face marketing challenges that lead to large volumes of food spoilage; in other words, the problem is not solely lack of capacity to produce enough food, but also an inadequate market in which to sell it. This point was made forcefully by the representative of PFAG:

> So that is why we are saying if you claim—because in the first place, we don't think the GMOs are the solution to the food situation in the country. Because there are a lot of, in fact, there are times in the country that we produce more than we even need, and there are lot of the food go waste, so is not about production, you understand? We have a lot of challenges maybe in terms of infrastructure, storage, transportation, a lot, okay?, so if you are limiting it to as if is the seed [is the problem], it like we are not tackling the bigger portion of the issue.

The PFAG representative's argument is valid because a substantial quantity of food already goes to waste in Ghana due to high post-harvest losses attributed to lack of storage facilities, transportation bottlenecks, and a lack of ready markets for farm produce (Alhassan & Kumah, 2018; Ansah et al., 2018). If these problems are not tackled, why then the need to introduce GMOs?

This study confirms findings of other studies in which participants argued that Ghana does not lack food to warrant the cultivation of GM crops (Ignatova, 2015; Rock, 2019). Writing on GM cowpea in Ghana, Ignatova (2015) found that even scientists who defend GMOs publicly in Ghana admit privately that GM crops are not necessary in Ghana. Hence, the introduction of GMOs could further aggravate the poor marketing situation of farmers in Ghana because they could be prevented from accessing the European market. Another challenge is the enforcement of GMOs regulations. In the United States where GM crops are produced on large scale, there are regulations to ensure GM crops and organic farming co-exists to offer consumers ample choices. Such regulations could be difficult if not impossible to implement in Ghana due to the fragmented land tenure system resulting in small farm sizes. According to the United States Department of Agriculture (USDA, 2019), the average farm size in the U.S. for 2018 was 443 acres compared to Ghana's 4.9 acres. Most of the farms in Ghana are not up to the size of recommended buffer zone between farms to prevent contamination with GM crops, which places Ghanaian farmers in a precarious situation.

There are also socio-cultural challenges that are presented by the introduction of GM crops in Ghana that merit further investigation. For instance, a majority of Ghanaians depend on herbal medicine (Boadu & Asase, 2017; Darko, 2009; James et al., 2018), and most of the food crops also serve as herbal medicine. So, to what extent do GM crops compromise the medicinal properties of these food crops? For instance, can the pesticide-producing GM crops be used for medicinal purposes? If not, how would the local farmers be aware of this information when the majority of them cannot read and write? Also, most parts of Africa practice a totem system that forbids them from eating certain crops or animals. In the case of gene transverse, to what extent can this affect the beliefs of the local people? These and other questions are worth investigating as Ghana is contemplating on commercial production of GM crops.

It is therefore necessary to address the prospects and constraints of GM foods in Ghana for many reasons. First, Ghanaians must explore indigenous food crops to address food security challenges. For example, numerous AIFCs, such as millet, sorghum, various varieties of yams, and a wide range of African indigenous leafy vegetables, are drought resistant (Mabhaudhi et al., 2017) and nutritive (Raschke et al., 2007). Second, Ghanaian consumers should be consulted regarding the decisions to either accept or reject GM crops in Ghana. Such consultation should be in the form of a referendum for every Ghanaian who wishes to exercise her/his rights to vote, to either accept or reject GM crops in Ghana.

Conclusion

This chapter explored the effects of GM crop introduction and commercialization on smallholder farming households in Ghana. The study found that although GM crops can present some advantages, they equally present certain challenges that are mostly ignored. It was revealed that a majority of farmers are not aware of GM crops, and those who are aware have little to no accurate information. Apart from the health effects that farmers are not sure of, farmers are equally worried about exorbitant prices of GM seeds and the poor taste of GM foods compared to their local varieties of crops. Additionally, farmers are worried about completely losing their indigenous seeds that could address most of the challenges such as drought, pest and disease infestation, and post-harvest losses. Also, farmers face challenges that are not addressed, such as lack of storage facilities to prolong the shelf life of farm produce along with a lack of ready markets. The study, therefore, recommends broader consultation with various stakeholders on commercialization of GM crops in Ghana.

References

Alhassan, N. B. & Kumah, P. (2018). Determination of postharvest losses in maize production in the Upper West Region of Ghana. *American Scientific Research Journal for Engineering, Technology, and Sciences, 44*(1), 1–18. https://asrjetsjournal.org/index.php/American_Scientific_Journal/article/view/4189

Amankwah, A. A. (2009, March 16). Ghana: Women lose their land to biofuel farms. *AllAfrica.* http://allafrica.com/stories/200903161744.html_

Angry farmers hit the streets over GMO. (2014, January 28). In *MyJoyOnline.* https://www.myjoyonline.com/news/angry-farmers-hit-the-streets-over-gmo/

Ansah, I. G. K., Ehwi, J., & Donkoh, S. A. (2018). Effect of postharvest management practices on welfare of farmers and traders in Tamale metropolis and Zabzugu District, Ghana. *Cogent Food & Agriculture, 4*(1), 1–16. https://doi.org/10.1080/23311932.2018.1475916

Banks, J. A. (1993). The canon debate, knowledge construction, and multicultural education. *Educational Researcher, 22*(5), 4–14. https://doi.org/10.3102%2F0013189X022005004

Baskin, C. (2019). Contemporary Indigenous women's roles: Traditional teachings or internalized colonialism? *Violence Against Women.* https://doi.org/10.1177%2F1077801219888024

Bello, W. & Baviera, M. (2009). Food wars. *Monthly Review, 61*(3), 17–31. https://monthlyreview.org/2009/07/01/food-wars/

Bertell, R. (1999). A pollution primer. In M. Wyman (ed.), *Sweeping the Earth: Women taking action for a healthy planet* (pp. 34–55). Gynergy Press.

Boadu, A. A. & Asase, A. (2017). Documentation of herbal medicines used for the treatment and management of human diseases by some communities in Southern Ghana. *Evidence-Based Complementary and Alternative Medicine.* https://doi.org/10.1155/2017/3043061

Braimah, J. A., Atuoye, K. N., Vercillo, S., Warring, C., & Luginaah, I. (2017). Debated agronomy: Public discourse and the future of biotechnology policy in Ghana. *Global Bioethics, 28*(1), 3–18. https://doi.org/10.1080/11287462.2016.1261604

Brandt, A. M. (1978). Racism and research: The case of the Tuskegee syphilis study. *The Hastings Center Report, 8*(6), 21–29. https://dash.harvard.edu/handle/1/3372911

Brookes, G. & Barfoot, P. (2014). Economic impact of GM crops: The global income and production effects 1996–2012. *GM Crops & Food, 5*(1), 65–75. https://doi.org/10.4161/gmcr.28098

Brown, P., Wilson, K. A., Jonker, Y., & Nickson, T. E. (2003). Glyphosate tolerant canola meal is equivalent to the parental line in diets fed to rainbow trout. *Journal of Agricultural Food and Chemistry, 51,* 4268–4272. https://doi.org/10.1021/jf034018f

Buah, J. N. (2011). Public perception of genetically modified food in Ghana. *American Journal of Food Technology, 6*(7), 541–554. http://dx.doi.org/10.3923/ajft.2011.541.554

Carson, R. (1962). *Silent spring.* Houghton Mifflin.

Carvalho, F. P. (2017). Pesticides, environment, and food safety. *Food and Energy Security, 6*(2), 48–60. https://doi.org/10.1002/fes3.108

Center for International Forestry Research. (2011). *Global biofuel information tool.* http://www.cifor.org/bioenergy/maps/

Dahleen, L. S., Okubara, P. A., & Blech, A. E. (2001). Transgenic approaches to combat Fusarium head blight in wheat and barley. *Crop Science, 41*(3), 628–627. https://doi.org/10.2135/cropsci2001.413628x

Darko, I. N. (2009). *Ghanaian indigenous health practices: The use of herbs* [Master's thesis, University of Toronto]. TSpace. https://tspace.library.utoronto.ca/handle/1807/18072

Davis, D. (2002). *When smoke ran like water: Tales of environmental deception and the battle against pollution.* Basic Books.

de-Graft Aikins, A., Kushitor, M., Koram, K. Gyamfi, S., & Ogedegbe, G. (2014). Chronic non-communicable diseases and the challenge of universal health coverage: Insights from community-based cardiovascular disease research in urban poor communities in Accra, Ghana. *BMCl Public Health, 14*(S3). https://doi.org/10.1186/1471-2458-14-S2-S3

Dei, G. J. S. (1986). *Adaptation and environmental stress in a Ghanaian forest community* [Unpublished doctoral dissertation]. University of Toronto.

Dei, G. J. S. (1989). Hunting and gathering in a Ghanaian rain forest community. *Ecology of Food and Nutrition, 22*(3), 225–245. https://doi.org/10.1080/03670244.1989.9991071

Demi, S. M. (2014). *African indigenous food crops: Their roles in combating chronic diseases in Ghana* [Master's thesis, University of Toronto]. TSpace. https://tspace.library.utoronto.ca/handle/1807/68528

Demi, S. M. (2017). Using African indigenous food crops as local remedy against chronic diseases: Implications for healthcare systems in Ghana. In J. Kapalanga & A. L. Fymat (eds.), *Science research and education in Africa: Proceedings of a conference on science advancement* (pp. 198–226). Cambridge Scholars Publishing.

Demi, S. M. (2019a). *Assessing indigenous food systems and cultural knowledges among smallholder farmers in Ghana: Towards environmental sustainability education and development* [Unpublished doctoral dissertation). University of Toronto.

Demi, S. M. (2019b). Reclaiming cultural identity through decolonization of food habits. In N. Wane, M. Todorova, & K. Todd (eds.), *Decolonizing the spirit in education and beyond: Resistance and solidarity* (pp. 117–136). Palgrave Macmillan.

Domingo, J. L. (2007). Toxicity studies of genetically modified plants: A review of the published literature. *Critical Reviews in Food Science and Nutrition, 47*(8), 721–733. https://doi.org/10.1080/10408390601177670

Fanon, F. (1963). *The wretched of the earth.* Grove Press.

Freestone, D. & Hey, E (1996). Origins and development of the precautionary principle. In D. Freestone & E. Hey (eds.), *The precautionary principle and international law* (pp. 3–15). Kluwer Law International.

General Council for the United Church of Canada. (2003). *Genetically modified food—General principles (2003G255).* https://tinyurl.com/ufavtcv

GMOs, EPAs signs of neocolonialism; farmers cry. (2014, May 19). In *Modern Ghana.* https://www.modernghana.com/news/542006/gmos-epas-signs-of-neo-colonialism-farmers.html

Holm, S. & Harris, J. (1999). Precautionary principle stifles discovery. *Nature, 400,* 398. https://www.nature.com/articles/22626

Howell, J. (2017). Race and U.S. medical experimentation: The case of Tuskegee. *Cadernos de Saúde Pública, 33*(Suppl. 1). https://doi.org/10.1590/0102-311x00168016

Ignatova, J. (2015). *Seeds of contestation: Genetically modified crops and the politics of agricultural modernization in Ghana* [Doctoral dissertation, University of Maryland, College Park]. DRUM. https://drum.lib.umd.edu/handle/1903/17287

International Service for the Acquisition of Agri-biotech Applications. (2017). *Global status of commercialized biotech/GM crops in 2017* (ISAA Brief 53). https://www.isaaa.org/resources/publications/briefs/53/executivesummary/default.asp

James, C. (2012). *Global status of commercialized biotech/GM Crops: 2012* (ISAAA Brief No. 44). ISAAA.

James, P. B., Wardle, J., Steel A., & Adams, J. (2018). Traditional, complementary and alternative medicine use in Sub-Saharan Africa: A systematic review. *British Medical Journal Global Health, 3*(5). https://doi.org/10.1136/bmjgh-2018-000895

Kriebel, D., Tickner, J., Epstein, P., Lomons, J., Loechle, E., Quinn, M., Rudel, R., Schettler, T. & Stoto, M. (2001). The precautionary principle in environmental science. *Environmental Health Perspective, 109*(9), 871–876. https://dx.doi.org/10.1289%2Fehp.01109871

Kushitor, M. K. & Boatemaa, S. (2018). The double burden of disease and the challenge of health access: Evidence from access, bottlenecks, cost and equity facility survey in Ghana. *PLoSONE, 13*(3). https://doi.org/10.1371/journal.pone.0194677

Mabhaudhi, T., Chimonyo, V. G. P., & Modi, A. T. (2017). Status of underutilised crops in South Africa: Opportunities for developing research capacity. *Sustainability, 9.* https://doi.org/10.3390/su9091569

Mannion, A. M. & Morse, S. (2013). *GM crops 1996-2012: A review of agronomic, environmental and socio-economic impacts* (University of Surrey, Centre for Environmental Strategy (CES) Working Paper 04/13). https://tinyurl.com/rgcxxzl

Marzband, R., Moallemi, M., & Darabinia, M. (2017). Spiritual nutrition from the Islamic point of view. *Journal of Islamic Studies and Culture, 5*(2), 33–39. https://doi.org/10.15640/jisc.v5n2a4

Moellenbeck, D. J., Peters, M. L., Bing, J. W., Rouse, J. R., Higgins, L. S., Sims, L., Nevshemal, T., Marshall, L., Ellis, R. T., Bystrak, P. G., Lang, B. A., Stewart, J. L., Kouba, K., Sondag, V., Gustafson, V., Nour, K., Xu, D., Swenson, J., Zhang, J., ... Duck, M. (2001). Insecticidal proteins from *Bacillus thuringiensis* protect corn from corn rootworms. *Nature Biotechnology, 19*(7), 668–672. https://doi.org/10.1038/90282

Ministry of Food and Agriculture. (2010). Medium Term Agriculture Sector Investment Plan (METASIP) 2011–2015. Accra, Ghana: Author.

Murphy, D. (2007) *Plant breeding and biotechnology: Societal context and the future of agriculture.* Cambridge University Press.

Mutva, V. (1999). *Indaba, my children.* Grove.

Myhr, A. I. & Traavik, T. (2002). The precautionary principle: Scientific uncertainty and omitted research in the context of GMO use and release. *Journal of Agricultural and Environmental Ethics, 15*, 73–86. https://doi.org/10.1023/A:1013814108502

Parent, K. & Vandelac, L. (Directors). (2000). *The genetic takeover or mutant food* [Film]. National Film Board of Canada.

Pufall, E. L., Jones, A. Q., McEwen, S. A., Lyall, C., Peregrine, A. S., & Edge, V. L. (2011). Perception of the importance of traditional country foods to the physical, mental, and spiritual health of Labrador Inuit. *Arctic, 64*(2), 242–250. https://doi.org/10.14430/arctic4103

Raab, C. & Grobe, D. (2003). Labeling genetically engineered food: The consumer's right to know? *AgBioForum, 6*(4), 155–161. https://tinyurl.com/v4ggzho

Raman, R. (2017). The impact of genetically modified (GM) crops in modern agriculture: A review. *Biotechnology in Agriculture and the Food Chain, 8*(4), 195–208. https://doi.org/10.1080/21645698.2017.1413522

Raschke, V. & Cheema, B. (2007). Colonisation, the new world order, and the eradication of traditional food habits in East Africa: Historical perspective on the nutrition transition. *Public Health Nutrition, 11*(7), 662–674. https://doi.org/10.1017/S1368980007001140

Raschke, V., Oltersdorf, U., Elmadfa, I., Wahlqvist, M. L., Cheema, B. S. B., & Kouris-Blazos, A. (2007). Content of a novel online collection of traditional East African food habits (1930s–1960s): Data collected by the Max-Planck-Nutrition Research Unit, Bumbuli, Tanzania. *Asia Pacific Journal of Clinical Nutrition, 16*(1), 140–151. https://tinyurl.com/t5htoyl

Robertson, B. (2010). Global land acquisition: Neo-colonialism or development opportunity? *Food Security, 2(3)*, 274–283. https://doi.org/10.1007/s12571-010-0068-1

Rock, J. (2018). Complex mediascapes, complex realities: Critically engaging with biotechnology debates in Ghana. *Global Bioethics, 29*(1), 55–64. https://doi.org/10.1080/11287462.2018.1480253

Rock, J. (2019). "We are not starving": Challenging genetically modified seeds and development in Ghana. *Culture, Agriculture, Food and Environment, 41*(1), 15–23. https://doi.org/10.1111/cuag.12147

Royal Society of Chemistry. (2014). *Royal Society of Chemistry response to the Science & Technology Select Committee inquiry on GM foods and application of the precautionary principle in Europe.* www.rsc.org

Shiva, V. (2008). *Soil not oil: Environmental justice in a time of climate change.* South End Press.

Speaker suspends GMO deliberations. (2014, January 28). In *MyJoyOnline.* https://www.myjoyonline.com/news/speaker-suspends-gmo-deliberations/

Steingraber, S. (2010). *Living downstream: An ecologist's personal investigation of cancer and the environment* (2nd ed.). Da Capo Press.

Stote, K. (2012). The coercive sterilization of Aboriginal women in Canada. *American Indian Culture and Research Journal, 36*(3), 117–150. https://doi.org/10.17953/aicr.36.3.7280728r6479j650

Tannor, E. K., Sarfo, F. S., Mobula, L. M., Sarfo-Kantanka, O., Adu-Gyamfi, R., & Plange-Rhule, J. (2019). Prevalence and predictors of chronic kidney disease among Ghanaian patients with hypertension and diabetes mellitus: A multicenter cross-sectional study. *The Journal of Clinical Hypertension, 21*(10), 1542–1550. https://doi.org/10.1111/jch.13672

United Nations General Assembly. (1992, June). *Report of the United Nations conference on environment and development: Annex I—Rio Declaration on Environment and Development.* https://tinyurl.com/qqh9ejv

United States Department of Agriculture. (2019, April). Farms and land in farms 2018 summary. National Agricultural Statistics Service. https://www.nass.usda.gov/Publications/Todays_Reports/reports/fnlo0419.pdf

Vain, P. (2007). Trends in GM crop, food and feed safety literature. *Nature Biotechnology Correspondence, 25*(6), 624–626. https://doi.org/10.1038/nbt0607-624b

VoPham, T., Bertrand, K. A., Hart, J. E., Laden, F., Brooks, M. M., Yuan, J-M., Talbott, E. O., Ruddell, D., Chang, C. H., & Weissfeld, J. L. (2017). Pesticide exposure and liver cancer: A review. *Cancer Causes & Control, 28*(3), 177–190. https://doi.org/10.1007/s10552-017-0854-6

Vorster, H. J., Pichop, G. N., Maro, F. & Marealle, R. (2007). Indigenous vegetable supply chain in South Africa: Significance, constraints and opportunities—Case of Soshanguve (City of Tswane). Unpublished Indigenous vegetables survey report.

Watson, J. P. & Crick, E. H. C. (1953). Molecular structure of nucleic acids: A structure for deoxyribose nucleic acid. *Nature, 171*(4356), 737–738. https://doi.org/10.1038/171737a0

Whitman, D. B. (2000, April). Genetically modified foods: Harmful or helpful? *CSA Discovery Guides.* http://artsci.ucla.edu/biotech177/reading/GMO_Harm_or_Help.pdf

World Health Organization. (2002). *WHO answers questions on genetically modified foods.* https://www.who.int/mediacentre/news/notes/np5/en/

Author Biographies

Coly Chau has a Master of Education in Social Justice Education from the Ontario Institute for Studies in Education, University of Toronto. Her research interests include race, gender, sexuality, migration, anti-colonial thought and spirituality. Coly is interested in the unearthing and reclamation of knowledges for imagining and working toward decolonial and liberatory futures. She is often working, organizing and learning in her communities.

Cherie A Daniel has been a lawyer in the Province of Ontario since 2005, who has also taught at both College and University level law and related courses across the GTA. Cherie is also among the 100 Accomplished Black Canadian Women honourees for 2020. She obtained her Master of Laws in 2019 from Osgoode Hall Law School, the same year she graduated from the University of Toronto (OISE) with a Master of Education. In Fall of 2019, she began a Ph.D. in Social Justice Education at the University of Toronto (OISE)

Ghanaian-born **George Sefa Dei** is Professor of Social Justice Education & Director of the Centre for Integrative Anti-Racism Studies at the Ontario Institute for Studies in Education of the University of Toronto (OISE/UT). He is a Fellow of the Royal Society of Canada. In June of 2007, Professor Dei was installed as a traditional chief in Ghana, specifically, as the Gyaasehene of the town of Asokore, Koforidua in the New Juaben Traditional Area of Ghana. His stool name is Nana Adusei Sefa Tweneboah.

Suleyman M. Demi is a Postdoctoral Fellow at the Department of Health and Society at the University of Toronto at Scarborough. His research interests are multidisciplinary but currently focusing on health equity, social and environmental justice, food systems analysis and rural and international development.

Arthi Erika Jeyamohan is an artist and student in Ph.D. Cultural Studies at Queen's University. She completed her M.Ed. Social Justice Education at the Ontario Institute for Studies in Education of the University of Toronto (OISE/UT).

Heba Khalife is a Lebanese, Canadian-born Human Resources and Equity, Diversity, and Inclusion Professional. She recently completed her Master of Education in Social Justice Education at the Ontario Institute for Studies in Education at the University of Toronto.

Kenyan Born **Hellen Chepkoech Komen Taabu** is a Registered Nurse in Ontario, Canada, currently pursuing her Ph.D. studies at the Department of Social Justice Education. She is also an educator and a community activist who actively champions black immigrants and nurses' rights in her community. Hellen's work revolves around disrupting power imbalances, inequities and injustices that are deeply entrenched in the schools and healthcare system in Canada. Hellen calls for the interrogation of varied perspectives and exposing colonizing rhetorics and characteristics in a bid to expose, resist, transform liberate the spaces we inhabit from the persistent presence of colonialism.

Izza Tahir is a doctoral student in the Educational Leadership and Policy program at the Ontario Institute for Studies in Education at the University of Toronto. She holds a bachelor's degree in Philosophy and English and a master's degree in Public Policy, both from the University of Toronto. Her research interests include education system reform and education policy in developing countries, with a special focus on teacher change and teacher effectiveness.

Sri Lankan born **Thanuja Thananayagam** is a human resources professional with over 15 years of professional work experience in Sri Lankan and Canada. Thanuja holds an MBA from the University of Leicester and MEd in Social Justice Education from the University of Toronto – Ontario Institute for Studies in Education of the University of Toronto. Thanuja is a second-year Ph.D. Social Justice student working under the guidance and supervision of Professor George Dei.

Ciro William Torres Granizo was born and raised in Quito, Ecuador, where he worked as an educator and translator. While in Ecuador, he studied Business and Engineering at an international business school and the Pontifical Catholic University of Ecuador. Ciro travelled extensively in Europe and South America before settling in Canada. Since his arrival, he has earned a BAA in Paralegal Studies from the Humber Institute of Technology and Advanced Learning and an MEd, Social Justice Education from the University of Toronto. Ciro lives with his spouse in Toronto, Ontario.

Zainab Zafar, Pakistani-born, is a graduate in Bachelor of Science from Ryerson University. Zainab completed her Master of Education in Social Justice Education at the Ontario Institute for Studies in Education at the University of Toronto. (OISE/UT). She is currently an Ontario certified teacher in the Adult Education at Toronto District School Board, teaching science with an equity-focused lens. She is a proud mother of two girls.

Index